Manga Studio 5 Beginner's Guide

An extensive and fun guide to let your imagination loose using Manga Studio 5

Michael Rhodes

D1310748

PUBLISHING

BIRMINGHAM - MUMBAI

Manga Studio 5 Beginner's Guide

First published: April 2014

Production Reference: 1170414

Published by Packt Publishing Ltd.
Livery Place
35 Livery Street
Birmingham B3 2PB, UK

ISBN 978-1-84969-766-8

www.packtpub.com

Cover Image by Michael Rhodes (mike@crtoons.com)

Credits

Author

Michael Rhodes

Reviewers

Heldrad

Dawn Blair

Melissa Darkshore

Mark Egan

Acquisition Editors

Edward Gordon

Subho Gupta

Content Development Editor

Balaji Naidu

Technical Editors

Rosmy George

Krishnaveni Nair

Pratish Soman

Copy Editors

Roshni Banerjee

Sayanee Mukherjee

Karuna Narayanan

Laxmi Subramanian

Project Coordinator

Kranti Berde

Proofreaders

Simran Bhogal

Maria Gould

Ameesha Green

Paul Hindle

Clyde Jenkins

Indexers

Hemangini Bari

Tejal Soni

Graphics

Ronak Dhruv

Production Coordinators

Kyle Albuquerque

Conidon Miranda

Cover Work

Kyle Albuquerque

Conidon Miranda

About the Author

Michael Rhodes took apart grocery bags at the age of five to create pads of drawing paper. Decades later, he still hasn't stopped, although he has switched from grocery bags and crayons to charcoal, paint, pen, ink, and computer. He has taught web designing at Silicon Valley College and has conducted cartooning classes for elementary school children. He has illustrated *Tales of The Living Room Warrior*, an eight-part fable following the epic adventures of cats from the creation of the world to the domestication of humans.

He is also the creator of *Thingies*, a fantasy comic book series that details the adventures and perils that a reporter experiences while she uncovers secrets of her universe. His books and art work are carried by Fantastic Comics in Berkeley, Heroes and Villains Comics in Pleasanton, and Solo Comics in the Napa wine country. He holds a Bachelor's degree in Digital Design. His cartoons and artwork are displayed at www.crtoons.com and www.quatumgumbo.com.

I would like to dedicate this book to Janet, my wife, my partner, and *my always*.

About the Reviewers

Heldrad is a freelance web comic artist who has been posting her work online since 2004. She writes and draws her own stories, and lately, she has begun self-publishing her comics at local conventions and participating in the international manga contest, The Morning International Comic Competition.

Dawn Blair has a passion for telling stories about noble hearts and fantastic places. Though she started out writing novels, her life expanded into art and photography. She created Morning Sky Studios to support all of her creative endeavors: writing, painting, illustrating, and photography. She is currently teaching herself how to animate. She began using Manga Studio 3 and Anime Studio 5 and has loved the Smith Micro line of products since then.

She has two fictional series in publication: *Sacred Knight* and *The Loki Adventures*, published by *Morning Sky Studios*, as well as a non-fiction editing book for authors titled *The Write Edit*. She has won numerous awards for writing, painting, and photography, and has collectors of her art in Canada, Spain, Australia, and the United States.

You can find out more about Dawn Blair and her work on her websites www.dawnblair.com and www.morningskystudios.com.

Melissa Darkshore is a self-taught artist who enjoys sitting down and bringing her imagination to life through various mediums.

> I would like to thank Smith Micro for bringing us needy artists such a wonderful and versatile app for drawing and painting.

Mark Egan is a web cartoonist based in Oslo, Norway. He is an Irish expat and originally comes from the Dublin region of Ireland, but has since lived in China as an English teacher before settling in Oslo.

He graduated from Griffith College, Dublin with a Bachelor of Science degree in Computer Science in 2004, and following his time in China, started his career in the Telecom industry in Ireland, working as a call center agent. He later progressed to technical roles prior to the economic downturn in Ireland, after which he migrated to Norway, where he continues to live and work.

Having been actively cartooning since 2003, he focuses on producing manga-style web comics. His main noteworthy works are *Back Office*, an office comedy based in a call center, and *Bata Neart*, a magical girl web-manga set in Ireland.

Both the comics are published online via `rawrtacular.com`, which is the main portal of his studio, RAWRtacular Productions.

www.PacktPub.com

Support files, eBooks, discount offers and more

You might want to visit www.PacktPub.com for support files and downloads related to your book.

Did you know that Packt offers eBook versions of every book published, with PDF and ePub files available? You can upgrade to the eBook version at www.PacktPub.com and as a print book customer, you are entitled to a discount on the eBook copy. Get in touch with us at service@packtpub.com for more details.

At www.PacktPub.com, you can also read a collection of free technical articles, sign up for a range of free newsletters and receive exclusive discounts and offers on Packt books and eBooks.

http://PacktLib.PacktPub.com

Do you need instant solutions to your IT questions? PacktLib is Packt's online digital book library. Here, you can access, read and search across Packt's entire library of books.

Why Subscribe?

- ◆ Fully searchable across every book published by Packt
- ◆ Copy and paste, print and bookmark content
- ◆ On demand and accessible via web browser

Free Access for Packt account holders

If you have an account with Packt at www.PacktPub.com, you can use this to access PacktLib today and view nine entirely free books. Simply use your login credentials for immediate access.

Table of Contents

Preface

Manga, comics, sequential art, cartoon strips, and graphic novels are all the same, they tell stories with pictures and words. While the style, manner, and packaging of these stories have changed, the process of creating them has remained relatively stable. The artist draws on paper, the pages are sent to a letterer, an inker renders the pencil marks so that the pages can be reproduced for printing, and finally, the pages are sent to the colorist for coloring. The system has remained basically the same (with occasional flourishes) and lasted since the beginning of comics as we know them, from the 1940s to the 1990s.

Then, computers came along, and as the saying goes "everything changed."

Way, way back in 1988, Mike Saenz drew a comic called Shatter. It was the first comic entirely drawn on a computer. Using an, now ancient to us in the new millennium, original Apple Macintosh with MacPaint, I read it and my world changed. Sure, I still drew on paper, but programs like Photoshop, Painter, and Illustrator became more robust and I was able to do so much on my trusty Mac IIsi with an incredible 32 MB of RAM.

Things evolved very quickly, because of you know, Moore's Law (go ahead and do a search on it if it's new to you).

Malibu comics was the first publisher (that I know of) to incorporate digital coloring in all their comics. Then, letterers got into the digital game. Graphic tablets became the norm.

However, the process of comic creation, in this new frontier of digital production, was still piecemeal. Everything was so page-centric that the story became hard to see. There were dozens upon dozens of files, some for pencils, others for inked work, and then copies of files that were lettered and colored. Different applications were used, sometimes, for each step of the way. The system remained the same while the tools changed. Is your head spinning yet?

What comic creators needed was a new tool. What we got was Manga Studio. And everything changed.

I heard about this program lurking in various forums. Soon, I had Manga Studio EX 3 installed on my Mac. Ever did something that you got right from the start? I grokked Manga Studio the moment I first used a pencil tool in it. I could create pages within stories; no more dealing with dozens of files or hunting around and being fixated on filenames or directory structures as much as before. Here was a program that got comics in a way that no other program did before. Instead of having to work the way a program wants you to, Manga Studio allows the artist to determine how to work. No more hacks, add-ons, or manually using masks to make panels, Manga Studio does it all, in one place.

Manga Studio was my Star Wars. It changed everything.

My wife says that I'm a brain-dumper, meaning that I get the structure of a story first and then fill in details. With Manga Studio, I was able to sketch out an entire story, roughly, and then go in and add, delete, or move pages as it fit the story. I could see the entire story, in thumbnails before me—on the computer! This was big stuff for me. No longer was I a prisoner of filenames. No longer did I have to sketch out my story on paper and scan the sketches to individual files. I only had to worry about the art of comics.

Now with Version 5, drawing, inking, and coloring comics is even more elegant. Heck, you can even skip the inking and just paint your comics if you're so inclined. The engine that drives the various marking tools (pencils, pens, and brushes) has been overhauled to make customizations even easier. If you're not the type to roll your own, there are many pre-made brush sets for penciling, inking, and painting for Manga Studio 5 that you can purchase (go to http://www.frenden.com, see some examples of Frenden's work, and check out his Manga Studio 5 brushes).

In this book, I tried to cover the really important aspects of comic creation using Manga Studio. It's done in such a way that we can see how Manga Studio fits into the production process of comic creation. I've put in some exercises for neophyte creators to get us all used to this app. My approach was to introduce this app to not only those who are budding comic creators, but to those who are new to Manga Studio and want to know how to use it in their workflow.

No app is perfect, nor is there truly an application that can really "do it all." The previous statement notwithstanding, neither is Manga Studio perfect. I'm a lettering, calligraphy, and font nut, so I come down hard on Manga Studio's lettering abilities. But instead of just whining about it, let's consider a work-around. Be sure to check out the free e-book where I introduce you to Comic Life 3, whose only job is to letter comics. It does that job very well, and in the e-book, I'll show you a method of using it in conjunction with Manga Studio (and other graphic apps if you've not seen the Manga Studio light).

It's quite possible that in the next five, ten, or more years, it'll be the next big thing in creating comics. It will probably change our world. But for now, we have Manga Studio 5. With it, we can change the world. One story at a time.

What this book covers

Chapter 1, Installing and Setting Up Manga Studio 5, is where it all begins. Installing and registering Manga Studio 5 is covered in this chapter. Getting started with creating a new file and using a pencil tool is also covered.

Chapter 2, Messing Around with Manga Studio 5, is a walkthrough of the basic interface of Manga Studio, from the dreaded blank page to the plethora of palettes in this program. The marking tools of Manga Studio are covered.

Chapter 3, Formatting Your Stories, covers creating presets for comic pages or comic strips and more. A brief taste of the Material palette and the text tool is also included.

Chapter 4, Roughing It, examines the crucial step between story idea and putting that story down in comic storytelling. Aspects of layers are covered, as are Auto actions—a way of recording steps that can be replayed anytime.

Chapter 5, Putting Words in My Mouth, covers the captivating craft of calligraphy or lettering our comics. The limitations of Manga Studio 5 are candidly examined and work-arounds are investigated.

Chapter 6, Pencil Mechanics, explains tool creation to using rulers and perspective guides.

Chapter 7, Ink Slingers, focuses on tools, techniques, and more to render artwork in Manga Studio. Do not miss the shocking secrets of the Material palette explained in this chapter.

Chapter 8, Coloring the World, displays the wide spectrum of color, painting, and brushes in Manga Studio.

Chapter 9, Adding a Third "D", covers the 3D abilities of Manga Studio and some ways to work with the models, from placing one on the canvas to posing it.

Chapter 10, Caring about Sharing, explores the nuances of exporting for print and pixel. From printing out to your home printer to a faraway print on demand service and out to the outer regions of the Internet, this chapter covers it all.

Chapter 11, One More Thing, explores the features of Manga Studio 5 EX, stories of Manga Studio EX, batch processing of story files, and the page manager.

Chapter 12, Along for the Ride, is an online chapter that has sections and exercises that the physical book just didn't have room for. It contains information on vectors in Manga Studio, and more about color palettes and rulers. You can find this chapter at `https://www.packtpub.com/sites/default/files/downloads/7668OT_Chapter_12.pdf`.

Chapter 13, Lettering Comics with Comic Life 3, is an online chapter that details introduction and methods to use Comic Life for comic lettering; layout is the focus of this free e-book. You can find this chapter at `https://www.packtpub.com/sites/default/files/downloads/7668OT_Chapter_13.pdf`.

What you need for this book

To make the most of this book, you need to have a copy of Manga Studio 5 and a computer that can operate this application. Although not required, a graphics tablet is good to have as so much functionality of Manga Studio comes to life with a tablet in ways a mere mouse cannot.

Who this book is for

This book is for anyone who draws, wants to create their own comics, and wishes to do it digitally. For novices, the exercises within are designed to stretch their artistic muscles. And for comic pros, the Beginner in the title means a beginner's user guide of Manga Studio.

Conventions

In this book, you will find several headings that appear frequently.

To give clear instructions of how to complete a procedure or task, we use:

Time for action – heading

1. Action 1

2. Action 2

3. Action 3

Instructions often need some extra explanation so that they make sense, so they are followed with:

What just happened?

This heading explains the working of tasks or instructions that you have just completed.

You will also find some other learning aids in the book, including:

Pop quiz – heading

These are short multiple-choice questions intended to help you test your own understanding.

Have a go hero – heading

These practical challenges give you ideas for experimenting with what you have learned.

You will also find a number of styles of text that distinguish between different kinds of information. Here are some examples of these styles, and an explanation of their meaning.

Folder names, filenames, file extensions, pathnames, dummy URLs, user input, Twitter handles, and Secret Identities are shown as follows: "We want to name our file `Too_Many_Minions` inside the `Stories` directory."

New terms and **important words** are shown in bold. Words that you see on the screen, in menus or dialog boxes for example, appear in the text like this: "On the **New** dialog box, click on the **Paper Color** check box to set the color of the canvas in the new document."

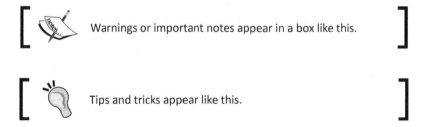

Warnings or important notes appear in a box like this.

Tips and tricks appear like this.

Reader feedback

Feedback from our readers is always welcome. Let us know what you think about this book—what you liked or may have disliked. Reader feedback is important for us to develop titles that you really get the most out of.

To send us general feedback, simply send an e-mail to `feedback@packtpub.com`, and mention the book title through the subject of your message.

If there is a topic that you have expertise in and you are interested in either writing or contributing to a book, see our author guide on www.packtpub.com/authors.

Customer support

Now that you are the proud owner of a Packt book, we have a number of things to help you to get the most from your purchase.

Downloading the example files

You can download the example code files for all Packt books you have purchased from your account at `http://www.packtpub.com`. If you purchased this book elsewhere, you can visit `http://www.packtpub.com/support` and register to have the files e-mailed directly to you.

Downloading the color images of this book

We also provide you a PDF file that has color images of the screenshots/diagrams used in this book. The color images will help you better understand the changes in the output. You can download this file from `https://www.packtpub.com/sites/default/files/downloads/7668OT_ColorImages.pdf`.

Errata

Although we have taken every care to ensure the accuracy of our content, mistakes do happen. If you find a mistake in one of our books—maybe a mistake in the text or the code—we would be grateful if you would report this to us. By doing so, you can save other readers from frustration and help us improve subsequent versions of this book. If you find any errata, please report them by visiting `http://www.packtpub.com/submit-errata`, selecting your book, clicking on the **errata submission form** link, and entering the details of your errata. Once your errata are verified, your submission will be accepted and the errata will be uploaded to our website, or added to any list of existing errata, under the Errata section of that title.

Piracy

Piracy of copyright material on the Internet is an ongoing problem across all media. At Packt, we take the protection of our copyright and licenses very seriously. If you come across any illegal copies of our works, in any form, on the Internet, please provide us with the location address or website name immediately so that we can pursue a remedy.

Please contact us at `copyright@packtpub.com` with a link to the suspected pirated material.

We appreciate your help in protecting our authors, and our ability to bring you valuable content.

Questions

You can contact us at `questions@packtpub.com` if you are having a problem with any aspect of the book, and we will do our best to address it.

1
Installing and Setting Up
Manga Studio 5

This chapter is the beginning of our adventure creating comics with Manga Studio 5. We'll install Manga Studio 5, snoop around at what was installed and where it is, set up our tablet, create our first page, and see some examples of work done with Manga Studio. If you can remain conscious through the first part of this chapter, we'll explore and learn how Manga Studio 5 has been used by other comic artists, and introduce a project that we'll be working on throughout this book.

In this chapter, we will cover the following topics:

- ◆ Computer requirements for Manga Studio
- ◆ Installing Manga Studio
- ◆ Registering Manga Studio and registration number tips
- ◆ Introducing the Manga Studio 5 interface and document creation
- ◆ Drawing on a document canvas
- ◆ Setting up a tablet for use with Manga Studio

Preparing for installation

If we purchased our copy of Manga Studio from Smith Micro, it will currently be on a DVD. When Manga Studio 5 was ordered from Smith Micro, the serial number should've been included in the e-mail that has the link to the download URL. Make a note of this, copy it as a text file, and put it in your document folder. This is the number that Smith Micro will require so that you can download updates and patches to Manga Studio. For now, we'll need a serial number so that we can install Manga Studio 5.

Computer requirements

Manga Studio's computer requirements are pretty basic. If you're using a relatively modern computer (manufactured within the past 10 years or so) and can run at least a version of an operating system released within that time frame, you should be good to go. But here's a list of the minimum requirements, just to be sure:

◆ A desktop or laptop computer that's using Windows XP or Macintosh OS X 10.6, or newer versions of either operating system.

◆ A minimum of 256 MB of video RAM on the video card. If your machine is at least five years old or newer, this should be no issue.

◆ At least 2 GB of RAM that can be used by Manga Studio 5. Like with many things in life, more is better. The more RAM your computer has, the more documents you can open in Manga Studio 5 concurrently.

◆ If you have more than 2 GB of hard disk space, you'll do just fine. Like with RAM, more space is a good thing. Hard discs, especially external USB drives, are relatively inexpensive right now and getting one to store backups of your work is never wasted money.

◆ A DVD drive attached to your computer, if you received a boxed version of Manga Studio 5.

Monitor

A good bright monitor that has accurate colors is important. A good resolution is 1920 x 1080. If you have a second monitor, that'll be great for all the palettes that we'll be bringing up and using. However, only having one isn't a show-stopper because Manga Studio has a very intelligent way to handle palettes.

Tablets or input devices

There are many different kinds of tablets that can be used with Manga Studio 5. We'll show you how to set up a **Wacom Tablet**. If you have another model, the principles will be the same. Although I have seen people use Manga Studio without a tablet, to make use of everything this program can do, get a tablet. For me, it was the single best computer purchase ever made. I will assume that you're all using tablets with Manga Studio for all the descriptions and exercises in this book. If you are using just a mouse, then most of the instructions can be performed, but the options about pressure sensitivity can be ignored.

Workspace

Between the chair and the keyboard, there is a part of this whole affair that just gets ignored or given cursory attention: **you**. In the mad energy of creation, it's so easy to let hours go by like minutes. Take breaks. Set a timer to go off every 40 minutes or hour. Then get away from the computer. Take a little walk outside or in your home. Your bones will thank you by not getting all achy and stiff. If our bodies aren't hurting when we create, we can put more effort into our work without being distracted by pain. Search for hand, wrist, and forearm stretches on Google. Do these prior to drawing and during your breaks. Our hands and arms are crucial to doing our art and getting tendonitis isn't fun at all.

A few artists have their desks raised so that they can draw while standing. This is great as our bodies are getting some exercise and the human form is built to stand.

As silly as this seems, don't forget to blink. It prevents our eyes from drying out and getting eye strain faster. Every so often, look at things farther away than your monitor, like outside your window. This will exercise our eye muscles and reduce some eye strain.

We'll touch on this subject occasionally. Remember, it's more fun to write out tendonitis than it is to experience it.

Installation of Manga Studio 5

It's the same whether you install it from a DVD, DMG, or EXE file. Once your computer gets the DVD on the desktop and you open the DVD or you locate the downloaded installation file, double-click on the installation file.

Manga Studio will install not only the program itself, but a number of other files (brushes, pens, tones, color palettes, and more) in different locations. Unless you're really comfortable with such things, it's best to let Manga Studio install the files where it wants.

We'll be asked to agree to some Licensing terms. It's up to us to read these terms carefully and agree to them before we can install Manga Studio. This applies to everyone who installs this program, even if you're just installing an evaluation copy.

Where are those files?

On the Mac, the files are inside your `Documents` folder as shown in the following screenshot:

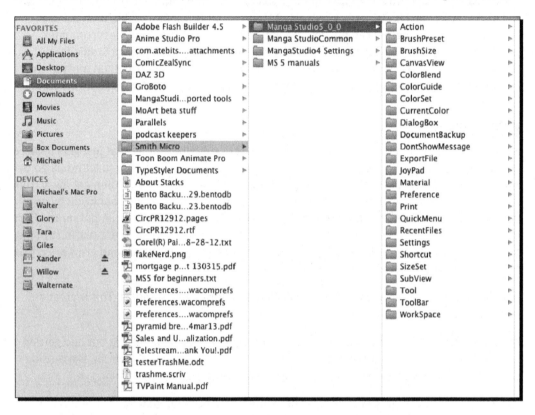

As we can tell, this is where all the cool stuff is located. If we ever need to reinstall Manga Studio, this folder should be backed up as it contains all the settings for preferences, keyboard shortcuts, customized tools, and much more. Fortunately, we won't have to directly install files into these folders; Manga Studio will do that for us.

To make it easier to look thing up and refer to the manuals, we can create a folder, name it `Manga Studio 5 manuals`, and put the `Installation Guide`, `Startup Guide`, the `Users' Manual` files, and the text file that contains our registration number in there. This way all the important documents are in a good and safe place. I have a pair of pocket notebooks that contain app names and their serial numbers. The notebook is stored in a storage locker with other important archival materials. It's better to have a number of duplicates and not need them, than to need them and not have a copy.

Like other graphic art programs, the Interface for Manga Studio 5 is huge and complex. To make things a bit more manageable, we'll just use screenshots of the sections of our workspace. We'll make sure that the area is identified and made clear. This way we'll focus in on the area of the program that we're concerned with. You can go to `https://www.packtpub.com/sites/default/files/downloads/7668OT_ColorImages.pdf` and download a ZIP file that has the color versions of all the screenshots in this book.

Starting up Manga Studio for the first time

Now that the computer's work is done, our work is just beginning. We'll be starting up Manga Studio for the first time and creating our first document. Let's begin!

Not your morning serial

There should be a shortcut to Manga Studio 5 on your desktop. Double-click on it and Manga Studio 5 will start up. If this is the first time it's being run, we'll have to tell it that we are legitimate users by giving Manga Studio a proper serial number. This is the only time that Manga Studio will demand an Internet connection, as it needs to validate the serial number with Smith Micro's servers. If we run into problems, we can try to register Manga Studio later. Keep in mind that this serial number contains both upper and lower case letters along with numbers.

Once we're all done with that, we can get down to some art! Finally! So let's grab something good to drink (I prefer tea, thank you) and we'll walk through just enough of the interface to create a new document template, and then play around with the pencil tool.

Palettes, toolbars, and documents

With Manga Studio open, take a look at the screen. This is going to be our home for our art. This interface has it all from pencils to pens, from paper to tones, from watercolor paints to oil paints. Instead of trying to redo Akira, Watchmen, or the Sistine chapel, let's just create a new document and put marks on it as a start.

The main Manga Studio 5 toolbar

The toolbar is mostly greyed out at this time, except for the two left-most icons. The one that looks like a dog-eared page with a star on the upper left is to create new documents, and the other with the open folder with the arrow curling out of it is to open new documents.

The toolbar looks like the following screenshot when you first install Manga Studio 5 (callouts for your learning enjoyment):

Palettes

Further to the left, we see that Manga Studio 5 has two rows of palettes. On the furthest left is the **Tool Palette**. What we see here on the page won't match what you see on the screen. That's because Manga Studio remembers which tool was used last and will display that tool within this palette. If you click-and-drag a tool icon up or down, we can see that a thick red line appears between icons. And if we release our mouse/stylus button, the tool will be dropped where we released our stylus. Move the tool icon back to where it was.

If we click on a tool, we'll see that the palette to the right is updated. That's the **Sub tool** palette. This palette shows us all the various related tools that we can use. In the following screenshot, we have the **Pencil** tool selected and in the subtool palette we see that we can choose from many options. Below the **Sub tool** palette is the **Tool property**. This is where we can determine just how the tool will work. Pay particular attention to the icon that looks like a wrench with a circle around the end of it. This is how we can go deep inside the tool and create variations that are distinctly our own.

Back to **Tools**, we can see that the tool bar is split into three sections. We can think of them as the object marking and refining parts. If you are familiar with Photoshop, then most of these icons look the same, and they do pretty much the same thing.

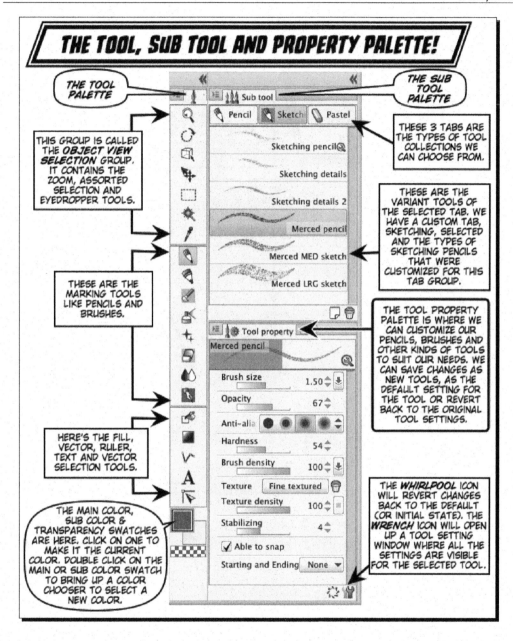

On the right-hand side of the screen are two more palette columns. The one that's made up of greyed square icons is where we'll get tones and 3D objects from. The last column is where the **Navigator**, **Subview**, **Layer Property**, and **Layer** palettes are.

We'll cover each and every one of these palettes and tools in time. Right now, let's go back to the Tool bar and create a new document.

That new document template smell!

Even though what we'll be covering may seem boring, this is setting the stage for the magic that we'll be doing with Manga Studio, so it'll be worth it.

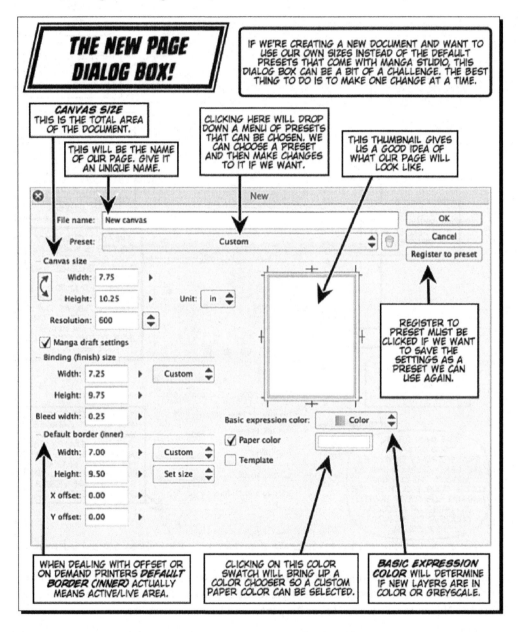

There's a lot of information here, so let's just focus on one area at a time and soon we'll have a customized page!

Time for action – creating a new document dialog box

The process of creating a new document dialog box is given in the following steps:

1. Click on the **New Document** button on the toolbar. A dialog box will pop up. The one on the screen will have different values than the one here. Being the heroes we are, we will create a new template that we'll be using for some tasks as we wind our way though this book. The template shown in the **New Document** dialog box is used for a Webcomic.

2. The top line is **File Name**. We can give our new document a name here.

3. The next section is labeled **Canvas size**. This is where we set up the full size of our document (in printing this is called the **Bleed** size). For our example, it's 7.75 x 10.25 inches. The resolution (dots per inch) is set at **600**. If our computer has limited memory or is a bit sluggish, set it to **300**.

4. Enter in 7.75 in the **Width entry** box.

5. Enter in 10.25 in the **Height entry** box.

6. We see that the **Preset** drop-down menu now says **Custom**. That's just what we want.

7. There's a double-headed button to the left of the width and height entries. This button swaps out the width and height.

8. **Unit** is set to **inches**. There are options for metric and pixel-based measurement in the drop-down menu.

9. The **Manga draft setting** should be checked. If unchecked, our page will not have borders and the binding and default borders will be greyed out.

10. In the **Binding (finish) size** area, enter the following values:
    - 7.25 for the **Width**
    - 9.75 for **Height**
    - 0.25 for **Bleed width**

Be sure to include the leading zero. Manga Studio doesn't like entries that begin with a decimal point without that leading zero.

If for some reason, the numbers in the previously mentioned area change, just go back and change them again. Sometimes Manga Studio is too helpful and we need to be adamant about what we want by repeating the information once or twice. It's always good to double-check the values in all the entry boxes to make sure that they haven't been changed.

11. The default border (inner) is called the live area outside of Manga Studio. This is the area where we'll be doing most of our work inside of this soon-to-be-created document. And all lettering must be within this area. Set the values to:

- **Width** is 7 inches
- **Height** is 9.75 inches
- The bottom two entries, **X** and **Y offset**, are for when you need to have your live area a bit higher or lower, or closer to one side or another. Just leave both of these at **0**.

12. There's a checkbox next to the text **Paper color**. This is where we can change the default paper color from white to another color or get rid of it. If we are doing a story that needs to have a solid color up to the edges of the page, then we will click on the **Color** bar and choose a color. But right now, we don't need to get fancy, besides we want to hurry up with this and get to drawing!

13. Double check the values. If we mistyped a number, Manga Studio will automatically recalculate other values and we could end up with some pretty strange pages.

14. Once we've made sure all our values are correct, let's save this as a `Preset`!

15. Under the **OK** and **Cancel** button there's a button labeled **Register to preset**. Clicking on this button will give us a dialog box as shown in the following screenshot:

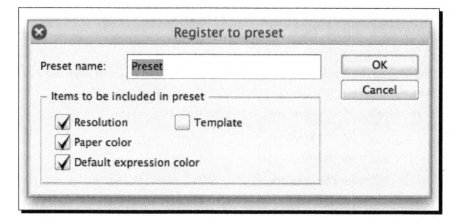

16. In the **Preset name** box, we can name it `Preset`. Type in `Webcomic w/Bleed`.

17. There are a number of checkboxes below where we named our preset:

- **Resolution**: This will save the set resolution as part of the preset. Usually if we're working on a series, we want the resolution to be consistent.
- **Paper color**: This is checked to be consistent.

❏ **Default expression color**: This sets the default way any new layers will be, either color, grey, or monochrome.

❏ **Template**: This will automatically load up any selected template. This is a bit advanced for us now, so leave it unchecked.

18. Click on **OK**.

19. We're back in the **New document** dialog box. Look closely at the **Preset** drop-down menu. It now lists the preset we just saved.

20. To the right of the drop-down menu is a trash can icon. If we create way too many presets and want to clear them up a bit, we can select the old templates one at a time, and click on the trash icon to delete them. We'll be given a dialog that asks us if we're really sure we want to delete the preset. We want to keep this preset, so click on **Cancel** if you pressed the trash icon.

21. Back in the New dialog box, click on the **OK** button and we're presented with a brand new document we can draw on.

22. Now take a few moments to mess around with the tools. What you do can be either undone or deleted. Go ahead, play around. You've earned it.

What just happened?

We went through, step-by-step, the creation of a new preset and made a new document based on that preset. We also encountered some odd things about Manga Studio, such as how it coined its own terminology for common print terminology. Here's a quick breakdown:

Manga Studio Term	Print Term	Description
Canvas size	Bleed size	The full size of the sheet that's being printed on
Binding (finish) size	Trim area	The size of sheet once it's been cut to this size
Default border (inner)	Active (or Live) area	All important drawings and text must be within this area

We will need to keep this translation table in mind, especially if we're going to talk to printers about printing our comic.

Have a go hero – creating a new document Dialog Box

Artists know faces. We'll recognize faces before we remember names. When we've created our first new document, fill it with faces of all kinds. Human, animal, or alien. Get used to moving around in the canvas area. Like with most other graphic applications, holding down the space bar will make your cursor a hand icon so that you can grab the canvas and move it around. *ALT/Command + =* will zoom in your view, *ALT/Command + -* will zoom out your view. Use these keyboard commands to move the canvas and zoom in or out and draw the faces in each of the four corners of your document, then zoom in and add details. In the toolbar, there's an icon that looks like an old style floppy disc, that's the **Save** button. Click on it and save your file with the name `practice_001.lip`. Remember where this file is as it can be helpful in warm-up exercises in the future. Experiment with the various marking tools. Get used to how the various tools work.

From your hand into the computer

Setting up the control panel for your tablet is one of those things that can seem like drudgery. It's worth doing because it can open up the full abilities of your tablet and make using aspects of Manga Studio 5 so much easier. We'll be covering how to set up a Wacom Tablet. These basic instructions are for an Intous 3 tablet, but can be adapted to a newer tablet model or to other manufacturers of tablets.

The Wacom tablet control panel

The Wacom control panel looks deceptively simple. There's a lot of functionality under those icons, buttons, and sliders. In my experience (and what Wacom recommends), the best results can be had by installing the drivers before plugging in your tablet. And this goes for installing updated control panel software. You should regularly save backups of your tablet settings.

When you first installed your tablet software, a folder named Wacom Tablet was created (on the Mac OS, it's in the `Applications` folder and in Windows, it's where applications are installed). Inside that folder is an application named `Wacom Tablet Utility`. This application is very simple: there's a button to remove, backup, and restore. First click on the backup button. Navigate to where you want to save your tablet settings. Save those settings. Remember where you have saved them. When it's time to update the tablet software, fire up Wacom Tablet Utility and click on the **Remove** button. This button does exactly what it says. Next, install the new tablet software. Once it's installed, run the Wacom Tablet Utility and click on the **Restore...** button. A dialog box will pop up and you need to navigate to where you saved your tablet settings when you clicked on the **Backup...** button. Select the backup file and click on the **Open** button. Now quit the Wacom Tablet Utility. We now return to the regularly scheduled instruction.

If you're using a Mac, open the **System Preferences** application. If you're on a Windows machine, go to your system and choose the **Wacom tablet control panel** option. The following screenshot appears:

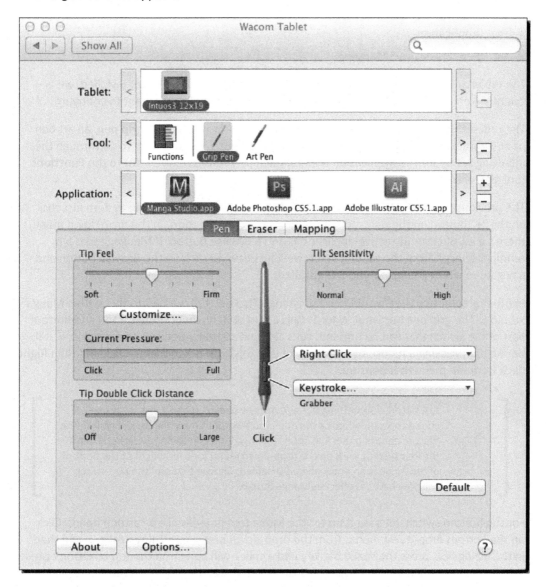

The control panel shown in the previous screenshot has four main areas:

- **Tablet**
- **Tool**
- **Application**
- **Pen**, **Eraser**, and **Mapping**

The tablet area is where you select your tablet. If there's only one tablet installed, we can move on. If there are two tablets installed, select the tablet you want to configure.

The tool settings have an icon for **Functions** and the pens you have (a grip pen, an art pen, or an airbrush pen). Select the pen you want to configure. You will have to go through the following set up for the **Application** area for each pen you have. We'll get to the **Functions** tool after the pen tool.

The previous image has Manga Studio already setup. To set it up on your system just click on the "+" button on the right side of the tier named **Application**. In the drop-down menu, there's a list of currently active applications and a **Browse** button. If Manga Studio 5 is running, select it from the list. If it's not, we'll just have to click on the **Browse** button and navigate to where Manga Studio 5 is installed.

In other graphic apps, we would need to change **Tip Feel**, but we can do that within Manga Studio 5. The grip pen has what Wacom calls a duo switch where there's a top and bottom part of the switch that can be pressed. Let's set it up so that when top part is pressed, it'll be like right-clicking a mouse by choosing, on the top drop-down menu, **Click** and then **Right Click** from the menu that pops up.

Just because something has a feature, it doesn't mean it has to be used. If you're constantly hitting the duo switch without meaning to, just go into the Wacom control panel and choose Manga Studio in the App scroller. Then in the **Pen** section, click on the drop-down menu for the switch. At the bottom of the menu is an entry named **Disabled**. Choose that and the duo switch will now have no effect in Manga Studio.

For the bottom switch, let's set it up for the **Move** tool (it looks like a cartoon hand). Click on the bottom drop-down menu, from the drop-down menu select **Keystroke...**, and then in the dialog box, press the space bar key and a space will appear in the top box. Don't press *Tab* (as that will add tab to the top box); just click in the textbox next to **Name:** and give your keystroke a name. I call this move tool the **Grabber** tool. Click on **OK**. We're now done here.

The eraser section usually doesn't need adjustment, so we'll skip it for now.

Now, click on the **Mapping** section button. If you have two monitors (like your author does), choose one to be the main drawing monitor. This is important so that it'll feel more natural. We can choose the monitor by clicking on the drop-down menu next to **Screen area**. Be sure to click on the **Force Proportions** checkbox. This is vital, in my opinion, because of muscle memory. We draw a circle on paper and we know it's a circle because of visual feedback. On a tablet (not a Cintiq or other display tablets), we don't have the single view of watching our hand draw a circle, we move our hand and watch it appear on our monitor. So if the tablet is stretched or squished in one direction or another, our hand draws an oval, but looks like a circle on the monitor. That's not good. Make things easy for yourself, click the **Force Proportions** checkbox.

Keep in mind that if things get out of control or you're a bit lost, don't fret. Just delete the application in the main control panel and start over again. It will make sense in no time. Just go slowly and make one adjustment at a time. Quit the control panel, open up Manga Studio 5, and test out the settings. This way, you can cement the new part of this a step at a time and learn it better.

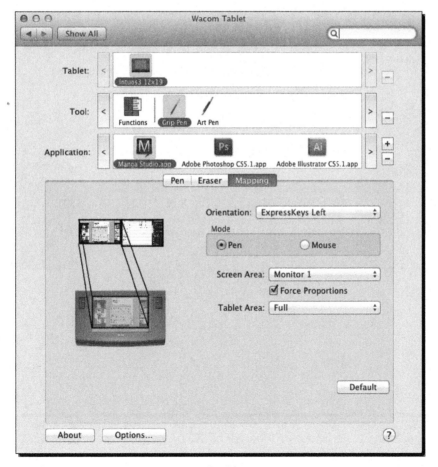

After this final set of settings, we can get back to Manga Studio 5 and have a bit of fun. In the **Tool** settings click on the **Functions** icon. Notice how the bottom part of the control panel changes?

We'll be making a few changes. Let's start with the **ExpressKeys**. On my tablet, there's a **Right** and **Left** side. I'm left handed, which means that in addition to being in my right mind, these buttons reflect that. This means that the buttons I use with my non-drawing hand are modifiers. The buttons on the left-hand side are the ones that I can use with the pen off the tablet, such as zoom in and out and swap colors.

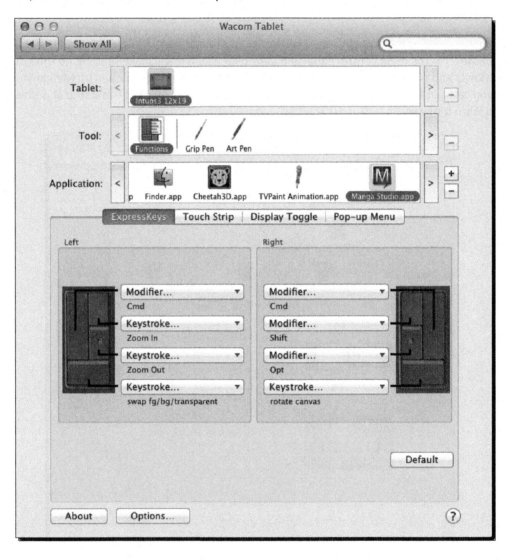

Assigning the keystrokes is exactly like what we did for the **Grabber** tool. Click on the drop-down menu and then choose the **Keystroke...** menu item. Here's a list of the names and the keyboard commands:

- For `Swap fg/bg/transparent` the **Keystroke** is a lowercase *z*
- For `rotate canvas` the **Keystroke** is a lowercase *r*
- For `Zoom in` the **Keystroke** is *+*
- For `Zoom out` the **Keystroke** is - (dash)

The rest are default settings.

The last **Wacom Tablet** setting we'll deal with is the **Touch Strip** setting. In newer models it's a circle, but the principle is the same. On one side of **Touch Strip**, we want to be able to **Undo** and **Redo**. On the other side of **Touch Strip**, we want to **swap colors**.

Even though I've put swap colors in two places, it's sometimes good to have more than one way to do something. If you find something that works better for you, go do it. Probably by the time we get to coloring, my tablet settings will have changed.

The **Touch Strip** part of the **Table Control** panel looks like the following screenshot:

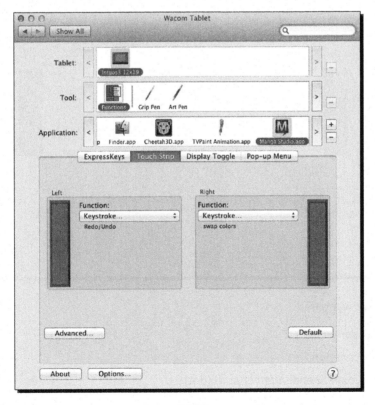

Each side can be set to have a top and bottom function. Usually, I try to make them related functions, such as zoom in and out, undo and redo, swap foreground and background colors. Click on the drop-down menu and follow the instructions carefully. Any or all keystrokes will be added to the command, so just press the keystrokes you want and use the mouse/ pointing device to move to a different area.

The keystroke entry areas are shown in the following screenshot. There's one area for the up arrow and one area for the down arrow. The control panel can detect when you type a key in the number pad (if you have an extended keyboard), so be careful.

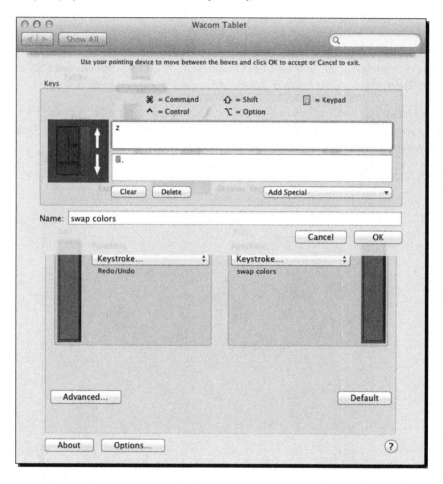

The settings we want are:

- Undo: *command* + *Z*
- Redo: *command* + *Y*
- Swap Colors: *z* and *(number pad)* (dot)

One thing that has helped me out is making a cheat sheet for the various buttons and keystrokes for the tablet's buttons. I made a drawing of the layout (left and right) of the tablet buttons and the Touch Strip and wrote down what the buttons do. I then wrote the name of the application it's for. So here's what it would look like for what we just did:

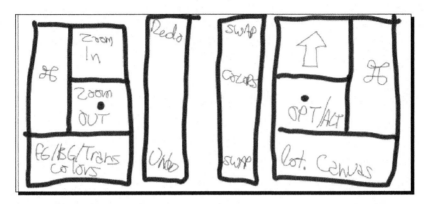

Manga Studio 5 Stylus settings

Finally, fire up Manga Studio 5 if it's not already running. Open a new document. From the Manga Studio menu, select the **Adjust Pen Pressure Adjust settings...** menu item.

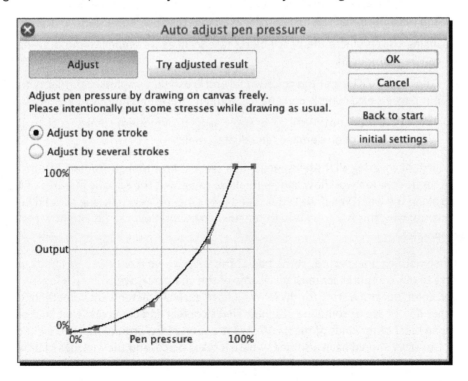

You can draw several strokes and the adjustment will be tailored to the way you draw. From experience, if the tablet has its pressure adjusted in the Control Panel and then in Manga Studio 5, the results are somewhat the same—the technical term is wacky. So it's best to adjust the pressure from within Manga Studio 5. The Wacom tablets I've used seem to be extremely sensitive on the light touch end, so you can see on the curve that it's very gradual at light pressure and then goes up and tops out at around 90 percent. This has worked well for me, but in your experience this may be different. So experiment. We can always go back to initial settings if we need to.

From a blank document to a finished page

The rest of this book will be about how to use Manga Studio. In addition to learning about page sizes, pencils, brushes and such, we'll cover the process of making a comic right from an initial idea to getting it ready for print.

This is how we'll roll for the rest of this book:

- **Idea**: The gem of a story. We'll tend to this seed and let it grow into a story.
- **Script**: This is where we figure out what follows what and address things such as pacing, characterization, and learn basic script formats.
- **Layouts**, **Penciling**, and **Lettering**: We'll layout pages, see how much text we have and make sure that the text and art work together.
- **Inking**: This is where the pencil marks take form as we embellish our drawing so it can be reproduced.
- **Coloring**: We'll look at the color wheel and brush up on some color theory to give our pages a nice complexion and make them interesting for our readers to look at.
- **Putting our work out**: We'll cover some aspects of modern comics, such as Webcomics, print on demand, and digital comics.

In the course of covering all these aspects, we'll see just how Manga Studio 5 fits into every possible comic creation workflow and learn all we can about the specific features of Manga Studio 5 along the way. Even if we're seasoned pros who are new to Manga Studio but not comic creation, this is a good way to see how your workflow can fit with how Manga Studio operates.

Now for something unexpected, at the end of this section, we'll put away this book, put our backs to our computer screens, take some of the characters we created a few pages back and come up with a story for them. We'll have each character want something that they either don't have or someone else has. That's conflict and comics do that kind of story better than most other kinds of media. We want a short story, around three to eight pages of comics. Our story should have a setting, where it takes place, and the makings of a three act play: beginning, middle, and end.

This is where our internal critic has way too much fun. Don't listen to that part of us. We're just doing this story for pure fun and to learn Manga Studio 5 in the process. We have to start somewhere and we can do this one story just for ourselves. If it is a stinker, it'll be our secret, okay? And if you're really stalled, just find a public domain play and use that as your story. The thing here is to have something that we can work on. If you can't come up with a story, just follow the examples in the exercises. There's a sample story (with characters, script, and so on) included in the downloadable ZIP file.

Pop Quiz

Q1. A pencil can be found:

1. In the toolbar
2. In the **Tool** palette
3. The last place we used it

Q2. A Wacom Tablet is the only kind of tablet we can use with Manga Studio:

1. True
2. False

Q3. In Manga Studio, the **Default border (inner)** is what printers would refer to as the:

1. **Trim area**
2. **Bleed amount**
3. **Active area**
4. **Slip region**

Q4. A tablet is necessary to use Manga Studio.

1. True
2. False

Q5. The **Command** bar is where we can find:

1. A **Save** document button
2. A **New document** button
3. A **Clear layer** button
4. All of the above
5. None of the above

Summary

Quite the quick tour, wasn't it? We learned the basic requirements that our computer should have to run Manga Studio 5 with and we installed Manga Studio 5. We learned that the registration number should be copied and stored in a few places so we don't lose this very important number. Then we toured the interface of Manga Studio, created a document, and drew on it with a pencil tool. With a tablet, we learned how to set it up for use with Manga Studio. Then we ramped down a bit and worked on some sketches for further work in Manga Studio that we'll be using in the forthcoming chapters.

Once we finish with the plot for our story, we can set it aside for a bit and head on over to the next chapter where we'll have some more fun with page presets and drawing.

2
Messing Around with Manga Studio 5

In this chapter, we'll go through a more in-depth overview of Manga Studio 5's interface, tools, and file formats. By creating customized workspaces and key stroke commands, we will make it possible to spend more time drawing and less time wrangling with the interface.

In this chapter, we will cover the following topics:

- Creating a new page and page preset
- Using Pencil tools and modifying them for sketching
- Duplicating a tool and creating a new subtool group
- Creating new layers, drawing on them, and transferring contents to the layer below the current layer
- The different kinds of marking tools we have in Manga Studio
- Types of file formats we can import and export from Manga Studio

The dreaded blank page

Before we can draw our page, we need to have a document to put it in. This means we need to create a new preset for comic book pages. Since we've already gone through the process in the last chapter, we'll breeze through the process here. For more information on the **New document** dialog, please read the *Chapter 12, Along for the Ride*, which is an online chapter.

Time for action – making our comic book page preset

If we were doing a comic on bristol board and analog pencils, we would start out on an 11 x 17 inch sheet. Although we could do the same with Manga Studio, we would have to convert a lot of measurements from the 11 x 17 inch size to the printed size of a comic. There's a better way and it's drop-dead simple: create a new document to the size of a printed page, with all the borders where they need to be. The trick is to make the document 600 dpi (or higher). Most print shops or print-on-demand places require the files to be 300 dpi, so the only conversion we need to be concerned with is the reduction of the resolution; no worrying about reducing the art by 67 percent and adding bleed or whatever. The less we have to calculate, the less chance there is of a mistake being made. Let's make a preset now, shall we?

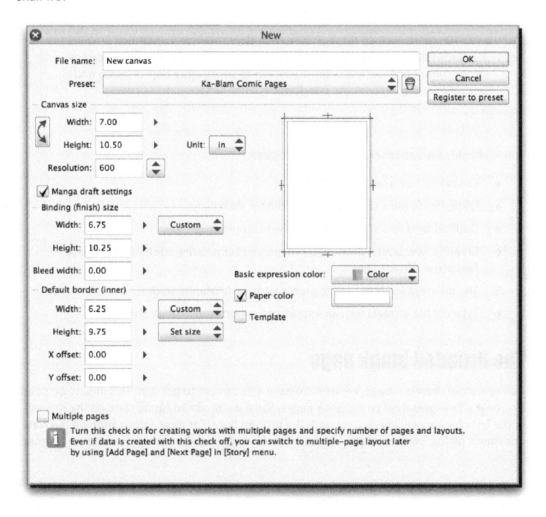

Perform the following steps to make our comic book page preset:

1. With Manga Studio running, click on the **New document** button in the command bar or go to **File | New**. The **New document** dialog appears.

2. Like in the previous chapter, we need to specify the dimensions of the canvas (or document).

3. Make sure Unit is set to **in** (inches).

4. Put 7.00 against **Width** and 10.50 against **Height**. This is the basic size of the untrimmed comic page.

5. Set **resolution** to 600 by using the drop-down menu, or just type in the value. If you enter 300, the pencils and other tools we'll be making through out this book will be huge; twice as large as needed. So, remember what your resolution for the file is (it'll be in the title bar of the document, by the way), and if it's not 600 dpi, you may want to adjust the size given accordingly.

6. Check the **Manga draft settings** checkbox. This allows us to set the borders below it.

7. As **Binding (finish) size**, enter 6.75 for **Width** and 10.25 for **Height**. This is our trim size; anything outside of this will be trimmed off in the printing process.

8. Make sure that the **Bleed width** is set at zero. This is a very fussy and unpredictable setting implemented by Manga Studio, and we don't really need it for this preset.

9. In **Default border (inner)**, set **Width** to 6.25 and **Height** to 9.75. If you don't see **Set size** (to the right of the **Height** entry, as shown in the previous screenshot), then click on this drop-down menu and select **Set size**.

10. **X offset** and **Y offset** should be zero.

11. Set the **Basic expression color** drop-down menu to **Color**.

12. Make sure that the **Paper color** is checked. It should default to white. If it isn't, click on the color swatch, and in the color chooser that appears, select white and click on **OK**.

13. Double-check the data. It should match with what's been entered in the image and in these steps.

14. Click on the **Register to preset** button.

15. In the dialog box that appears, name the preset as **Basic Comic Page**. The checkboxes for **Resolution**, **Paper color**, and **Default color expression** should be checked.

16. Click on **OK**.

17. Back in the **New** dialog box, the preset name should be visible in the drop-down menu. (In the previous screenshot, it says **Ka-Blam Comic Page**.)

18. Click on **OK**.

What just happened?

We just breezed through making a new preset. This preset will have all the borders we need to make most of every comic page we will work on. Although Manga Studio comes with many presets, mostly everyone is, sadly, not fit for western comics. This preset remedies that.

Making our marks

Manga Studio should be open, and we should also have a brand new document open using our spiffy new **Basic Comic Page** preset. The following is a screenshot of what should be on the left side of your monitor. There are callouts to areas that we'll be concerned with in this section. If what you see doesn't match with the following screenshot, we'll be sure to cover how to open and view each palette as we get to them:

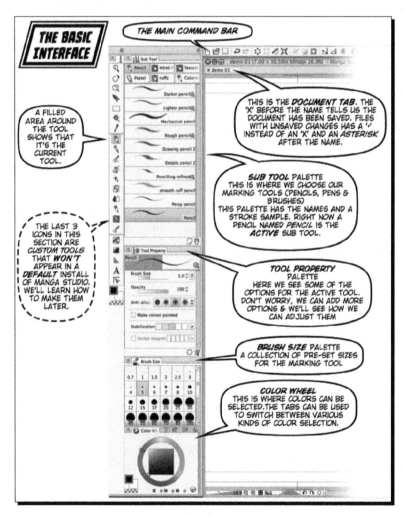

If we compare what you're seeing with the previous screenshot, we will find **Sub tool** tabs named **Sketch** and **MS4B**, which probably aren't on your screen. These tabs are created after installing Manga Studio. On your screen, the active tab and tool are highlighted with a bluish tint. This is a consistent interface feature of Manga Studio.

Manga Studio 5 allows us to customize the interface quite a bit. That's why, in some of the screenshots to follow, and for the rest of this book, the images are from my setup of Manga Studio 5. I've made a number of changes and additions to the interface, and these will be covered in the appropriate sections.

This is done to allow us to become comfortable with the basics of Manga Studio and not get too bogged down in details. We can (and will) learn how to make Manga Studio 5 work for us, rather than working for Manga Studio.

Right now, take a break. Put away this book and just doodle on your shiny new document. Use the pencil tool or any other tool. Just mess around. Notice what happens in the **Sub tool** palette and the **Tool** property palette when you click on a tool in the **Tool** palette. Have some fun, take as much time as you want. I'll be here when you're done. This is like breaking in a new pencil or brush. The more comfortable we are with our tools, the easier it will be to learn how to really use them.

Time for action - sketching and the digital environment

If we've set up our Wacom (or other manufacturer) tablet as shown in *Chapter 1, Installing and Setting Up Manga Studio 5*, we can refer to the cheat sheet (which you did make, right?) for shortcuts. If we're in a situation where using the buttons isn't possible, or if we're not using a tablet, we'll have one hand on the mouse and the other ready to perform keyboard shortcuts.

Although there is a tablet bias in this book, everything (save for pressure sensitivity) can be done with a mouse or a trackpad. If you're using a mouse or a trackpad, the terms stylus and cursor indicate the location of the mouse/trackpad input.

In this exercise, we'll be using any pencil to draw on the canvas, some keyboard shortcuts to zoom in and out, and transparency to erase. The following is a quick little exercise to get us familiar with drawing in Manga Studio and using shortcuts and layer commands:

1. Manga Studio should be open and a new document created. The new document should have a paper layer (if we're using a template we created, it will be the default).

2. Look at the **Layer** palette. It has two layers: **Paper** and **Layer 1**. The **Paper** layer is a special layer; it's there to give our canvas a color. It's handy to have, as we don't have to stare at the checkerboard pattern that indicates transparency. **Layer 1** should have a blue tint to indicate it's the current layer.

3. Choose a pencil from the **Tool** palette.

4. In the **Sub tool** palette, choose any pencil.

5. Draw a rough figure or face. Don't get into details.

6. Once we're happy with the rough sketch, go to the **Layer** palette and set the **Opacity** of the layer down to 30-40 percent. Our sketch should be greyed out.

7. On the bottom of the layer palette, there's a series of buttons that look like dog-eared pages. Hover the cursor over the first one. The tooltip should read **New Raster Layer**. Click on the icon.

8. A new **Layer** is created.

9. Use the same pencil or pick another one. If the size of the tool is too large, go into the **Brush size** palette and click on a smaller size.

10. Add details on the new layer. If there's hair, don't draw it now.

11. Create another layer and add hair details on that layer. This new layer should be automatically named **Layer 3**.

12. *Alt/Command + =* and *Alt/Command + –* will zoom in and out of our canvas, respectively, in steps that are mentioned in the **Preferences** dialog box under the **Canvas** category. *Alt/Command + 0* (zero) will fit the canvas to our view, so we can see the entire document at once.

13. Pressing the spacebar by itself will allow us to move our view around when zoomed in, and spacebar + *Shift* will allow us to rotate our view so we can turn the paper (so to speak) to a better angle for drawing. Try holding down the spacebar and pressing the *Alt* or *Ctrl* keys (Windows) or *Command* or *Option* keys (Mac OS) to see how to get the zoom in/out keys for as long as the keys are pressed.

14. When we're finished with the hair, we will go to the **Layer** palette and right-click on the layer with the hair (it should be named **Layer 3**).

15. The contextual menu that pops up has a number of menu items. We're interested in two of them, **Transfer to Lower Layer** and **Merge with Lower Layer**:

- ❑ **Transfer to Lower Layer** will send the contents of the current layer to the layer directly below. This will leave the current layer empty.

- ❑ **Merge with Lower Layer** will combine the contents of the current layer with the layer directly below, making the combined layer the active one.

16. Select **Merge with Lower Layer**.

17. Notice how we no longer have a **Layer 3** in the **Layer** palette, but **Layer 2** has all the drawings we did on **Layer 3** added to it. **Transfer** and **Merge** are handy to use if we want to try something out but don't want to mess up an existing drawing.

18. Continue drawing the details. Instead of using the eraser, try changing the current color to transparency. At the bottom of the toolbar, there are color options for the main, sub, and transparency swatches. Click on the transparency swatch (it's the one with the checkerboard pattern in it). Now use the pencil as an eraser. It behaves just like the previous pencil did, except that it draws with transparency instead of a visible color. This is a great way to add detail in shadowed areas.

What just happened?

We're getting used to working digitally and making the most of this virtual environment. We used one layer for our rough sketch and made a new layer for refining and adding details. We then created another layer to experiment with hair and combined it with the layer below. We also used the view shortcuts to zoom in and out and to rotate and change our view of the document. We'll be refining this process as we go along, but nothing beats practice.

The marking tools

To make things a bit clearer, we'll call the tools that we use for penciling, inking, and coloring marking tools, because they have a number of behaviors and settings in common. When we're talking about settings specific to a type of tool, we'll call it by name.

The following screenshot shows the marking tools with arrows pointing to the specific **Sub tool** tabs that appear in the **Sub tool** palette:

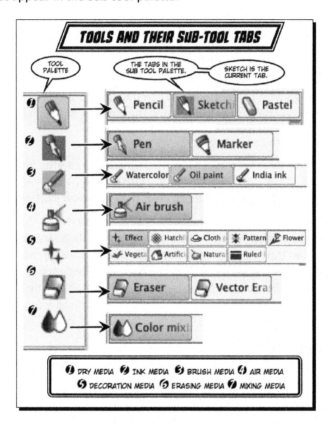

The icons on the tool palette are dynamic; they change according to either the current tool or the last tool used. Notice that the second icon (if we're looking at the color image from the ZIP file) has magenta as its background color. These colors are the colors that were chosen for the icon when a custom tool was created. The positions of the icons are consistent. From top to bottom, they are:

- **Dry media**: As we can see from the **Sub tool** palette, the tabs have **Pencil**, **Sketch**, and **Pastel** tools (note that the **Sketch** tab is a custom tab). When the cursor hovers over this icon's place, the tooltip reads **Pencil(P)**. No matter what tool is selected, this tooltip will always read the same. This is very helpful as we artists are visually oriented; even though the icon for the tool may change, its name remains the same. The letter within the parentheses is the single key shortcut to the tool. In this case, it's a *P*. Even though it's a shortcut that's shared with the Ink Media tools, just press the *P* key again (or a few times) and the Ink Media tool will be selected.

- **Ink media**: Here is where the various **Pen** and **Marker** tools are found. The tooltip reads **Pen(P)**.

- **Brush media**: We'll use these for coloring. The tabs are **Watercolor**, **Oil paint**, and **India ink**. The tooltip reads **Brush(B)**.

- **Spray media**: This only has an air brush in the **Sub tool** tab. It's so lonely. The tooltip reads **Air brush(B)**.

- **Decoration media**: As we can see, there's a wide assortment of different categories in this tool. This tool creates ribbons or swaths of patterns, both colored and greyscale (black and white). This tool can be used to create borders and shading patterns. We'll look at this tool more closely in the **Inking** section. The tooltip reads **Decoration(B)**.

- **Erasing media**: The sub tools are regular and vector erasers. As the saying goes, these tools are for a second chance at perfection. The tooltip reads **Eraser(E)**.

- **Color Mixing media**: This is used to sharpen, blur, or blend colors. It is very useful for coloring. The tooltip reads **Color Mixing(J)**.

Think of the **Tool** palette as a shelf for all your drawing tools and the **Sub tool** palette as compartments in the shelf. Similar tools are grouped together. If the grouping doesn't make sense to you, they can be changed, deleted, and new ones created. Let's do that to the Dry Media shelf now.

Inside a marking tool

Select the **Pencil** tool from the **Tool** palette. In the **Sub tool** palette, click on the **Pencil** tab. There's a list below the tab; these are the various pencils that have been made for us to use. Choose any one of them. Now look at the **Tool Property** palette. This is where we see some of the settings we can apply to the **Pencil** tab. There are more settings; click on the icon that looks like a wrench to see them, and the **Sub tool** detail palette window will open. The following screenshot shows these palettes with descriptions and some of the special icons in them:

On the **Tool Property** palette, click on the wrench icon visible in the lower-right corner of the palette. This brings up the **Tool Settings** floating palette. It's a floating palette because it cannot be docked with the other palettes. Generally, we'll only have this palette open when we're creating and drastically altering settings.

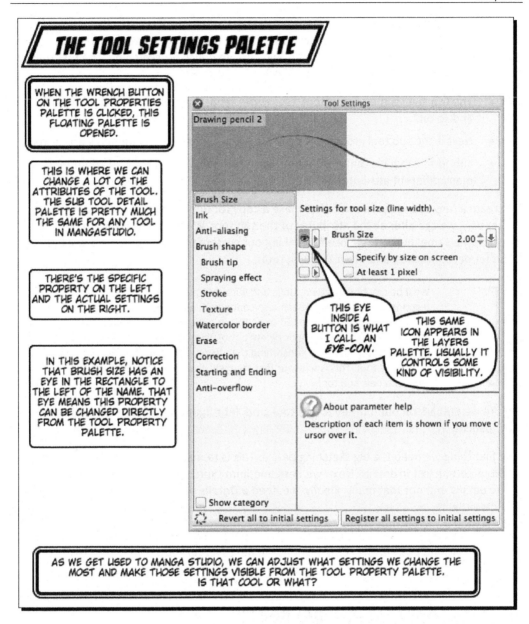

THE TOOL SETTINGS PALETTE

WHEN THE WRENCH BUTTON ON THE TOOL PROPERTIES PALETTE IS CLICKED, THIS FLOATING PALETTE IS OPENED.

THIS IS WHERE WE CAN CHANGE A LOT OF THE ATTRIBUTES OF THE TOOL. THE SUB TOOL DETAIL PALETTE IS PRETTY MUCH THE SAME FOR ANY TOOL IN MANGASTUDIO.

THERE'S THE SPECIFIC PROPERTY ON THE LEFT AND THE ACTUAL SETTINGS ON THE RIGHT.

IN THIS EXAMPLE, NOTICE THAT BRUSH SIZE HAS AN EYE IN THE RECTANGLE TO THE LEFT OF THE NAME. THAT EYE MEANS THIS PROPERTY CAN BE CHANGED DIRECTLY FROM THE TOOL PROPERTY PALETTE.

Tool Settings

Drawing pencil 2

Brush Size
Ink
Anti-aliasing
Brush shape
  Brush tip
  Spraying effect
Stroke
Texture
Watercolor border
Erase
Correction
Starting and Ending
Anti-overflow

Settings for tool size (line width).

Brush Size   2.00
Specify by size on screen
At least 1 pixel

THIS EYE INSIDE A BUTTON IS WHAT I CALL AN *EYE-CON*.

THIS SAME ICON APPEARS IN THE LAYERS PALETTE. USUALLY IT CONTROLS SOME KIND OF VISIBILITY.

About parameter help

Description of each item is shown if you move cursor over it.

Show category

Revert all to initial settings   Register all settings to initial settings

AS WE GET USED TO MANGA STUDIO, WE CAN ADJUST WHAT SETTINGS WE CHANGE THE MOST AND MAKE THOSE SETTINGS VISIBLE FROM THE TOOL PROPERTY PALETTE. IS THAT COOL OR WHAT?

What we're going to do is create a few customized pencils for sketching and drawing. First we need to know the variations we have at our disposal, and then we can alter them to fit our needs.

The **Pencil** tool should be selected by default; if not, choose any **Pencil** tool. In the **Tool Property** palette, click on the wrench icon to bring up the **Sub tool settings** palette. We can keep this palette open while we make our own custom pencil for sketching. The first thing we need to understand is how Manga Studio "looks" at tools:

- The top level is the type of tool. Like we've seen, they're Dry Media, Ink Media, and so on.
- Next is the sub tool groups or tabs. This is where the specific sub tools are stored.
- Sub tools can have their own name, icon, and background color, in addition to many different attributes.

To create a new sub tool, we can either make a copy (or duplicate) or create a new one. Either way, we can alter all the attributes of the sub tool. We are going in-depth here because the same methods we use for making our custom pencils can be (and will be) used for pens, brushes, and other marking tools.

We'll be creating our own tools, and with that great power comes great responsibility, because we can also change or delete tools. It can't be stressed enough that we need to do this in a measured and deliberate manner. Never ever create or delete a tool when in a hurry. Nothing is more annoying and time consuming than to recreate a mistakenly changed or deleted tool. This is why our first step will always be to create either a copy or a new sub tool.

Before we embark on our journey to sub tool land, let's figure out what we want in our new pencils.

The first thing we need is a big sketching pencil. This is to make it easier to rough in drawings without getting lost in details. Next, we need medium sketch pencils that will allow us to get a few details, but not that many. Finally, we need a **Details pencil**, which we'll use to add all our details with.

To create a new pencil sub tool, make sure that a pencil sub tool is selected. Then, click on the **Palette Menu** button. The screenshot in the next section shows what you should do and what you'll end up with.

Creating our first custom pencil

The following screenshot gives us an idea of the basic steps we'll be going through in detail in this exercise:

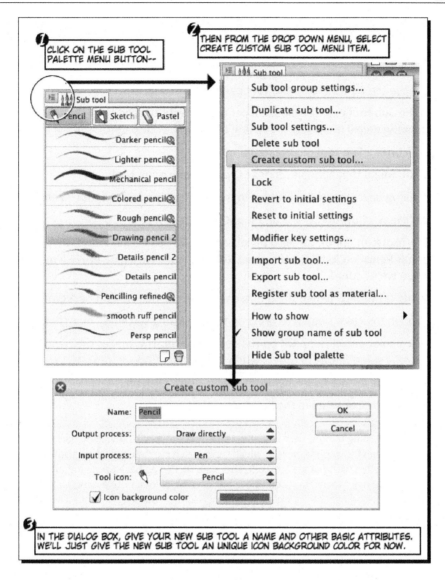

In the next few *Time for action* sections, we'll create a new pencil, modify it for our needs, and learn how to use it for creating rough sketches in our character sheet.

Creating our custom marking tool

It's always a good idea to keep originals untouched and make copies to change. Our steps here will be to duplicate an existing tool and then modify its attributes.

Time for action - duplicating an existing tool

Perform the following steps to create a duplicate copy of an existing tool:

1. Choose the pencil tool in the **Tool** palette.

2. In the **Sub tool** palette, choose a pencil you want to modify. In this exercise, the **Drawing pencil** is chosen. If you don't have it in your palette, choose any pencil.

3. Click on the **Sub tool** palette menu button.

4. In the menu that appears, choose **Create custom sub tool**.

5. A dialog box appears; we'll enter in the name of the custom tool, **Sketching Large**.

6. We'll leave **Output process** and **Input process** alone.

7. The **Tool icon** option can also be left alone. We can click on the drop-down menu (it has **Pencil** on it) to see the other kinds of icons we can use. We'll reselect **Pencil** when we're done.

8. To make our new pencil stand out, check the box before **Icon background color**.

9. Click on the color swatch to bring up the operating system's color chooser.

10. Pick a color and click on **OK** on the color chooser. This makes the pencil we're creating stand out from others when selected.

11. Back in the **Create Custom Sub Tool** dialog box, click on **OK**.

12. The new tool appears in the **Sub tool** palette.

One thing to note here is that we gave the sub tool its own icon background color. This is so we can see which tools we've created and which tools were installed with Manga Studio 5. This way, we can go back to the default tools if we need to, as they don't have background colors. I use a rainbow kind of color-coding. Cool colors (blue, green, and blue-purples) indicate a new pencil tool, one where the attributes are changed greatly. Warm colors (reds, oranges, yellows) are for pencils that are slightly modified (smaller brush size, different texture, and so on) from the parent tool. Always use the name of the tool to be very clear. For example, a copy of Sketching Large could be Sketching Med; its only change would be that the brush size is reduced.

When we click on the checkbox next to **Icon background color** and then click on the color swatch, we'll get a color chooser. Windows users will see the color chooser they are familiar with. Mac users will see theirs.

What just happened?

In our first step in creating a new custom pencil tool, we duplicated an existing tool. This is a crucial step, as we should always make changes to a duplicate of a tool. This way, we can have the original to go back to and still have a tool with the changes available to be used. We also used a color for the background of the tool's icon to give us a visual clue that this is one of our new tools.

Time for action – modifying the new Sketching Large pencil

Now, it's time to adjust the settings to get the look of this new pencil the way we want it to be, as shown in the following screenshot:

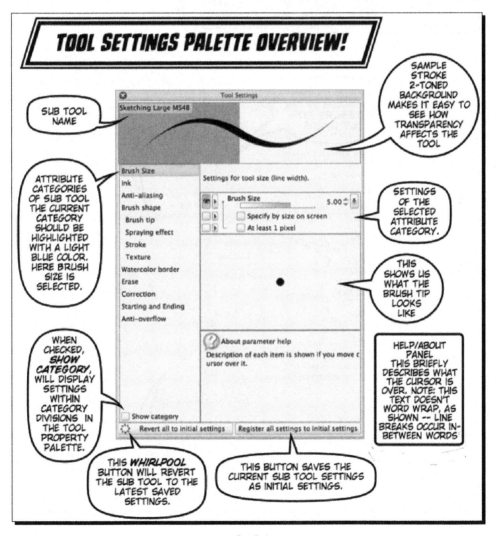

The previous screenshot shows the **Tool Settings** palette. This is where we change the tool's attributes, revert to what was saved as the initial settings, or save the current settings as the initial settings for the current tool.

This is a floating palette, so it can be kept open while we draw on the canvas. Right now, let's make changes so this pencil is a real **Sketching Large** pencil! Perform the following steps to modify the new Sketching Large pencil:

1. Click on the **Brush Size** category.
2. Set the brush size to large. In our example, it is set to **8**.

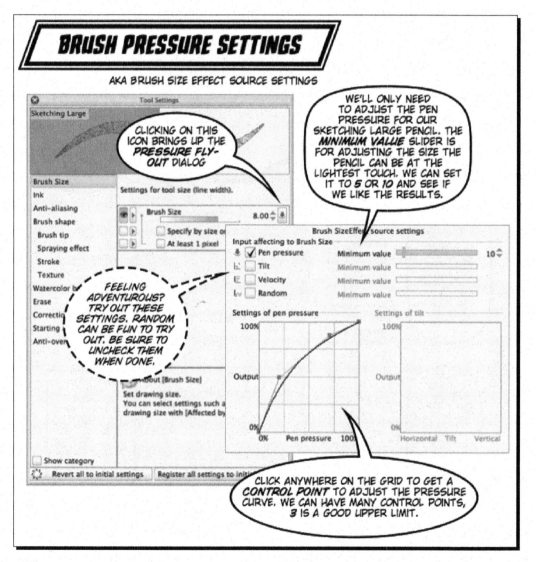

3. As the previous screenshot shows, click on the icon for the **Effect source settings** (**Pen pressure**) fly-out menu.

4. Check the checkbox for **Effect source settings (Pen pressure)**.

5. We want a curve like the one shown in the screenshot. To get a control point near the bottom end of the line, click on the line and drag the cursor up.

6. Towards the top end of the line, click-and-drag upwards.

7. To adjust the points, hover the mouse over them until the squares turn red. Click-and-drag them so there's a curve, as is shown in the next screenshot.

8. In the **Pen pressure** fly-out menu, set **Minimum value** to **10** by clicking on **0** and typing in **10**. The **Minimum value** option controls the pen pressure when the pressure sensitivity begins. The higher the number, the less the effect pressure sensitivity has on, in this case, the pencil size. This is similar to drawing with a slightly dull pencil.

9. Click on the **Tool Settings** palette to dismiss the fly-out menu.

10. Click on the **Ink** category.

11. Set **Opacity** to **65** by clicking on the number **100** and typing in **65**.

12. The next few steps will simulate pencil marks on a rough paper. Feel free to experiment with the settings.

13. Click on the **Spraying effect** category.

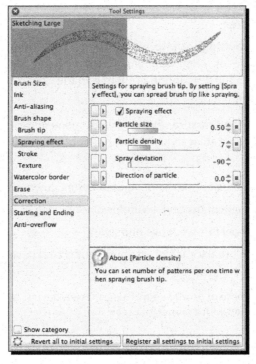

14. Check the **Spraying effect** checkbox.

15. Set **Particle size** to **0.50**, like we did for **Opacity** and **Brush size**.

16. Set **Particle density** to **7**.

17. Set **Spray deviation** to **-90**. You may have to enter the negative sign after typing in **90**.

18. Click on **Register all settings to initial settings** so that this sub tool will be saved as it is now. We'll be asked to confirm if we want to overwrite the current initial settings. We do; this is a copy of the original so it's all cool.

19. Move the **Sub tool** palette so that a larger part of the canvas (the page we will be drawing on) is visible. You can use the grabber hand to move the canvas over if needed.

Don't forget that if your tool works in an unexpected way, click on the whirlpool button to restore the brush to its previous state. Sure, the settings will have to be redone, but sometimes it's better to start with a blank page than to work with something that's not right at all. Reverting to the initial settings button (the whirlpool icon) is a great way to experiment with the many different settings that all tools have. We can always revert to the tool's original state by clicking on the whirlpool button. Just don't save the settings by clicking on **Register all to initial settings** by accident. There is no undo for that. This is why the exercises always have us start out by making a copy of a tool, just so that we can recover from an accident.

What just happened?

Going through the **Brush Settings** palette, we adjusted a few settings and made a custom pencil tool that we can use for rough sketching. There are many categories and settings we didn't touch on here; a full description of them is in the *Chapter 12, Along for the Ride*, which is an online chapter.

First though, let's look at the **Pressure settings** fly-out menu in a bit more detail. These settings allow us to have our tablet stylus' pressure affect the line being drawn. The pressure settings are:

◆ **Pressure**: This relates to how hard we are bearing down with our stylus

◆ **Tilt**: This is the angle of our stylus when we're drawing

◆ **Velocity**: This is how fast we move our stylus

◆ **Random**: This isn't really a tablet attribute, but is cool nevertheless

 For those of us who aren't using a tablet, the last two settings can be used with a mouse/trackpad.

The button that controls these attributes is usually on the immediate right of the setting. Manga Studio calls this button **Effect source settings**. We can think of this button as **Tablet setting**. The tablet attributes live in the fly-out menu that appears when we click on this button. We can have just one or any number of them active.

The little icon in this button may change to reflect what attributes are selected, so remember its placement in the palette.

The way **Pen Pressure** works in this exercise means it'll take just a bit of pressure to get the pen to full width (this is the brush size category), and as pressure increases, the width will grow more slowly. The reason why we're using this kind of curve rather than the one for the **Sketching Large** pencil is so we can do lots of detailing with a slower moving pencil that requires less pressure to get a clean, thicker line. We don't want to spend hours adding detail and having to press insanely hard on our pens now do we?

Drawing with our new pencil tool

We are leaving the **Sub tool detail** palette open so we can adjust the pencil's settings as we draw. Since we all draw differently (thankfully!), we all need different things from our tools. Once we get a good collection of customized sub tools, we'll only use this palette when we make new sub tools.

If we do create new settings that we really like but don't want to overwrite our existing sub tool, all we have to do is go to the **Sub tool** palette menu and choose **Duplicate sub tool**, like we did at the beginning. Then, give this duplicate a unique name and icon background color. Don't forget to register the settings of this new sub tool so the current settings become the initial ones.

We should still have our character sheet open; for the moment, we'll let that be our scratch paper to test out our new pencils. If your screen is filled up completely with the document, go to the **View** menu and choose the **Fit to Screen** menu item. Our zoom level should be somewhere between 10 and 20 percent (depending on the size and resolution of our monitor). If your pencil is still too large, make the size smaller, and be sure to save the settings.

One of the things to think about when creating art on a digital platform is that it is so very easy to get lost in details that the drawing itself loses some of its life. We'll do our best to avoid that by having a large pencil and zooming in the document to fit the screen of our monitor.

When I was starting out with digital art, it was disappointing to see that my sketches had lost something when done via a tablet and stylus rather than through pen and paper. Then, realization dawned that it wasn't so much the tools that were being used, but how they were used; I had been drawing like I would on paper; I didn't take into account that this was a new media and like using a new drawing tool, I had to get used to it.

Too much of the focus of drawing was devoted to the end result and not to the beginning sketches. It's those rough sketches that had the life that the detailing drained. I struggled with that for some time until I realized that it was the size of paper I was drawing on that helped to give the sketches the spontaneity that gave them life. Simply put, I was drawing too big on the monitor/tablet and got way too fussy in my line work. I solved this by zooming in to fit and by making special sketching pencils with large tips. This method works for me, and I hope for you too.

In Manga Studio, go to the **View** menu and select the **Whole Size** menu item. The shortcut for this is *Command/Alt + 0* (zero key). This is a good key combo to remember and use often. The analog to this is to step back from your drawing and look at all of it in one glance. This helps us to see how the composition is working and any glaring mistakes that sometimes creep into the drawings.

If we've been doodling on the open document (I do it all the time), the canvas is kind of all filled with scribbles and such. There's a quick way to clear the current layer. It's a button on the toolbar; the one that looks like a starburst.

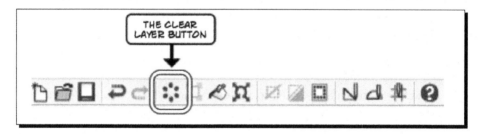

In the previous screenshot, the button that looks like a starburst (labeled **THE CLEAR LAYER BUTTON** on that icon) will clear everything from the current layer. This is what we call a destructive action, although we can undo it; it's an all-or-nothing action. For our needs, it serves us well. Click on it, and now we can proceed.

 One nice thing about Manga Studio is the consistency that it has about icons. This starburst icon will clear not only what's on the layer, but as we will learn, it will also clear the rotation of the canvas and tool settings. In fact, if you see that icon (or one like a whirlpool) anywhere, assume that it will clear/restore whatever you're doing at that moment.

The settings for the **Sketching Large** pencil are just a starting point. Play around with the assorted categories and their settings until you get something that feels right for you. Remember these settings; when changing them, go for extremes, and then settle for smaller changes. This is a good thing to experiment with, especially when there are a lot of variables to contend with.

When messing around with this new pencil, notice how it behaves kind of like a real pencil. If you go over lines, they become darker. Overlapping lines are darker where they overlap.

Give yourself a break now. Stretch your legs and do some finger exercises. Work on using this rough pencil for a while. Next up, the other two pencils: the Sketching Medium and Detailing pencil.

Duplicating sub tools

Now that we've used our new pencil tool for a while and, hopefully, adjusted it to suit our individual tastes, it's time to learn how we can save our tool and create new ones based on it.

Differences between Revert and Register

If Manga Studio isn't running, start it up and create a new document or open the character sheet document we've been using as our scratch paper so far in this chapter. Let's look at the **Tool Property** palette and see what we can do with it.

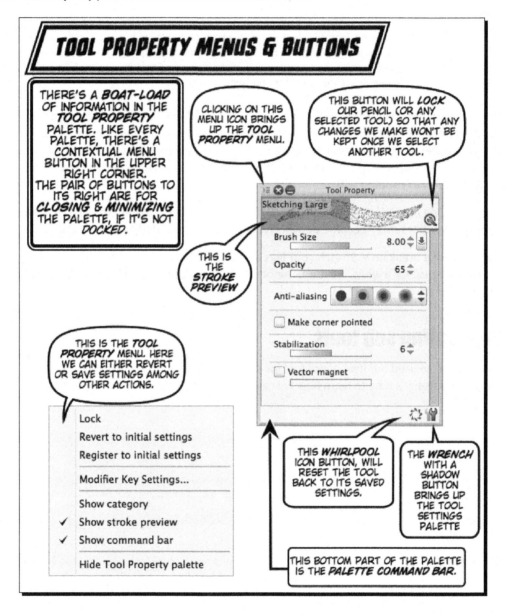

As with all other palettes in Manga Studio 5, in the upper-right side is the palette drop-down contextual menu button (we'll just call it the **Palette menu** button from here on). For the **Tool property** palette, there are just two menu items we're interested in:

♦ **Revert to initial settings**

♦ **Register to initial settings**

We're going to select each of these menu items and look at their respective dialog boxes. Be careful not to click on the **OK** button; this is just informational, so we will click on the **Cancel** button:

1. On the **Tool property** palette, click on the **Palette** menu button.

2. In the menu that appears, select the **Revert to Initial Settings** menu item.

3. The dialog box that appears has the text **Revert to initial settings of content of selected sub tool. Do you want to proceed?**.

4. What this dialog is trying to ask is **Do you want to discard all the changes you made and revert the sub tool to its previous initial settings?**.

5. Click on **Cancel**.

6. Go back to the palette menu and choose **Register to initial settings**.

7. The dialog that comes up says **Overwrite initial settings of selected sub tool with current content. Do you want to proceed?**. What it means to say is: do you want to overwrite the initial settings of the selected sub tool with the current settings?

8. Click on **Cancel**.

The main thing we should take away from this is that when we're saving or reverting a tool, we need to take our time and look at the dialog boxes closely. I've lost many tools because I didn't take my time and just clicked without looking at the dialog box.

The short version of this would be to **Revert** to go back to the saved settings and **Reset** to save new settings.

Time for action – duplicating a subtool for our second pencil

What do we do in those instances where a tool almost does what we want it to and we don't want to change the original tool? Easy, we make a copy. In this *Time for action* section, we'll create a new tool and then alter it so that it does what we want it to do. Perform the following steps to duplicate a sub tool for our second pencil:

1. Select the **Sketching Large** pencil we just created.

2. In the **Sub tool** palette, click on the **Palette Menu** button.

3. Choose the **Duplicate tool** menu item.

4. A dialog box named **Duplicate sub tool** appears.

5. In the name textbox, change **Sketching Large 2** to **Sketching Med**.

6. The icon background color checkbox is checked. Click on the color swatch. In the color chooser, select a darker color. Click on **OK** on the color chooser dialog. Double-check the information in the **Duplicate Sub tool** dialog box. Make any changes, if needed. Click on **OK**.

7. In the **Tool Properties** palette, change the size from **8** to a smaller number between **3** and **5**. Take a few moments and test the new size on the open document. What we want here is a finer tip so we can add a bit of detail, but not too much.

8. If the results are not acceptable, go to the spray settings and turn them off to see if that improves things.

9. When we are happy with the results, go to the **Tool Property** palette, click on the **Palette Menu** button, and choose the **Register to Initial Settings** menu item to make the new settings the initial (or default) settings.

What just happened?

We created a duplicate of an existing pencil so we can freely make changes without losing any default or other customized pencils.

Now we're going to create what we can call a **Details Pencil**. Think of it like a digital version of a 0.5 mm mechanical pencil.

Creating a details pencil

Like we've done a few times already, let's take a few moments to consider what we want in a details pencil:

◆   This pencil will need to be responsive to pressure.

◆   It can have variable opacity; more transparency when pressing lightly, and more opaqueness when pressing harder. That'll simulate how a real pencil works.

◆   Since we're in the digital realm, we can add some things that aren't in the real world, such as adjusting the thickness of the pencil according to pressure.

◆   We also want to have the line this pencil makes to be sharp, therefore easy on the anti-aliasing.

Take your time doing the following exercise. Play around with the settings and experiment with those that aren't mentioned. This is where we really learn what Manga Studio can do. It's a wild and wonderful thing to go down a path and come up with something totally unexpected and cool. You can always discard the changes by using the **Revert to initial settings** button (on the **Sub tool settings** palette) or menu command if things get really whacked out.

Time for action – making a detail pencil, our third pencil

We will create a custom pencil that should be good for us to use to add lots of details to our rough drawing. As in the previous exercises, we'll be doing a bit of work in the **Sub tool detail** palette. The following screenshot is an overview of the palette and the categories we'll be having some fun in:

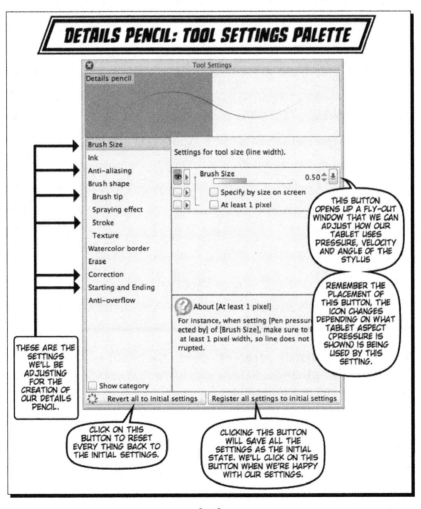

1. Go to the **Sub tool** palette and click on the palette menu button.

2. Choose the **Create Custom Sub tool** menu item.

3. In the dialog box, name this new tool **Details Pencil**. Give the icon background a grey color (or whatever color you want to).

4. Click on **OK** and make sure the new tool is selected; then, click on the **Tool Settings** button, the one with the wrench with a shadow. This is a toggle button; if the palette is opened when this button is clicked on, then the palette will close.

5. Click on the **Brush Size** category. Set the **Brush size** to **5**.

6. Click on the **Effect Source settings** button.

7. We want a sharper curve than in the **Sketching Large** pencil. This is shown in the next screenshot. Remember that when the control points turn **red**, we can click-and-drag them around.

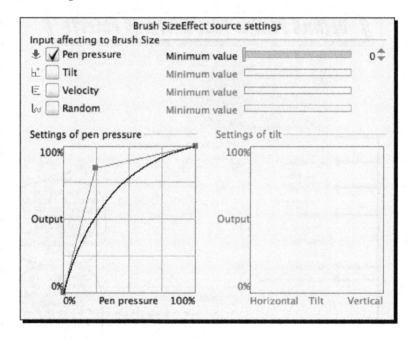

8. Click on the **Anti-Aliasing** category to dismiss the fly-out menu. Click on the up and down pointing triangles to bring up a menu so we can see the icon and names for the anti-aliasing settings.

9. Select **Weak** from the choices.

10. Click on the **Brush Tip** category. In **Tip Shape**, choose **circle**.

11. Set **Hardness** to **40**.

12. Set **Direction** to **5.0**.

13. Set **Brush density** to **80**.

14. Check the **Adjust brush density by space** checkbox.

15. Click on the **Correction** category. Set **Stabilizing** to **4**.

16. Set **Brush Stroke** to **2**.

17. Check the **Able to Snap** checkbox.

18. Click on the **Starting and Ending** category. In **Methods**, choose **By length** from the drop-down menu.

19. Check the **Starting** checkbox

20. Set the value of **Starting** to **20**.

21. Check the **Ending** checkbox.

22. Set the value of **Ending** to **20**.

23. Check the **Starting and ending by speed** checkbox.

24. In the **Sub Tool Detail** palette, click on the **Register all settings to initial** once to save our new brush.

What just happened?

We modified our rough sketching pencil to be a bit more refined and then made a final custom pencil that we could use to add details and fine line work to our drawings. We adjusted a number of settings in various tool categories. By having a clear idea of what we wanted before we started adjusting things, we made things easy for ourselves.

What about the brush category settings?

There are 13 categories in the **Tool Settings** palette. Each of these categories has its own settings. In order to keep things somewhat orderly, information is provided in the *Chapter 12, Along for the Ride*, which is an online chapter. In the online chapter is a listing of all the categories and settings for all tools, pencils, and brushes. This is intended to be a reference, and while not needed for this book, because we'll cover them as we need to, it's something that should be very handy in case you're creating your own customized tools.

If there's a setting that we're not sure about, we'll just hover our cursor/ stylus over it; in **About Parameter Help**, we will get a brief description that will, hopefully, make it clear what the setting does. If not, change it and see what it does on a doodle on the open document.

Making a custom sub group

Now that we've created three custom pencils (the Sketching Large, Sketching Med, and Detail pencil), why don't we create a group for them? That way, we can easily go to them and not waste time scrolling through a list containing dozens of tools to find the one we need.

There's no menu command to create a sub tool group. The only way to create one is to first drag a tool up to the tab group area at the top part of the **Sub tool** palette. The new group will be named for the tool. Since we'll be creating one for our sketching pencils, the new group will be named **Pencil** and will have the icon background color we choose for that sub tool. You can always change the icon background color by right-clicking on the sub tool and choosing **Sub tool settings** from the contextual menu.

Unlike most of the *Time for action* sections here, this one demands an almost visual step-by–step description, since there's a lot of dragging-and-selecting going on.

If we followed the steps from the screenshot, we should have made a custom group for our new pencils. This method works with any of the sub tools. Try to keep the names for each group meaningful and short. Remember that if you delete a group, the tools within it also get deleted.

It's very important to keep in mind that these steps are not undoable. They are permanent; at least until the developers change it. So be careful. If we accidentally drop a tool into the wrong tab, we can go to that tab and select the misplaced tool and drag it to the correct tab. If we delete a tool, it's gone. Be careful about using the Backspace or Delete keys when moving brushes around. That is, don't touch these keys!

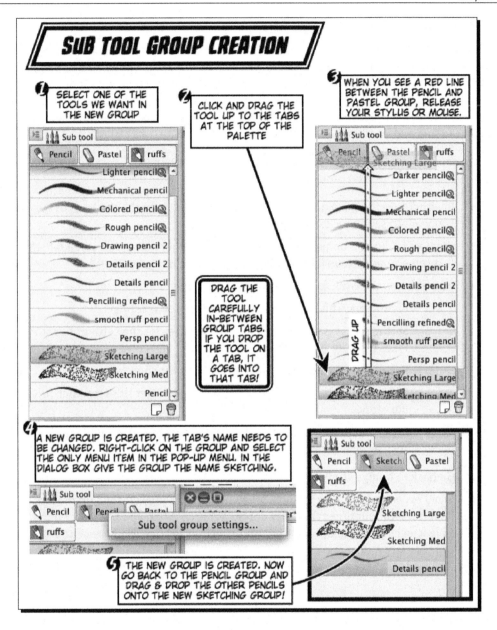

Now that we've created a page template, made a new document, and made some customized tools, the next step is to save files and create homes for them to reside in.

Making folders and saving files

Before we get into drawing and losing track of time, let's save our files. One of the things that can come back to mess us up is where we save files. We want to be able to find them quickly and get on with the drawing. Like most things digital, the time we spend preparing things will save us more time than it takes. Although at first the time it takes will be more than a moment, it will become second nature to us, will give us peace of mind, and will allow us to find and back up files easily.

Most creative comic/Manga artists have a multitude of ideas they're working on at any one time. Let's make things a bit orderly:

♦ In either Windows Explorer or the Mac OS's Finder, go to the top level of the drive you want to save your exercises in.

♦ Create a folder and name it MS4B work, or any other name that you'll remember. Just remember that we'll be calling it MS4B work in this book.

♦ Inside the MS4B Work folder, create a set of folders:

  ❑ **Characters**: This is where we'll put our character sheets.

  ❑ **Settings**: This is where we'll put the sketches for the settings our story takes place in.

  ❑ **Pages**: This is where we'll save the art for our comic story.

  ❑ **Reference**: This is where we'll put pictures we get from research for our story.

  ❑ **Exported Stuffings**: A catch-all for things we export from Manga Studio, such as pages, character sheets, and so on.

♦ Go back to Manga Studio.

♦ In my experience, Manga Studio 5 is very robust; it's only crashed on me less than three or four times. You may not be as lucky. When you first click on the **Save** icon in the toolbar, you'll see this dialog box (or one like it, depending on your operating system):

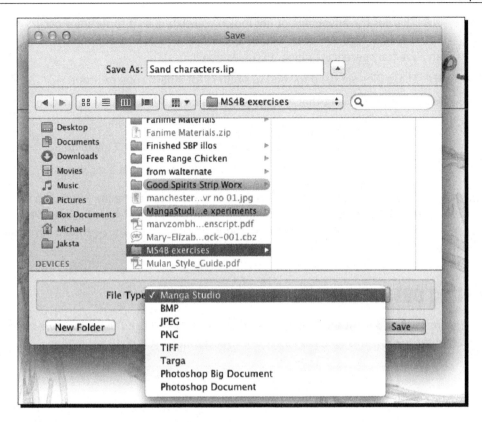

Most times we'll save our files as a native Manga Studio (`.lip`) file. There are other file formats as we can see:

- ◆ **BMP**: This is not really used much outside of Windows. If we're posting artwork on the Web for others to see, don't use this format, as it results in large file sizes, and a good number of people online won't be able to see the file. Basically, BMP is not really needed, since the formats that follow do a much better job at preserving the image and compressing it for speedy transfers.

- ◆ **JPEG**: This is used to export and share your work on the Internet. We can choose how much compression these files have; it's the standard for photographs and photorealistic art.

- ◆ **PNG**: This has the advantage of not looking pixelated, as it sometimes occurs with JPEG files with high compression. PNG files can have an alpha channel (that is, they can have transparency), which JPEG files don't.

- ◆ **TIFF**: These files are used to send to printers for a hard copy printout.

- ◆ **Targa**: This format isn't that widely used outside of a few 3D and animation programs, such as:

  - ❏ The regular Photoshop Document is for files under 2 gigabytes
  - ❏ The Photoshop Big Document is for files larger than 2 gigabytes

In the top of the dialog box, type in a descriptive name for your character sheet. I'm working on a series titled "Sentinels of Sand", so calling it "Sand Characters" makes sense to me. Navigate to where your MS4B Work folder is and go into the Character folder. Save your file in there.

Testing out the pencils

Here's what my first pass at roughing in a character looks like. I used the pencils we created in this chapter to draw this on a page that uses the character template we made:

It's very rough and gives just a hint of clothing and body form. As we can see, the top part of the sheet is used to contain the character's name and the (misspelled) story title. There's even a blocked-off area in the lower left where biographical information can be put. There's a three-fourth front view and a smaller rear view of the character, so the costuming can be figured out. There are two more-or-less neutral faces of the character. Character sheets are very important when first creating a story. This is where we get comfortable with the character instead of figuring out what they look like on the fly while drawing the story itself. We may find out that in the process of creating multiple character sheets, an idea occurs to us, and since it's character sheets, we have the luxury of going back and adding in that idea to older sheets or even the script itself.

In animation, there's something called off-model; this means when a character is drawn differently in some frames when compared to other frames. Comics, especially cartoony ones, can be considered to use visual shorthand. This means that every single line has to count. The more characters we have figured out visually, the more consistent they will look from panel to panel and from page to page. It's okay to figure out better ways to draw them, or even different ways to render them. That's growth, and if it's intentional, readers will pick up on it and go with you. If it's nothing but accidents, we could disturb the reader and could lose them.

We can now create new page templates, new documents, and pencils. We even know a bit about changing the interface of Manga Studio. If there's a section that stumps you, that's fine. Manga Studio is what we can call a deep application in the sense that a lot of the power it has is buried under the surface. The rivers of Manga Studio may be deep, but its waters are refreshing. So we'll keep wading into it, and soon we'll be swimming.

So, if we've been following the exercises here, in addition to the new page template and marking tools, we have a basic story we want to tell and some characters that are in that story.

Now, we'll draw them using the character template with our sketching pencils and detailing pencil.

If you're using a tablet stylus with an eraser tip, it should always use the last-used eraser. So if you're doing rough sketching, use a large-sized eraser; to clean up, use a smaller one. Just click on the eraser tool, select the sub tool you want, adjust the size, and click back on the pencil tool, which will automatically be the last pencil tool you used. Now when you erase using the eraser tip on the stylus, Manga Studio will use the eraser you just used. Well played Manga Studio, well played.

One more thing, every marking tool can use transparency to draw with. Basically, this means that you can use a sketching pencil or the detailing pencil as an eraser. Now that's something that most other programs don't let us do.

To use transparency, go to the color section of the **Tool** palette (it's on the bottom) and click on the area that has the ultra-retro checkerboard pattern. To go back to black, just click on the black square swatch.

Pop quiz

Q1. What is a page or document that's taller than it is wide?

1. Landscape
2. Portrait
3. Wide-screen

Q2. Paper color gives us a base color that our document will always have and cannot be changed once set.

1. True
2. False

Q3. What is the expression of Color Manga Studio's way of telling us?

1. How is color going to be dithered in the document?
2. If a layer is going to be in color, will it be grey or black and white?
3. The saturation of colors in a document.

Q4. What do most print on demand services require the Dots Per Inch (DPI) to be?

1. 72
2. 150
3. 300
4. 350
5. 600

Q5. Icons in the toolbar change to show the last-used tool.

1. True
2. False

Q6. If we want to save a tool's current settings, what do we want to choose?

1. Revert to initial settings
2. Register to initial settings

Q7. Saving files that belong together in a named folder is...

1. Hard to do.
2. Annoying and a waste of effort.
3. A way to save us time.

Q8. Legacy file formats are out-of-date and not-widely-used formats. Which of the following could be thought of as being a legacy format?

1. JPG
2. PNG
3. GIF
4. BMP
5. PSD
6. TIFF
7. TARGA

Q9. Is it a good workflow if you have different layers for the Rough Sketch, Refined Sketch, and Finished pencils?

1. Yes
2. No

Summary

We're still not slacking off. There's a lot covered in this chapter. We revisited page presets to make new ones for our character sheets. We then proceeded to make new pencil tools that we can sketch with. We learned a bit about file formats as they relate to Manga Studio and some ways to save our files.

Now, take the time to do some drawing and don't forget to take breaks, because in the next chapter, we'll be getting into different ways to format a story, a bit about what Materials are in Manga Studio, and some general storytelling methods.

3
Formatting Your Stories

This is the chapter where we begin to think about not only what we want to do, but how to do it. We'll cover some story theory and storytelling methods unique to comics. We'll explore how we want to present our story (web, tablet, print, or a combination of these) Passive sentence, and we'll create some new page presets marking tools to aid us in this.

When we have characters drawn in rough or fully detailed and a story idea percolating within our minds, then comes the most important part of any comic creation. What format do we want to tell this story in? Do we want to format our story as a comic strip, comic book, or as a graphic novel? Then, do we want to publish it as a print comic or as a Webcomic? Each of these formats has its own specific quirks and requirements, and we'll create yet more page presets to cover these diverse ways of telling a comic story. To help us with repeating the same graphics or text, a visit to the Material palette and our initial use of the Text tool in Manga Studio will be in store. There are several topics to cover so let's get to them.

In this chapter, we will cover the following topics:

- ◆ Creating specific page presets for comic strips and comic book pages
- ◆ Using the tabs when we have more than one document open
- ◆ Using the grid feature
- ◆ Saving layers as materials

Story formats

With the advent of the Internet and web-based comics, the variety and ease of publishing comic stories has exploded and never been easier.

Comic strip

We all know what this is. A few examples are Garfield, Calvin and Hobbes, Foxtrot, Evil Inc., and so on. The conventions of this format require a structure:

1. **Set up**: This introduces the character(s) and conflict

2. **Follow through**: This is where the conflict is escalated

3. **Punch line**: This is the ending of the strip's joke

The classic "knock, knock" and "how many ... does it take to change a light bulb..." joke structures help us understand how to do this kind of strip, whether it's a humor, satire, or adventure strip. While it's possible to do a continued story in this format, each installment (or episode) needs to end with a punch line of some sort or a cliffhanger to entice the reader to read the next strip. In the past, strips such as Gasoline Alley and Brenda Starr used the four-panels-a-day strip to tell stories that spanned months (if not years). If we decide to do this kind of strip, we've got the advantage of being web-based. The reader can always go back and re-read older strips to understand what's happening. Just keep in mind that this doesn't excuse obtuse storytelling.

Comic book

This format is rapidly approaching its centennial. For it to still be around means that there's something to it. Modern monthly comics are published once (or a few times) a month and have a page count somewhere between 20 and 30 for each story in each issue.

Like with comic strips, comic books can be "done in one", where the issue tells a story that's complete with beginning, middle, and end, all within the 20 to 30 pages of story allotted. The comic book could also be a limited series that consists of a continued story that spans between 2 to 20 or more issues.

As with comic strips, comic books require pacing and setting up of the story. However, the follow-through can be the bulk of the story. Usually, in the case of limited series or an ongoing serialized comic book, each issue ends on some kind of cliffhanger that must be placed near or on the last page of a story of any issue.

Graphic novels

If comic books are like TV shows, then graphic novels are movies. The structure is the same; set up, follow-through, and punch line. Just like what we learned in composition or creative writing classes, graphic novels too have a beginning, a middle, and an end. Pay attention to this trio of requirements of storytelling. The three-act-play structure is all around us. Sure there may be some stories that don't adhere to this, but like with any craft, we have to know the rules before we can break them.

Graphic novels can be pretty much any length, thirty pages to well over a hundred pages. Where they differ from comic strips and comic books is in the pacing of the story, which is based on how the creator wants to tell the story. It's not limited to a rhythm of four panels a day or multiple pages per installment.

Some creators will serialize a graphic novel as a comic book and release the compiled comic book as a trade paperback. Others will post a page, a week or so, on a website, and when the story is concluded, release a print version as a graphic novel. There are many different ways of getting to a comic convention; the important thing is to get there, and the best way to get there is to begin with a plan.

Publishing

Really, there are just two ways to do this: **web-based digital comics** and **printed comics**, pixel or paper. As artists, we don't have a lot of disposable cash that we can use to print on paper outside of a print on demand (**POD**) service. Usually, this means that we want to publish our comics on the Internet. We won't be getting into the mechanics of putting a Webcomic up on a website, since that's a topic worthy of a book by itself. In the bibliography, there are links to books and websites on this topic.

We'll be focusing on how to create and export our comics in the best way for both print and web.

We'll be focusing on a comic strip and comic book format for the rest of this book. We can take a break now and search the Internet for different comic strips or book sizes and formats. What you'll find may be different from what we'll be doing here. The good thing is that all formats have few things in common:

- **Trim area**: This is where the artwork on a page goes to the edge, and when printed, will get some trimmed off.
- **Margin or bleed area**: This is the area that will not be trimmed. However, nothing of real importance should be within this area.

◆ **Live area**: All lettering and essential artwork goes here. This area will always be printed. For pages that don't use bleed (that is, artwork that goes to the edge of the page), the margin of the live area is where the outside borderlines of panels are established.

 By making our presets the printed size and putting our dpi to 600, we allow ourselves the luxury of being able to downsample (reduce the resolution of our page) to 300 dpi and double the size of the page to the standard 11 x 17 inch (tabloid size) original art comic page size, without losing any detail. I've done this for several projects, and it's been so much easier than any other method I've tried out.

Next up, we'll be creating more page presets and will get to know how to transfer the information we get from a printer to Manga Studio's preset dialog box.

Making the page presets

Our task in this section will be to create some presets for various kinds of comics. For the comic strip and comic page presets, the information here is as accurate as I can make it. Sometimes other sizes aren't used, so go out and search for sizes and page requirements, and follow along using the dimensions you've found.

While it may seem like a rehash of the page presets we've created so far, it's important that we know how to create these presets and also know how pages are set in Manga Studio if we want to reliably export our artwork to web-friendly formats or to a printer. Having a set of consistent presets to create our comics with will save us a lot of time and effort when publishing them. We wouldn't want to create a comic book from pages that are all different sizes and proportions, would we? Reformatting all these sheets would take almost as much time as we spent in creating the artwork in the first place. Since we should be very familiar with the **New document** dialog box, there's a table following the brief discussion of each kind of document.

The comic strip

The original size for comic strips is 4 x 13 inches. When printed, the strips are 6 x 1.84 inches. There are no bleeds or such for a straight comic strip, just the live area of 4 x 13 inches.

There's an additional comic strip column, this one is for comic strips that need a logo or title above the actual comic strip itself. To do this, we use **Y offset** to drop the active area of the comic strip down a half inch to give us a good amount of room for a logo or title. Experiment with the use of **X offset** and **Y offset** to have different looks and arrangements for left-sided and right-sided pages.

The double-decker comic strip

In the mid 80s, there were a few comic strips that were double-decker strips, that is, each strip was as tall as two comic strips. A number of Webcomics use this format, as it's not as large as a full comic book page but gives more design possibilities than a single-tier comic strip.

What we want to do is to create a new preset based on the comic strip we just created, and add an additional tier to its size. Note that it's not even doubling in size from the single-tier comic strip. This is to include space for a possible horizontal gutter that divides the active area in half. The settings in this column allow for a logo or title. Set **Y offset** to **0** to counter this if you don't want space for a logo above the comic itself.

The comic book and graphic novel

This is based on the template given out by Ka-Blam, a POD comic book printer. They are a good printing place with reasonable prices, and I've been very happy with them for some time.

Ka-Blam and other POD printers have presets of all kinds of sizes and differing bleed, margin, and live areas; if there's one that you like, use their dimensions instead. You will notice that in the following example, bleed still isn't being used. It's because, from my experience, using bleed for some presets in Manga Studio can be rather useless and make the page a bit more complex than it needs to be.

Settings for the new document dialog box

Here's the table with information on the comic strips, double-decker comic strips, and comic book pages. We should know our way around the new document dialog by now, so consider the following table a recipe of sorts to begin making your own custom presets for all comic-making needs. To maintain some brevity, in the parentheses that tell us what type of setting the **Setting name** is, **Textbox** is shortened to **Text**, and **Drop Down Menu** is shortened to **Menu**.

So, look through the following table, and let's get cooking!

Setting name (type of setting)	Comic strip	Comic strip with space for logo	Double-tier comic strip (Webcomic)
File name	N/A	N/A	N/A
Preset (Menu)	N/A	N/A	N/A
OK (Button)	N/A	N/A	N/A
Cancel (Button)	N/A	N/A	N/A

Setting name (type of setting)	Comic strip	Comic strip with space for logo	Double-tier comic strip (Webcomic)
Register to preset (Button)	Click on this button only when all the settings are adjusted the way we want them.		
Canvas Size			
Double-headed arrow (Button)	N/A	N/A	N/A
Width	14	14	14
Height	6	6	11
Resolution (Menu)	600	600	600
Manga draft settings (Checkbox)	Checked	Checked	Checked
Unit (Menu)	in	in	in
Canvas thumbnail (Dynamic updated graphic)	N/A	N/A	N/A
Basic expression color (Menu)	Color	Color	Color
Paper color (Color swatch button)	White	White	White
Template (Checkbox)	Unchecked	Unchecked	Unchecked
Binding (Finish) Size			
Width	13.5	13.5	13.5
Height	5	5	10.5
Bleed width	0	0.25	0.25
Custom (Menu)	N/A	N/A	N/A
Default border (Inner)			
Width	13	13	13
Height	4	4	8.5
X offset	0	0	0
Y offset	0	0.5	0.5
Custom (Menu)	N/A	N/A	N/A
Set size (Menu)	N/A	N/A	N/A

While this dialog box is a bit cluttered and oddly arranged, the visual representation of the page is very helpful. Manga draft settings, when checked, will show us the various borders of the binding size and default border (not to mention the entry boxes for these sections). When dealing with printing shops and POD services, remember the following:

- Canvas size is the raw size of the sheet that's being printed on
- Binding (finish) size is the trim size
- Default border (inner) is the active area

This has been mentioned a few times already, but it's important to keep the terms that Manga Studio uses in sync with the terms that printers expect. Of course, this wouldn't be necessary if Manga Studio actually used the terminology that's commonly in use.

For full bleed pages, draw up to the very edge of the document. By doing this, the artwork on the printed version will go to the edge of the physical page, because we've included some wiggle room (aka bleed or the register mark area).

There are pre-made presets for comic strips and pages that you can download or purchase. While these presets are good to use and can come in very handy at times, they do have a cost that should be mentioned.

They are files that we import into our document as a new layer. They will increase the file size of our comics, and when we get to coloring comics, this increase could slow down our work. In my humble opinion, these presets are good to learn from; nothing beats the Manga Studio presets that we've been using in this and other chapters. These have no real overhead as far as the file size goes. If these downloaded or purchased templates are used, make sure that the document size in Manga Studio is the size the template describes.

Comic sizing isn't rocket science, a good search on the web can give you many different sizes and approaches to setting up your page. Pick one that makes sense to you. Alter it to fit your needs. If a page has more than document size, trim and live areas in it, chances are it's more complex than it needs to be.

Tabs in the canvas area

If we've all been following the previous steps, we should have two documents open. Save them in your MS4B folder. Then, open the character sheet from the previous chapter.

The following screenshot is what appears on the monitor:

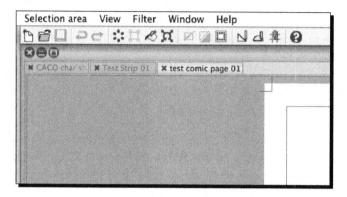

There's my CACO character sheet (stands for Cape and Cowl Opera, a satire series), Test Strip 01, and test Comic Page 01. Like in most other tabbed interfaces, we can click on the tab and the document comes forward.

Notice how much information these filenames have though they are named Untitled 1, Untitled 2, and so on. One of the most important things while working digitally is to give anything that can have a name, a meaningful one. This can make the difference between finding a file we want to work on within seconds or spending minutes to find that specific file amongst a sea of generically named files. If I used the CACO as an acronym for Cape and Cowl Opera, and wanted to find the third page of the second story, it would be the file named CACO_02_03.lip, where the first set of numbers refers to the story number and the second set of numbers tells me the current page number. With character sheets, the main numbering always has a leading zero, and secondary (supporting) characters have a leading 1. The thing is to come up with a titling method that makes sense to you and stick to it.

Manga Studio allows us to move these tabs around. Click-and-hold the tab and move it around the canvas area. There's a red line or area where the tab will appear. We can split the tabs, so one half (either horizontally or vertically) of the canvas has a tab and the other half has the other tab(s).

I have had up to thirteen pages open on the tabs at one time and Manga Studio didn't get sluggish or balky. This is a great feature as it allows us to go from page to page when getting details consistent, such as for backgrounds, characters, and page flow considerations.

 If you move a tab so it's a stand-alone window, and then click outside it, the window disappears. Don't panic. Click on one of the visible tabs and then go to the Windows menu, select the canvas menu item, and look out for a list of all open documents in the pop-out menu. Choose the lost document and it'll pop up in front. Now, just click-and-drag the tab back to the tab area in the other window. Crisis averted!

Now take a break from reading all these words. Draw on the documents you've made so far in this chapter. There are still more words to come.

Modifying older page presets or the character sheet revisited

Let's pay one more visit to the **New** dialog box and tweaking a page preset.

We've made a character preset and its landscape (wider than tall). While it serves its purpose and all, we find ourselves wanting a character preset sheet that's portrait (taller than wide). What do we do?

Well, let's make a new document and look at the dialog box with the character sheet preset chosen:

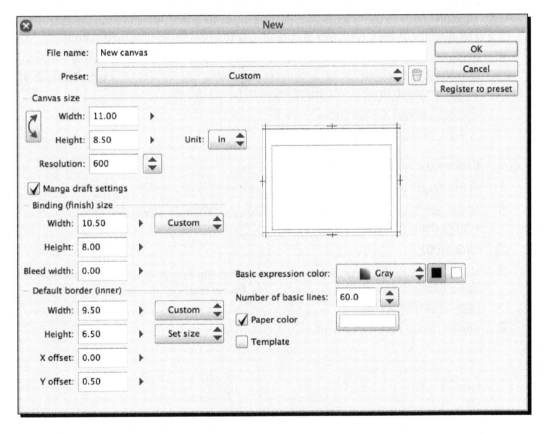

Time for action – modifying an existing page preset

Here we're going to make a few changes to an existing preset and learn a few new things about the **New** dialog box. We should note that we'll end up with another preset at the end of this exercise. The instructions are succinct, as we should be familiar with this dialog box. The instructions are as follows:

1. In the **File name** textbox, give the new document a name such as `char sheet test portrait`.

2. In **Basic expression color**, click on the drop-down menu and choose **Gray**. Notice the two boxes that appear to the right of the **Gray** text. This is to determine whether we'll see both black and white in the gray layer or just one among the two. Black is selected (it'll have a blue tint), so that white won't show up. This is good if we're importing black and white or grayscale scans into our document. With this setting (which can also be changed per layer in the layer palette) adjusted in this manner, we won't have to use a multiply blending mode to make the white transparent. The number of basic lines (set automatically to 60) is for tones and dithering.

3. Click on the double-headed arrow in front of the **Width** and **Height** setting. This flips the **Width** and **Height** for all sections in this dialog box, except for **X offset** and/or **Y offset**. We have to deal with them separately, as follows:

    -   Change **X offset** from 50 to 0
    -   Change **Y offset** from 0 to 25

4. Click on the **Register to preset** button.

5. In the **Preset name** textbox, type in `Character Sheet Portrait`.

6. Make sure that the **Resolution**, **Paper color**, and **Default expression color** boxes are checked.

7. Click on **OK**.

8. Now go back to the **New** dialog box; notice that the **Preset** drop-down menu has the name of the preset we just created. In the **Name** textbox, give this new document a name and click on **OK**.

9. Enjoy a brand new document.

What just happened?

That double-headed arrow button in front of the **Width** and **Height** settings will swap the **Width** and **Height** settings. Since we like the dimensions of the page itself as it'll be printable on almost every printer, we just want to change the height and width.

Now, we have a portrait character sheet and the offset is still the same. Notice that **X offset** and **Y offset** have also been swapped. The 0.5 offset is now in **X offset**. We zeroed it out and set **Y offset** to a smaller amount of 0.25. When we did this, the default size menu changed from **Character Sheet** to **Custom**. What this tells us is that swapping **Width** and **Height** still leaves us with the same preset, but the moment we change any value, the preset listed in the **Default size** drop-down menu changes to **Custom**.

Something important to remember about the double-headed arrow button—we can change our preset from landscape to portrait without losing any of our settings. Manga Studio will remember this swap until we create another new document and hit the swap button again. For instance, we may want to have a landscape page in our otherwise portrait-formatted story. All we have to do is click on the double-headed arrow swap button. The page will still print out fine and we won't have to do a lot of new stuff.

Now what about adding some title text and other bits of information on our character? Read on.

Using grids for display lettering

Grids, formerly known as evenly-spaced lines positioned at right angles to one another, have been used by artists since time immemorial. They've been used for proportions, perspective, composition, and many other uses. That's why any graphics program that's worth anything has a grid feature. Manga Studio's among this august crowd.

We'll be using grids on our character sheet to place information in specific places, so we can have uniform placement from sheet to sheet without a lot of copying and pasting.

Manga Studio's grids are saved with the file, so when you reopen it, the grids will be the same as when you set them up. Since grids are something we view, the settings menu for them is within the **View** menu. Go to the **View** menu and choose the **Settings of grid ruler** menu item, as shown in the following screenshot.

There's a lot of power in this simple-looking dialog box. Grids can be used for many things in Manga Studio, from placement (like we're doing now) to doing hand-lettering for titles and dialog balloons.

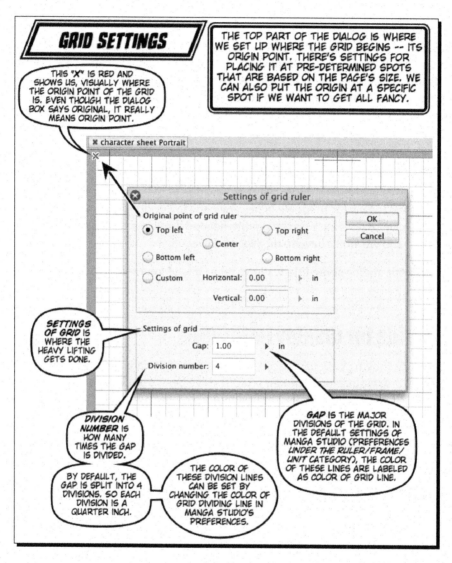

If we set **Gap** too small or have too many divisions, we'll end up with a page with unusable grids. That's just not going to be much fun. Let's say we want a grid measuring one-eighth inch squares. We could either set **Gap** to 0.5 inches or **Division number** to 8. I've opted to go with setting **Gap** to a half inch. This gives a good balance between having a small grid that is still usable and a large grid that is only good for rough placement.

After we make our changes to the grid, click on **OK** and you'll be surprised to find that the grid isn't visible. That's because we need to, as a famous captain would say, make it so.

Go to the **View** menu and choose the **Grid** menu item. There's our grid, waiting for us to use it; we shall use it.

By this time, we should have a name for our story and some of the characters. If not, just follow along and make them up as we go. It's all good. Here's a screenshot of my character sheet for the "Sentinels of Sand" story with callouts to where titles and other text will be placed:

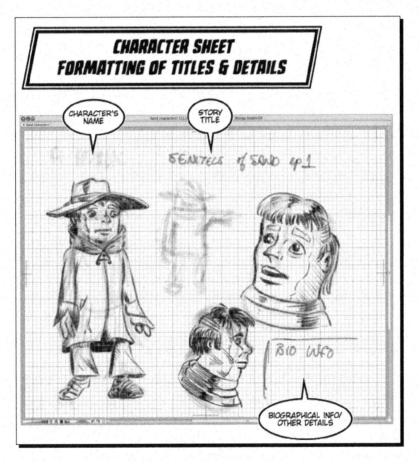

As far as roughs go, this isn't that bad. Looking it over, wouldn't it be better if the placement of the character's name and story title were swapped? As we westerners tend to read from left to right, it makes sense to go from the general (story title) to specific (character name). This also gives us the benefit of having the details text block below the name.

This is one of the advantages of working rough and digitally. We can make changes like this to make the work better and it really doesn't cost us much in time or effort.

If you don't know where to put the text or what the text is, take a moment and sketch out ideas on a character sheet. Take a bit of time, don't worry about perfection, this is a learning exercise. Sometimes, failing and making a big mess teaches us much more than getting all fussy about getting things just right. Right here and now, you have permission to make mistakes and totally mess things up, as they pertain to Manga Studio. Now let's get to work.

Using text for the first time in Manga Studio

Text in Manga Studio is somewhat limiting and confusing. We'll touch on it a bit here, and go into much more depth later in *Chapter 5, Putting Words in My Mouth*. The following screenshot is what I ended up with, so we'll have an idea of where we're going with this.

Click on the **Text** tool icon in the **Tools** palette. You'll see, in the **Tool property** palette, the basic text attributes we have in Manga Studio.

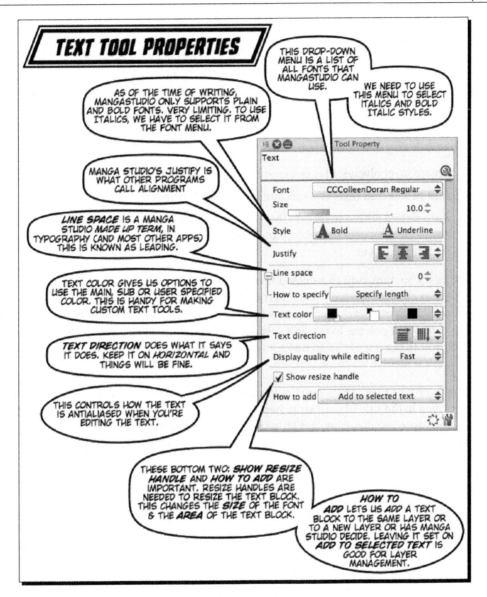

Using the previous screenshot as a guide, set up your font size and justification to fit what's wanted in your character sheet. In the previous example, only two fonts were used: one for the title and character name and another for the biographical info text block. We'll be putting in some brief text that we'll add to as we get to the lettering chapter. This is just to get acquainted with using text.

The font CCColeenDoranRegular is a real font available from ComiCraft (`http://www.comicbookfonts.com`). While not necessary for the completion of this chapter, it is a really excellent dialog font. We'll touch on where to get great comic fonts in *Chapter 5, Putting Words in My Mouth*.

Near the bottom of the **Tool property** palette is a drop-down menu labeled **how to add**. This determines how Manga Studio will add a new text block to your canvas. The three settings are:

- **Create layer always**: This will create a new layer for every text object we create
- **Add to selected text**: This will add the new text object to the text layer
- **Auto detect where to insert**: This gives Manga Studio the decision power to either create a new text object and layer or to add the new text object to the current text layer

The middle menu item, **Add to selected text**, is what we want to use. This way, both our story title and character name will be on the same layer. If you don't see **How to add** on the **Tool properties** palette, click on the wrench icon at the bottom of the palette to bring up the **Text sub tool detail** palette. In the **Edit setting** category, there's the **How to add** setting. Click on the button to the left of this to make it appear in the **Tool properties** palette, so it'll be there when we need it.

Now click on your canvas area. We should see a blinking cursor and a light cyan blue outline. Now, just type in the title of your story here. If the text is too small, finish typing in the title and use the resize handles (they are little square and round blue dots on the corners and middle of the text block outline). This is a quick (and somewhat inaccurate) way to resize text to fit an area.

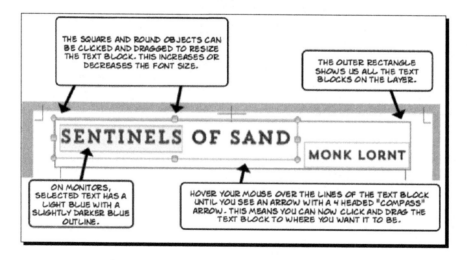

Now just make a mental note where the title text block is in relation to the grid. This will be important in a short while when we begin using the **Material** palette.

If we need to reposition the text, we can choose the **Operation** tool (the third tool down from the very top of the tool bar). It looks like a cube with an arrow in the lower right. This allows us to select an individual block of text and move it around without worrying about accidentally changing the text itself.

Take your time with this. If something isn't right, you can hit the *Esc* key to get rid of an unwanted insertion cursor and use the undo command to step back from what you did. If you don't have a title for your story, just use a title from anywhere, or just put in My Awesome Story.

The example character sheet's layer palette looks like the following screenshot at this moment:

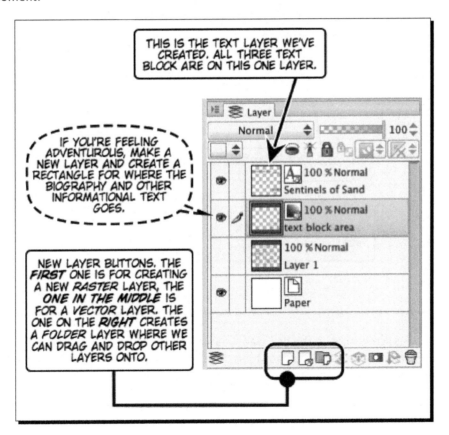

After the three text blocks (all on one layer because we set the **Add to** menu to **Add to selected text**) were created, a new vector layer was also created. A rectangle was made using the **Direct draw** tool to enclose the biographic text.

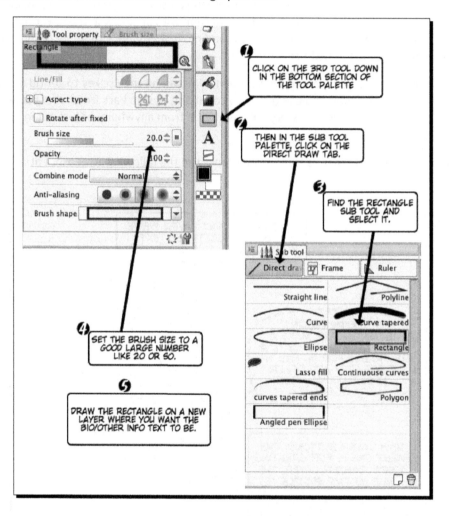

In the previous screenshot, in the first step, be mindful that Manga Studio remembers the last subtool used for all the various tools. So, the icon for the third tool down in this last section may be different. Like in real estate, location is key.

After making our text block rectangle, rename the layer by double-clicking on the name in the layers palette and typing in text block area. When that's done, click on the new folder layer button on the layer palette. This new layer can be renamed to Character sheet text. Now, click-and-drag on the text layer and drag it on top of the folder layer. This moves the layer into the folder layer. Repeat with the text block area layer.

Adding content to the material palette

Manga Studio has what it calls material. They are stored in, surprisingly, the **Material** palette. In other graphic apps, this could be called templates, symbols, or presets. In Manga Studio, **Materials** can contain anything from textures for paper to panel breakdowns.

What we want to do here is create a custom material that we can reuse for other character sheets. We've done the difficult part by creating the text layers and vector lines for the biographic information. Now, we'll just do a bit of work and the titles will be just a drag-and-drop away.

Time for action – making new materials

For making new materials, perform the following instructions:

1. Go to the **Windows** menu and select the **Material** menu.

2. From the hierarchical menu, select one of the **Material** menu items (there's quite a few of them, any one will open the **Material** palette and we can choose the exact one we want, no matter how we opened this palette).

3. This will open the **Material** palette.

4. We want to create a new folder called `Character sheets` and have it within the `Manga material` folder.

5. Click on the disclosure triangle of the `Manga material` folder.

6. With the folder open, right-click on the `Manga material` folder.

7. In the contextual menu, choose the **Create new** menu item.

8. This creates a new folder. It's named the `New` folder. Not very descriptive, is it?

9. Right-click on the `New` folder. Choose **New name** (or change name) from the contextual menu.

10. Type in `Character sheet`, and click on **Return** when done.

11. The folder is now created and has been given a meaningful name. Make sure that the new folder is selected. Notice the area to the right. That's the content pane for the folder. This is the target area where we'll be dragging things into.

12. In the **Layers** palette, select the `Layer` folder that contains the character text and rectangle.

13. Now click to drag the folder from the layer palette to the target area.

14. Well done! You're on the way to being a material maven in Manga Studio!

What just happened?

Although we opened up the **Material** palette via the menu, we can also open it from the interface by clicking on the open/close drawer buttons. So, provided the **Material** palette is still open from the exercise, the following screenshot should be close to what's on your screen:

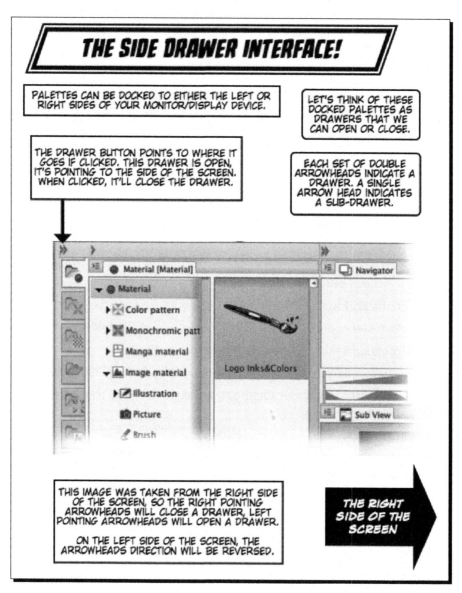

At the top of all the palette columns are these arrowhead icons. Both sides of your monitor or display screen has these drawers. The arrowheads point to the direction they'll go, if clicked. As in the previous screenshot, the arrowheads point to the right. Since they are on the right side of the screen, clicking on them will close the drawer. When closed, the arrowheads will now point left. Click on it again and the drawer opens. The arrowheads point in the opposite directions when on the left side of the screen.

When you don't have any documents open, when you create or open a new one, the document window will expand to the area that's not filled by the drawers. The **Material** palette isn't one that we use a lot, so it stays closed most of the time. This way, we have as much free space as possible when we open or create a document.

When we go into creating our own workspaces in the next chapter, we'll cover these drawers in a bit more detail. Just get used to them for now.

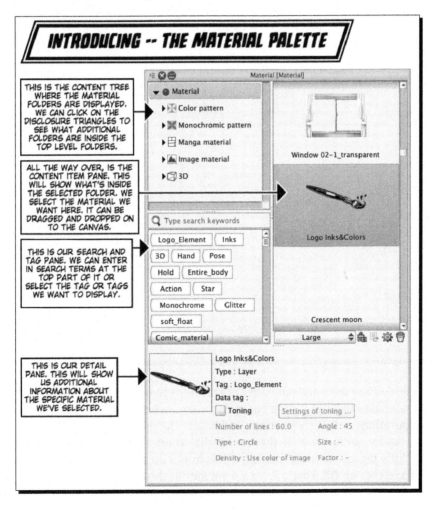

The **Material** palette has a number of panes, as shown in the previous screenshot. The **Content tree** pane only shows folders. Clicking on the disclosure triangles will show the folders that the parent has within it. The **Manga material** folder contains folders for balloons, sound effects, and the character sheet folder we created.

To the right of the **Content tree** pane is the **Content item** pane. This pane will show the materials based on what's selected in **Content tree**. In the previous screenshot, the top level `Material` folder is selected, and the **Content item** pane shows all the materials inside of the `Material` folder and all the folders inside it. By selecting and opening folders, we can narrow down what's displayed.

The pane below the **Content tree** pane is the **Search and tag** pane. We can type in a keyword or tag at the top part where the magnifying glass is. A quicker way is to click on the **Tags** pane. We can see from the previous screenshot that on my system, there's **Logo-Element**, **Inks**, **3D**, **Hand**, and more. More than one tag can be selected. The more tags that are selected, the narrower the results in the **Content item** pane are. From this, we realize that **Tags** are used to categorize the many materials that Manga Studio has installed by default.

Adding a tag to a material item is easy. In **Content tree**, click on the `Character Sheet` folder. Double-click on the `Character sheet` material and a dialog box will pop up.

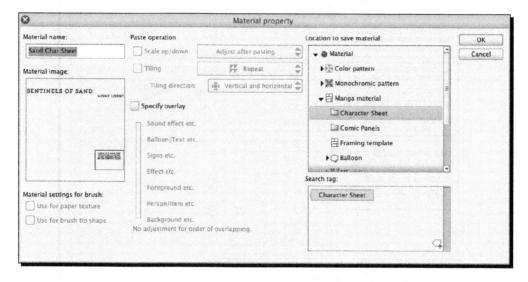

This dialog box allows us to add a number of attributes to our humble material. Since we want this material to be used for the entire document, we don't need to be concerned with the **Paste operations** or **Specify overlay** checkboxes. The only thing we're interested in is setting up a tag for our material. In the lower right, where there's a label called **Search tag**, click on the little tag icon with the plus sign. This brings up an empty tag. Type `Character Sheet` in it and click on **OK**. That's it. Now if we look at the **Item details** pane of the **Material** palette, we see that our material now has a tag added to it.

By creating a new tag, **Character Sheet**, we have a category that we can perform searches on and see all the materials that has that tag. Materials can have many tags. Remember to be as specific as possible with these tags. If you use too many in one material, it defeats the purpose of them.

Have a go hero – making new materials

We've covered some boring basics in this chapter. Now reward yourself by working on a few more of your character sheets. Use some of the presets and don't forget to save them in the `MS4B exercises` folder on your hard drive.

Get used to the pencil tool and play around with some of the other marking tools. If you mess up, there's always the undo or revert tool to return to the initial state.

If you don't mind losing any custom brushes or the page presets, you can hold down the *Shift* key as Manga Studio starts up, and it will restore the interface, tools, and page preset to the original installed state. This helps to isolate problems. There are bonus points if you can figure out how to export and save brushes. (Hint: Find menu items named **Export sub tool** and **Import sub tool** in the **Sub tool** palette.)

While working on the characters, don't neglect the story. It should have some form of conflict, each character should want something, and it's the interaction between the characters' desires that fuels exciting drama.

Pop quiz

Q1. Comic strips can only have 4 panels.

   1. True
   2. False

Q2. Which of the following describes what **X offset** or **Y offset** does?

   1. Shrinks the size of the active area
   2. Moves the active area up/down or left/right
   3. Takes the place of setting the bleed amount

Q3. The grid's origin point can't be adjusted.

   1. True
   2. False

Q4. In the Material palette, tags allow us to find specific materials with the same tags.

1. True
2. False

Q5. Layer folders can hold Text layers.

1. True
2. False

Q6. Which of the following are not kinds of layers in Manga Studio?

1. Vector layers
2. Text layers
3. Gradient layers
4. Onion skin layers

Summary

We covered page presets (or templates) in depth and learned a bit about text and materials in Manga Studio. We're done with page presets, but we will revisit text and materials later. We used the grid in Manga Studio for help in arranging our text blocks. Different kinds of comic storytelling formats were touched on: comic strips, double-tier comic strips, the regular comic book, and graphic novels. Actual storytelling in comics is a book-length topic in itself. The *Chapter 12, Along for the Ride*, which is an online chapter has some leads on some pretty good sources of information on this.

Now that we have created pages and drawn in rough our ideas, let's level up and get into penciling a bit. In the next chapter, we'll learn about panels and auto actions.

4
Roughing It

When creating a comic page, no matter whether it's for a comic strip, comic book, or graphic novel, we need to have an idea of what the page/strip will look like as a whole. In this chapter, we'll go from very rough to a basic layout drawing in order to see our page with an artistic eye. We'll learn about creating different kinds of layers, their attributes, and how to create actions for specific robotic-type tasks. We'll learn about how to create a simple and easy way to create non-photo blue pencil-type pages. This chapter will wrap up with planning and making frame layers in Manga Studio that serve as panels. Roughing it doesn't mean sleeping on the ground, not when we can enjoy the comforts of the fine lodging that Manga Studio 5 provides.

In this chapter, we will cover the following topics:

- Creating roughs for our pages
- Using the zoom tool
- Layer properties and how to use them
- Layer color effects
- Frame layers
- Introducing auto actions in Manga Studio

What are roughs?

Ask ten artists or designers what roughs are and we'll get ten different answers. What everyone agrees on is that roughs are basic drawings of what is to be drawn and rendered. Roughs can be as simple as stick figures to complete-looking drawings of the page's form. The level of detail in our roughs is determined by the person who will be seeing them. If it's for our eyes only, then they need to be understood by us. If the roughs are to be seen by a writer or editor, then they'll need to be a bit more complete.

You want to know why creating roughs is a perfectly acceptable question? The answer is in storytelling. We all have tics (things that we say or do that we rely on), from beginning a sentence with "like" to pulling on our earlobes when thinking. This happens in art. As we draw more, we will gravitate to certain types of compositions and panel arrangements that we are comfortable with. That's not bad in itself. It gets annoying if it becomes a routine thing. By distilling down our pages into roughs, we can see the essence of a page and compare it with other pages to see how the story flows and whether the story stalls anywhere or skips over important points.

That's where using roughs is very important. We can see the bare-boned structure of our story and make improvements before we invest a lot of work into something that may very well end up being either changed or removed. We want to make every moment of drawing work for us, and losing hours of work because of something we would've corrected in the roughs stage isn't something that works for us, is it?

From script to panels

If we all have been following the exercises in the comic story so far, we should have a plot and basic script figured out. Unlike scripts for movies and television, there's no set standardized format for comics. Usually, a modified movie/TV script is used. For comics, the script is first broken down into pages and then further into panels. That's where some people have problems: how much can one panel have? There's a simple and possibly annoying answer: a panel can have as much information as it can handle. The larger the panel size, the more it can contain. The smaller the panel size, the less it can have. This is where page roughs or breakdowns show us how important they are.

There are a number of good writing apps that can create comic scripts. One open source solution is Celtx (`https://www.celtx.com`). Other apps such as Scrivener (`http://www.literatureandlatte.com`), Writer's Café (`http://www.writerscafe.co.uk`), or Storyist (`http://www.storyist.com`) can be purchased. Some apps provide ready-to-use comic script templates (for example, Scrivener). Other apps require some modifications of the existing screenplay template. An app that is due to be released after the publication of this book is ComiXwriter (`http://www.comixwriter.com`), specifically designed to only create comic scripts. However, a simple text editor such as Notepad or simpleText can be just fine to create our scripts.

Time for action – breaking down the page

When we're presented with a script, we need to figure out panel breakdowns, even if the writer has given us guidance. Although every page is different, there are some things that are constant. Be sure to work loose and don't get bogged down in details, there's time for that later. Here's the way to transfer a script into a rough layout:

1. Read the script for the page. Mentally break down what happens on the page in simple declarative sentences. If need be, write this down or add it to the beginning of the page in the script.

2. Each one of these sentences can be a panel. Ideally, we should have between four and eight sentences. If there are more, then either there's too much happening, or a number of panels are wordless.

3. On a piece of paper, just draw the panel outlines (don't draw anything inside the panel) for the page we've been working on. Make each panel as similar in size as possible.

4. Chances are if you have an even number of panels, the panels are pretty static looking, probably two columns and either three or four tiers (rows).

5. On a new sheet of paper, redo the panel breakdowns, only this time make the importance of the panel determine its size. The more important the panel is, that is, the more dramatic it is, the larger it is in comparison with the other panels. Don't hesitate to have a tier with a single panel or with three. Break up the structure, keep your tiers on an even height, but it's okay to break up the columns so there's not a "river" of gutter running from the top to the bottom of the page.

6. Compare the two breakdowns. The second one probably looks more interesting.

What just happened?

We just observed a basic occurrence that will follow us for the rest of our cartooning life; sometimes, the second (or third or fourth) try will get us something we like more and something that will work better for our characters and story. This is part of looking at a page as a whole and deciding which parts to emphasize over others. That's the beginning of comic page composition—the page has to be broken down into interesting and dynamic shapes and arrangement of panels. A movie can have montages and slow motion to convey things. We comic artists use the same shape, size, and number of panels, because our story dictates us to do the same things that are done in movies.

Examining a page breakdown for the sample story

The following screenshot shows the basic breakdown for the page. It's done in Manga Studio, using the rough sketching pencil (don't hesitate to adjust the size if you feel it's too big or small).

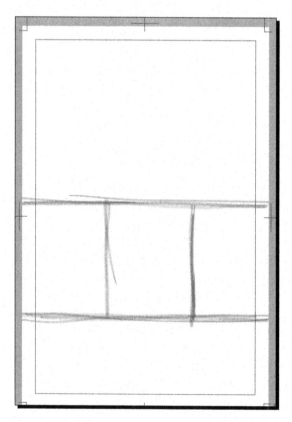

The following screenshot shows the rough drawings. These drawings were done in a separate layer. (Go to **Menu** | **Layer** | **New Layer** | **Raster Layer** to create a new layer. We'll be getting to working on the layer palette in no time.)

This was drawn with the same large sketching pencil as the panel borders after adjusting the view to fit the window (*Alt/command – 0*).The image shown in the previous screenshot is the basic panel layout of the first page of my story "Making a Splash." The sentence breakdown is:

A monk, Lornt, was meditating while listening to the ocean. A female figure appears over the water. He hears the scream from her. The female figure falls into the water. He dives into the ocean to rescue her.

Five sentences and five panels; each sentence is simple and says just one thing, nothing complex. Since this is the first page of a story, there are some basic things that need to be in this page:

1. We need to have some form of establishing shot. This is so that the reader has a sense of place. Your story may need the location to remain unclear until the final panel; just hang on and you'll see how we use these things in this specific example, then you can apply them to your story. It's that "learning the rules before breaking them" concept again. I opted to have a large first panel to really show the ocean and the coastal headlands to indicate the scale of things.

2. The middle tier, with its three panels, will show the monk hearing the scream and the woman appearing in air and beginning to fall. The last panel shows the monk diving into the ocean. Now here, I changed the order of the sentences a bit in order to heighten the drama. Incidents in these three panels happen pretty much at the same time. It's at this point that I think it'll be a good idea to have some kind of energy burst in the first panel to herald the woman's appearance.

3. In the last panel, there is a big splash of the woman hitting the water and the title. I prefer having the second panel in the above tier (the one with the woman falling) and the last panel being borderless, so it will appear that these panels are similar and indicate quick passage of time.

4. Lastly, since I have a penchant for puns (my wife would say weakness), I had to put the title of this story ("Making a Splash") on the last panel. One of the best things about comics is that we don't have to worry about not being subtle.

As we can see, Lornt is meditating on the headlands in the first panel. There's that energy burst in the middle (above the middle panel of the next tier). The second panel shows him reacting to the screams; this is also a good character shot of him that gives the reader a face to give to the character. The third panel shows the woman beginning to fall. The fourth panel shows the monk jumping off the cliff. The fifth panel shows the splash the woman makes as she hits the water.

There are some issues with the drawing of this page. The first panel may not be clear where the monk is, since the view is too far away from him. So, that'll have to be adjusted. The female falling in the third panel may also be a bit too small, but I do like the arc that it makes with the second and fourth panels. Therefore, may not need to be changed.

So far we've looked at a way to reduce a comic script for a page into sentences, and then give weight to each sentence according to the narrative needs of the story. Next, we break down the page into panels. We then rough in the contents of the panels. With minor tweaks and modifications (such as, the writer of the script breaking down the page into panels, that we need to conform to), this is how a comic page begins.

Zoom in and Zoom out

The previous two screenshots were done within Manga Studio. Notice how the lines aren't fussy or overly detailed? That's because they were drawn with the page being zoomed out, that is, the page is small on the monitor and the **Large Sketching** pencil (that we created earlier) was used to draw the panel borders and contents of the panels.

The one thing that just got me when I first started doing art digitally was that I had a heck of a time getting that initial rough sketch down. It wasn't until I came across the analog world of pencils and paper that I used a really big, dull carpenter's pencil for my rough drawings. You know the kind of pencil, rectangular lead that's somewhat soft so it leaves a mark on the paper with a light touch.

When I realized this, it dawned on me that all I needed to do was make a really big digital pencil and sketch with it. Still, the rough sketches were not as spontaneous as I was used to seeing them. I looked at the monitor with frustration, then I looked at the view—it was 50 percent or some such number. I realized what I had to do: zoom out more and make the canvas fit the screen. The keyboard shortcut is *Alt/command – 0*, or select the **Fit to screen** option from the **View** menu. Once I did that, life returned to my rough sketches.

Simply put, zoom out to sketch out and zoom in to add details in. Don't be afraid to experiment with new ways of approaching or doing things. A little shift of process and lots of practice can open up better ways of doing things.

Before we start putting down panel lines and rough sketches, we need to create our page, modify a pencil, and learn about layers in Manga Studio.

Our next steps will be to:

- Create a new Manga Studio comic page document
- Make a new layer and set its properties
- Adjust and save a new sketching pencil
- Draw out our panels
- Make a rough sketch inside the panels

Let's do this!

Making our page

Start up Manga Studio 5 and create a new page from the comic book template we created in the last chapter. Name this page with the name of your story (or an abbreviated version) and with `pg_01` after the story name. The story we're using as an example in this chapter has the title "Making a Splash", so the file is named `MakeSplash pg_01`.

> The capitalization used in the title `MakeSplash` is called camelback capitalization (or that's what I was told). This is a good way to make concise titles with fewer spaces. I found that my eye got used to seeing this very quickly, and it's great for doing a quick search for a misplaced file as I'll get fewer hits (which I want) by searching for `MakeSplash`, rather than for `Make` or `Splash` by themselves.

Now we're going to take a look at layers in a segment.

Life with layers

In every graphics program that is worth using, there's a layer. Manga Studio 5 is no different. What is different is the many kinds of layers, attributes of layers, and things we can do with layers in Manga Studio.

Since we only really just glanced at the **Layer** palette, let's go a bit deeper and see more things we can do with layers in Manga Studio. There's a lot of information about layers in Manga Studio. This is because layers are analogous to paper. And we all know that paper has many, many different attributes from tooth to thickness and from being for charcoal to being for watercolors. Layers are how our marking is interpreted by Manga Studio.

We probably won't use all the different kinds of layers, as we all have our own way of creating art, so let's explore some of the important kinds of layers and attributes that the Manga Studio 5 have and see what we can use.

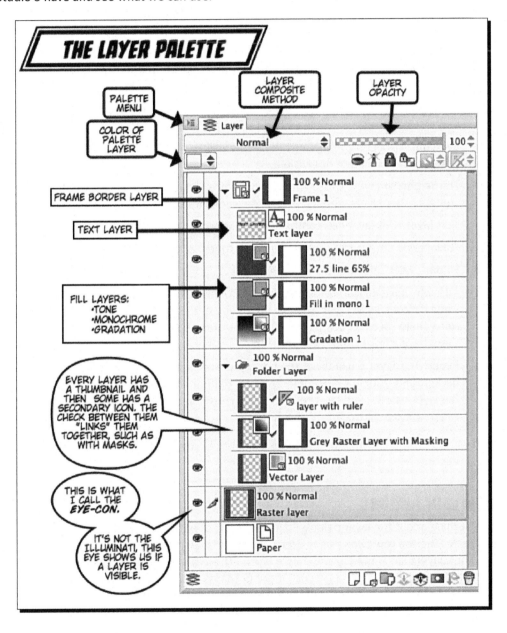

- **Palette menu**: This drop-down menu is where we can select items that are already icons in this palette as well as choose from various **Layer** settings. The one layer setting we're most interested in at this time is **Set as Draft Layer**. Choosing this menu item will put an icon of a pencil in the layer's name. What setting as draft layer will do is make this layer to not be printed or exported. A draft layer can be changed back to a regular layer via the layer palette menu.

- **Layer composite method**: Like with other drawing/photograph/painting programs, this controls how the current layer interacts with other layers.

- **Layer opacity**: This is still the cheapest and best way to simulate glass, thin cloth, and cranky ghosts.

- **Eye-con**: This open eye means the layer is visible. If the eye isn't there, or greyed out, the layer's hidden or invisible.

- **Frame border layer**: This is what we can call a group layer in the sense that it can contain other layers within it and those layers are controlled by this layer's settings.

- **Text layer**: This layer can contain one or more text objects.

- **Fill layers**: Entire layers can be filled with tones, colors, and so on.

- **Folder layer**: This can contain other layers.

- All layers have an icon reflecting the type of layer it is. Sometimes there are two icons if it's a special layer (such as text, ruler, or vector). If the layer has a mask or ruler, there's a checkbox to the left of that icon, such as with the fill layers (all of them have a mask) and the layer with ruler layer.

- **Paper**: This layer is usually at the bottom of the layer list. This gives our page a background color. It's currently set to the default color, white. You can look above the layer palette, and see the layer properties palette and the color swatch that can be clicked on to choose another color.

When we start working with layers, we will look at the properties palette and the things it allows us to do.

Know your buttons

One last thing about the layer palette is the two rows of buttons at the top and bottom of the palette. The top row allows us to do tasks on the layers; the bottom row allows us to create new layers, layer masks, and delete layers. These buttons can be a bit confusing to understand the first time, but as we use more of Manga Studio, especially for inking and coloring, the full power of these buttons will be clearly understood.

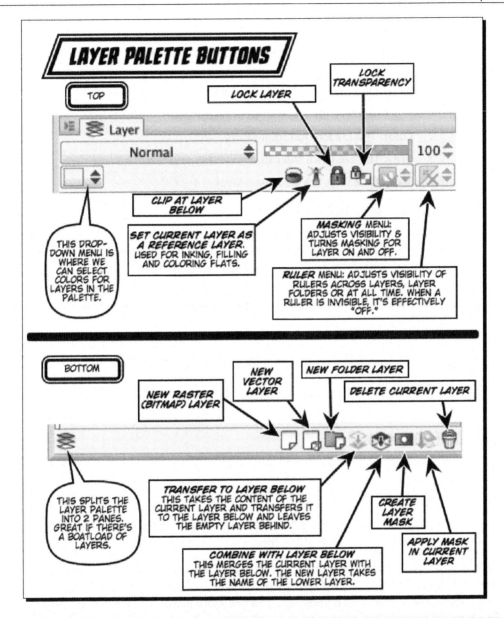

LAYER PALETTE BUTTONS

TOP

LOCK LAYER

LOCK TRANSPARENCY

Layer

Normal 100

CLIP AT LAYER BELOW

THIS DROP-DOWN MENU IS WHERE WE CAN SELECT COLORS FOR LAYERS IN THE PALETTE.

SET CURRENT LAYER AS A REFERENCE LAYER. USED FOR INKING, FILLING AND COLORING FLATS.

MASKING MENU: ADJUSTS VISIBILITY & TURNS MASKING FOR LAYER ON AND OFF.

RULER MENU: ADJUSTS VISIBILITY OF RULERS ACROSS LAYERS, LAYER FOLDERS OR AT ALL TIME. WHEN A RULER IS INVISIBLE, IT'S EFFECTIVELY "OFF."

BOTTOM

NEW VECTOR LAYER

NEW FOLDER LAYER

NEW RASTER (BITMAP) LAYER

DELETE CURRENT LAYER

THIS SPLITS THE LAYER PALETTE INTO 2 PANES. GREAT IF THERE'S A BOATLOAD OF LAYERS.

TRANSFER TO LAYER BELOW THIS TAKES THE CONTENT OF THE CURRENT LAYER AND TRANSFERS IT TO THE LAYER BELOW AND LEAVES THE EMPTY LAYER BEHIND.

CREATE LAYER MASK

APPLY MASK IN CURRENT LAYER

COMBINE WITH LAYER BELOW THIS MERGES THE CURRENT LAYER WITH THE LAYER BELOW. THE NEW LAYER TAKES THE NAME OF THE LOWER LAYER.

Time for action – using layers

In previous chapters, I introduced the concept of "focused play", wherein we just messed around with a clear direction in mind. This relaxes us and makes learning a bit more fun and allows what Bob Ross would call "happy accidents" to occur.

Here's the game plan:

1. Create a new comic book page from the comic template in the new file dialog box.

2. Create a number of new layers via the palette menu. Go to the **New layer** menu and choose **Raster layer** from the hierarchical menu.

3. In the dialog box, there are three kinds of raster layers:

   ❏ **Color**: This creates full color layers

   ❏ **Grey**: This creates a layer that only has greyscale

   ❏ **Monotone**: This is a black-only layer

4. Create a layer of each of these types.

5. Draw on each layer a bit; use a thick marker or inking pen tool. Use different colors on each of the layers. To change a color, go to the color palette and then go to the **Color set** tab and choose a color from the set that appears.

6. Notice that on the Monotone layer, no matter what color you choose (even white), the line is always black. However, you can erase lines with transparency, as with other lines.

 The monochrome layer will produce a dithered tone for any color other than black; the grey layer will give you a grey line if any color other than black is used. The color layer will display any color you choose.

What just happened?

Each of these layers can be used in specific situations. The monotone layer is great for inking, the grey layer is excellent for most rough sketching and penciling tasks, and color is what we use for (duh!) coloring and some fancy penciling or inking.

Now keep in mind that each layer will add to the file size and complexity of our page. Each kind of layer will add to the weight of the file.

Think of each layer in our file as a dollar. We want the file to be as light as possible. A monotone layer is like two fifty cent pieces, pretty light and not many pieces to worry about. A grey layer is like ten dimes, a bit heavier and a few more pieces to track. A color layer is like a hundred pennies, lots to keep track of and pretty heavy. In this metaphor, where it says "heavy", think of "increased file size and complexity." If we're working on a file with just a few layers, it doesn't matter. Now, if we're working on a page with a dozen or so layers, making our layers as simple as possible is key to keeping our files as compact as possible and not making Manga Studio lag.

This is another reason why we should plan out our story before we start drawing it. If we know that the story will be just in black and white with grey tones, then we don't want color layers.

Layer properties

Before we head off and start drawing, we need to look at the **Layer Properties** palette. This is where a number of features and settings live.

If you click on a plain old raster layer to make it active, and then click on the **Layer color** button, you'll see something much like the following screenshot in your layer properties:

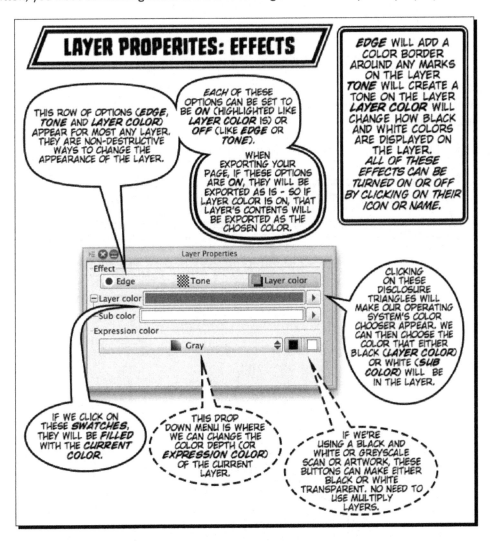

The three effects (**Edge**, **Tone**, and **Layer color**) are useful, depending on what we're doing. Since we're sketching for the time being, the most important is the **Layer color** effect. Click on the icon for this effect and notice that if there's anything drawn on the current layer, it will now be given a blue color.

That particular shade of blue is close to what we refer to as "non-photo blue" in the analog world. It's still in use by graphic artists and cartoonists who kick it old school on paper. When a page is drawn in non-photo blue pencil and either scanned or photocopied, the blue pencils won't be picked up by the scanning devices. The fact that it doesn't have to be erased is very attractive to comic production as it saves on time. However, for one who has erased his share of penciled pages after inking, time wasn't the only thing that was saved by not erasing pages.

In animation circles, blue, red, and sometimes green pencils are used to correct model drawings and design in-betweens and key poses.

Using this effect when we ink our pencil work makes it very easy to see what we've inked and what we haven't. It also gives us a good idea of how our page looks like without having to mess around with making layers hidden.

If you don't have a vector layer, create one and look at the properties for that layer.

Other layers, such as text layers or layers with rulers, have something analogous to what we see when we have a vector layer active. Those four tools are the major tools to adjust lines we draw with vectors. Make some inked lines with a pen or marker tool on a vector layer and see what each tool does. We'll get in depth with vectors in Manga Studio as we proceed. Right now, let's get back to drawing.

Drawing our rough page

All the previous exercises and info dumps have been leading us to this point. We just need to take a bit of inventory to see if we have all our materials together.

- We should have a story with characters. This can be in the form of a detailed plot or a full script. Whatever makes us most confident with, we can proceed with that. This is vital to have, as it's the map of our story. We need to know how/where it begins and ends. Ray Bradbury once said that plots of stories are like footprints in snow. It's our job to show the reader how those footprints got there.

- We should have some form of comic page breakdowns on the script itself or on paper. This is just for panel size and very, very rough content of the panels.

- There should be a few character sketches of our main characters. Usually, these are done well in advance of the actual drawing of the story, but we'll do them concurrently. I won't tell if you don't.

- Get your favorite beverage in hand. Put any snacks on the other end of the room, or leave them in the kitchen. It's good to get off your chair every now and then. We don't want to take root at your computer area.

- Turn off cell phones and quit any Facebook or Twitter app (I know, it's hard at first, but it's something we'll get used to).

Time for action – making our mark on the page

Now comes the fun part, what we've been patiently waiting for, making a rough of our story. In your MS4B exercises folder, make a new folder with the name of your story. Mine is called Sentinels of Sand. Now, mentally name your pages. I'll use the prefix `SentinelOfSand` and end the name with `_pg0X` (where the X is the page number). This rough page is included in the downloadable files that you can access by following the instructions in the beginning of this book. So you can feel free to follow along using this example page if you want:

1. Within Manga Studio, make a new file, use the comic page template, or the one that fits your story. Give the new file a title using the method mentioned previously or one that makes sense to you. Be sure to end it with the page number.

2. Repeat until you have a new document for all the pages in your story (remember that it was suggested that it be no longer than 8 to 10 pages. If it is, then just make pages for the first eight pages or so of the story).

3. The pages we made should be in our document window; each tab is a page file.

4. Using our script as a guide, make a new greyscale layer and name it Roughs.

5. Make sure that the entire page is visible. The key thing is to work up our page evenly. Like properties in Monopoly, we want to build each part of the page up at the same time. There's nothing worse than having one panel that's wonderfully rendered and drawn and all other panels sticking figures and squiggles. If we zoom in, we increase our chances of having a page like that. We'll get to detailing our pages in due time.

6. Now use your big layout pencil and draw out the panels in the page. If we hold down the *Shift* key, the pencil will draw a straight line from the last point you drew to where your cursor goes. This helps in doing boxy panels.

7. Keep mindful that we're just making empty panels to put our drawings into. Now's not the time to get lost in details.

8. Think about what's going into each panel and how important it is or isn't to the story itself and for the flow of art on the page. Don't be afraid of making a mistake, it can be changed real easy since we're working digitally. Better put down a wrong line than no line at all.

9. Repeat for all the pages that are open. When you're done, go across the room and grab a snack. Thumb through some comics. It's good to take a breather after steps in comic creation. This keeps us from exhausting ourselves. When we return to work, we're refreshed and can look at things with a new eye.

10. Earlier, we looked at (and hopefully messed around with) the layer color effect that layers have in Manga Studio. On one of the rough pages, click on the layer that has the rough panel layouts, and click on the **Layer color** icon.

What just happened?

Everything turned blue!

That's the way it's supposed to work. What if we want to have our rough panel lines to be red and our rough sketches to be blue? The simplest way to do this is to have one layer for our panel lines and another for our rough sketches.

Using the layer color effect

To change the color of the layer color, click on the right pointing triangle on the right side of the blue color swatch (the one labeled layer color). This will bring up your operating system's color chooser.

If you're on a Macintosh, there's a number of different color sets you can use. I use the crayon set myself. It has a large number of colors and I can be consistent on which red or other colors I use. I like either maroon or cayenne for this.

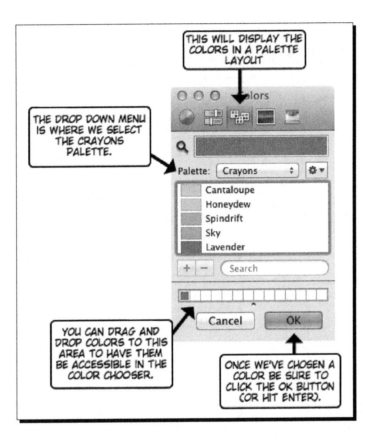

Choose a red that's not too vivid (we will spend quite a bit of time looking at this, so a bright color can become a distraction) and click on the **OK** button on the chooser. Now, our panel layout lines are in that red color and will be distinct from our rough drawings.

We just have to repeat this for every single page in our story.

What a time sponge this is! Not to mention, boring! If only there was a way to make this thing simple, like a button we could press to change the layer color.

There is a way.

Time for making actions

If we're still using the default workspace in Manga Studio, on the same area where the **Layer** palette is, there's a tab called **Auto actions**. Click on it. All names here are for automated actions that will do things to the current layer or document.

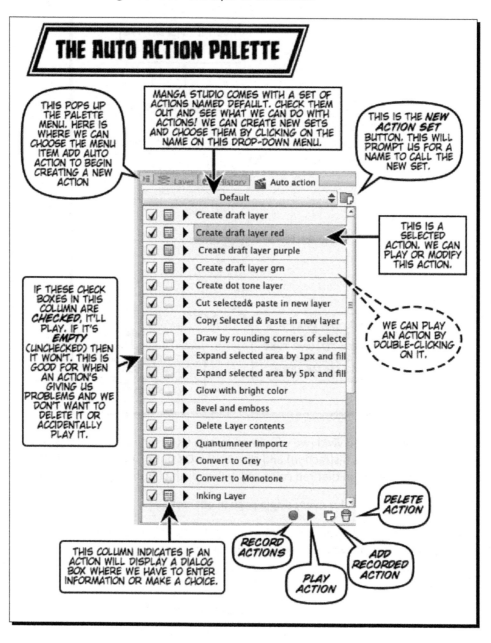

What we're going to do is create an action that will change our layer color from blue to red. This is a great use for actions, something that is used a lot and doesn't require many (if any) changes in it.

Here's some information to create good, usable actions:

- Complete the action via menu commands a few times. You'd be surprised how this really helps with creating an action. Some steps can be eliminated and others introduced. Just know that the time we spend doing this will benefit us in the time the action saves. This also has the benefit of getting us more familiar with Manga Studio's menu commands.

- An action should be looked at as something that performs menu commands on something that already exists. However, there are some settings and commands that actions cannot record; the marking tool size, for instance. So, if a tool or layer is changed via a palette setting, this may not be recorded.

- We can look at what an action does by clicking on the disclosure triangle to the left of the action's name. If an empty square appears in the dialog column, clicking in that square will make an icon of a dialog box appear. Now when that action is played, it will stop and display a dialog box. When you either enter new information and/or click on **OK**, the action will continue to play until it's finished.

Time for action – making actions

While, for the most part, actions are helpful, if they do things such as deleting layers, they can really be destructive. When starting out, use copies of your pages; this way, if things really get messed up, we've lost nothing but time. We'll start off by creating a simple action, as follows:

1. Go to the palette menu and select the **Add auto actions** menu item.

2. A new action appears in the palette. The name should be selected (if not, double-click on the name), so just type in a short name that summarizes what this action will do when you're finished with it. We can call this action Layer Color - Red.

3. Go to the bottom of the palette and click on the round red dot icon to begin recording the action.

 When recording, I find it's best to use menu commands and not keyboard shortcuts. Things are less prone to have errors that way and it's easier to remember what needs to be done in case the action has to be modified.

4. On the **Layer property** palette, if the **Layer color** isn't on, click on it.

5. Click on the triangle to the right of the color swatch labeled **Layer color**.

6. In the color chooser, pick out the red color we used previously, or choose a color you like better, as long as it's not blue. Click on **OK** on the color chooser.

7. On the bottom of the **Auto actions** palette, the round red record button has changed into a red square. This button changes shape depending on whether we're recording an action. Now that we're recording an action, it's changed to a stop recording button. Click on it and we're done.

What just happened?

In other programs, this could be called a macro. All the steps we took to change the layer color are now just a single button. Try out this new action on other layers and see what it does. Remember to either double-click on the action's name or single-click on the right-pointing triangle to play the action.

Time for action – adding existing actions

As we get used to making our own actions to speed up our work, we'll want to add to existing actions. It's quite easy and intuitive. Let's make this action set the layer to be a draft layer.

A draft layer won't be printed or exported unless we check the options in the print or export dialog boxes. This adds a pencil icon to the layer's entry in the **Layer** palette.

1. Select the **Layer color – Red** action.

2. Click on the red dot to begin recording the action.

3. Now click on the **Layer palette** tab.

4. With the **Layer palette** tab visible, click on the **Palette menu** button in the upper-left corner of the palette.

5. In the pop-up menu, go to **Settings** and select the **Set as Draft Layer** menu item.

6. Click back on the **Auto actions** palette and click on the **Stop recording** button.

7. In the **Layer Color – Red** action, click on the disclosure triangle to the left of the name. Scroll down if you need to. See how there's an entry for **Layer color change** and **Set as Draft Layer**.

What just happened?

Clicking on palettes to bring them forward isn't recorded, but menu commands from any menus are. New recorded actions are put after the last recorded action. Entries under an action can be moved up or down. Try this on the set as draft entry. Click on it and drag it up so it's between the **Layer color change** entry and the name of the action. When you see a red line between these two, release your stylus or mouse. Gaze at the awesome thing you did. I prefer to have a few colors for my layer colors, such as green for backgrounds and perspective drawings, purple for props, and orange for special effects.

To make things somewhat easy for us, Manga Studio allows us to duplicate commands within an action. Right-click on a command and select **Duplicate Command**. Then, click on the command and drag it to the action we want to be duplicated.

To get used to actions, make a few changes to the layer color in the way we just did. Once the color changes are tested and work like you want them to, just copy the entry for **Set as Draft Layer** to the new color layer actions.

Have a go hero – adding existing actions

I found it useful to make a set of actions that'll change the mode of the selected layer to monochrome, grayscale, or color. These menu commands are in the layer palette menu. Go ahead and make some actions. Add a command to change the palette color for the draft layer to yellow or some other color. You won't break anything and it'll be fun.

Filling in the panel contents

Now that we have our pages roughly paneled out, the next step is to fill in the panels with roughs for the artwork. We can choose to draw our rough contents on the layer where the panel lines are, or use a different layer.

Using a different layer allows us to erase (and we will) without losing the paneled lines or spending time redrawing them. This is also one reason why we use a red layer color for the panel lines and the default blue layer color for the rough layers. We can tell as soon as we start drawing whether we're on the right layer for what we're doing. Just make sure that the **Layer color** button is active on the **Layer properties** palette.

Use a nice thick pencil for this. Don't hesitate to make changes to the pencil's settings. We want to make Manga Studio work for us, so we can work the way that feels best for us.

These are roughs, so don't worry about details at this point. Keep the **Zoom** at **Fit in window**. Get in and get the basic shapes of the contents of the panels down. Dots are okay for eyes. A squiggle is fine for hair. We want to capture some immediacy and life with these drawings. They're like gesture drawings that we would do in life drawing classes. It's only for the entire panel and not just for a figure.

The best tool for doing roughs quickly and with a minimum of fuss is to use a timer. I have an old egg timer that I just set to five minutes or so. I start it and have that amount of time to finish the roughs for one page. This helps to keep the layouts fresh and keep its energy. Use a microwave's timer or one on your computer. Don't use the one on your cell, as the temptation to check twitter may be a great way to suddenly lose a half an hour or more. Remember, we have our phones either off or muted to avoid such occurrences of lost time.

Now go to Manga Studio and do these roughs, or as they are called, layouts. This is just a first pass, so if a panel's giving you the stinky eye, just put something in the panel and move on. Our minds are great for working out problems in the background while we move on to other things.

When all the pages are laid out, get off the computer chair and walk over and grab a snack. Have a cup of tea, coffee, or anything. Do a few stretches. Check your twitter feed. But don't lose track of time (use the timer to give you 10-15 minutes of break time), as we've got lots to do and, as usual in comics, not much time to do them.

Refining the roughs

In painting, part of the process is called the ugly stage. This is when the painting looks like trash and we all think it may be best to just abandon it and start with a new canvas. This is when it's important to carry on with the painting. Time and work will make this fuzzy caterpillar into a beautiful butterfly. Sometimes, it may be better to start over again. That kind of judgment comes with experience. But it always comes after wrestling with a drawing that just won't work. As much as we want to always do our best, we're getting used to a new program here, and it's okay to sacrifice quality over learning. With the art we're creating, as it's digital, it's easy to redo panels as our skill evolves.

It's quite probable that at this point, this is what we think of our roughs. Let's start fixing this thought.

Time for action – refining the line

At this point, we're going to go over our roughs and make line drawings (or wireframes, as some call them). Now, it's fine to make major corrections. Let's get our lines in gear.

1. Create a new greyscale layer and name it pencil outlines.

2. Select a default drawing pencil, a lighter pencil will work just fine.

3. Set the rough's **Layer color** to blue and the current layer, pencil outlines, to normal; no effects are required.

4. Use your roughs as a guide to make simple outlines of the panel's content. Don't worry about shading or lighting. Focus on drawing the form of what's in the panel.

5. Make sure that all panels get the same amount of attention. This doesn't mean the same amount of time, each panel should look as developed as the others.

What just happened?

In the previous screenshot, half of the panel is shown with refined pencils and the other half in rough sketching. Think of the rough sketch as being close to what we want and the pencil outlines being closer. There are areas where we're indicating shadows and gradations that may be done with color or tone. We'll be going over this drawing when we start the penciling process. Right now, we need to finish all the pages of our story. You could get along by choosing a page that has a bit of dialog, so when we get to lettering, we'll have something to work with. Just work on the dialog page for now.

Our goal here in the outlining phase is to make a basic line drawing that's clear and readable to the viewer. We want a dead line (one that doesn't vary in width) and we pay no attention to shading or shadows. Just focus on composition of the panels. If some panels aren't working, make a new rough sketch layer and redo that panel using the big rough pencil.

One of the purposes of making a pencil outline layer is to gain more confidence in our lines. When I was first starting to draw comics, my line was hesitant and scratchy. Over time, my line got more confident and expressive. Part of that was just getting experience in drawing. It was when I started doing this outlining stage when my line really got good. By not worrying about shading or shadows, we focus on the form. The lines of the clothes our characters are wearing, the shape of the window in the room, and other elements are figured out in our mind's eye. These details become more real to us, and it leads to better finished pencils; also, inking becomes much more fun. This leads us to have better areas of shadow, and we rely less on using "chicken scratching" to hide the fact we aren't sure about where the shadows are.

When we're finished with the outlining, we can break the page down into panels.

The process so far

Just so we can see our journey, so far we've:

- Created characters
- Written a story for them
- Written a script
- Made pages in Manga Studio
- Laid out the panel shapes for the pages
- Drawn rough sketches inside the panels
- Drawn refined pencil outlines from our sketches

Now, our next step is to create panels inside Manga Studio.

Panels in Manga Studio

In the analog world, the comic pages would be fully penciled and then handed off to the letterer, who would then rule the panels and letter the page. In the digital world, this part can be done by the pencil, before the pages are fully penciled. The main reason for this is that when the page is lettered, we can see how much room is used by the words, and we can then scale down or enlarge our pencil outlines to better fit the entire contents of the panel, which now includes word balloons and text. At this point, we haven't invested much time (comparatively speaking) in the drawing, so if we have to crop out parts or add more to panels, it can be done quickly and pretty painlessly. Ah, the advantages of working digitally!

> With the perks of working with digital comes a price in the use of terminology. What we've been calling panels are called frames in Manga Studio. I've learned to mentally translate frames into panels.

With all that in mind, panels in Manga Studio are peculiar animals. In this digital world, panels are outlined by vectors and the areas outside the panel are masked. What this means is that we can draw beyond the panel borders, and visually, the lines (or colors) stop at the border. Pretty nice when it comes to giving a panel a nice finished look. Like with most good things, there's a price to be paid.

That price is the need for planning. Now all that brouhaha about making a separate layer for panel borders makes sense. We needed to really know how we want the page to be broken down into panels, so this step of making the panels can be done quickly because we've done our homework.

In the *Time for actions – creating and setting up a frame folder layer* and *Time for action – cutting frames out of the frame folder layer* sections, we'll be creating panels in two different ways:

- All panels on a single layer
- Each panel in a separate panel group

Along the way, we'll be making a new **Auto action** palate to help us with this process, so things are all set up automatically in the way we like to work. We will use the grid, make new sub tools, alter the panel's shape and size, and learn a few tricks to make panels in Manga Studio work for us.

So, choose a page and let's get started.

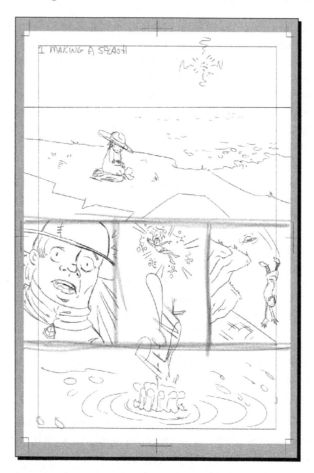

Time for action – creating and setting up a frame folder layer

The page I'm working on looks like the previous screenshot. It's a simple grid panel layout. The special thing is that the middle panel on the second tier and the bottom panel are one panel. It looks like an upside-down "T" shape.

1. To make sure that we're all on the same unit of measurement, go to **Preferences**, and in the **Ruler/Frame/Unit** section, set the **Length** unit to **MM**. PX is pixel and will change quite a bit between a page that's 300 dpi and 600 dpi. MM (millimeters) will give us consistent widths no matter the resolution. Unfortunately, since Celsys decided not to include inches in preferences, any conversion between inches and millimeters has to be done with a calculator of some kind. Time to use your preferred search engine, don't you think?

2. We need to start off with what Manga Studio calls a frame folder. This is a single page panel that extends only to the active area of our canvas. This was called the basic frame when we were setting up our page templates. See, it's all coming together.

3. Go to the **Layer** palette menu (top-left corner of the layer palette) and go to the **New layer** menu item. From the hierarchical menu, choose the next to last item: **Frame folder layer**.

4. In the dialog box, type in `panel 1` against **Name**. Make sure that **Draw border** is checked. **Line width** can be any value you want. In this example `1.00` mm (millimeter) was chosen to give a medium thickness to the panel border. This value can be changed on a panel-by-panel basis later. **Anti-Aliasing** can be set to **No** (meaning none), **Weak**, **Mid**, or **Strong**. If we are just dealing with straight lines, with no special effects on the borders, **No** or **Weak** is fine. If we want to have curves, rounded corners or emulate a brushstroke on the borders, then **Mid** or **Strong** would be best to choose.

5. Click on **OK**.

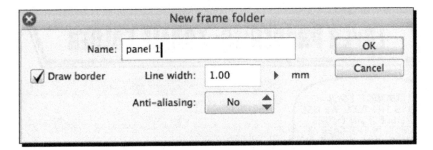

 Take a moment to look at the canvas now. The white area is what will be visible; the bluish area is what will be hidden or masked from view. Now, click on one of your pencil layers. Notice that all the fancy coloring is gone, we just have a border. Now we have to create layers to put in that frame folder. This way, when we split the main panel into smaller panels, the smaller panels will have copies of the layers we'll be making.

6. Click on the **Frame folder** layer named **Panel 1** to make it the current active layer.

7. Go to the **Layer** palette menu and make a new layer, or just use the new layer action we created a while back. Just make sure this layer is greyscale to conserve file size.

8. Notice that this new layer is within the **Frame folder** layer. This layer is now a child of the **Frame folder** layer and will inherit behaviors from the parent. In this case, the effects of the mask will be observed on this new layer. Any layer folder, including frame folders, can have masks added to them.

9. Choose a marking tool, pencil, or pen, and just scribble on this new layer. Go past the active area and see how the lines just stop at the border's edge.

What just happened?

By using the **Create frame folder** menu item, we created a frame folder complete with a mask that'll hide anything outside the frame. We also created a layer inside this folder layer that we can draw our roughs onto.

 Save your work, especially after creating a number of layers. Do this often, and if you have to deal with a zombie apocalypse, you won't lose much work.

Now we're going to split this **Frame folder** into panels. We won't be creating new groups, just dividing up this one honking huge panel into smaller ones.

Using the cut frame border tool to make panels

First, we should look at the **Frame folder** properties.

Like with some other layers (looking at your vector layers), there's a group of tools under the label **Tool navigation**. These are tools that we'll find real handy to use; we won't have to go to the **Tool** palette.

Since we want to create new panels, let's focus on the second tool, the cut border tool. Click on it to select it; let's take a look at the **Tool** properties and see what kind of mayhem we can do with it.

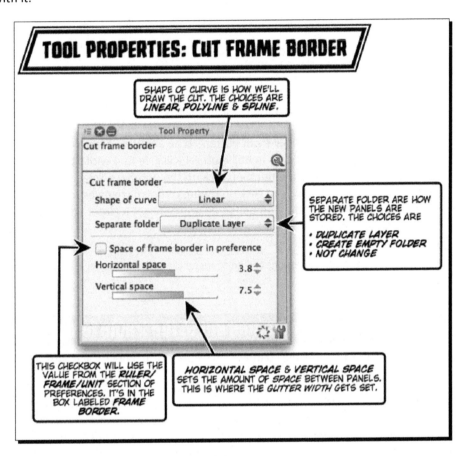

No sharks with laser beams here. But there are a few options that can make creating panels really fun and easy. They are:

- **Shape of curve**: This is where we choose how to split the frame.
    - **Linear**: This will draw a straight line.
    - **Polyline**: This can draw straight lines, so we can do an exploding type panel border or make inset panels.
    - **Spline**: This enables us to make curvy lines. Great for flashbacks.
    - **Polyline and Spline**: This will create a point to change the direction of the panel cut with a mouse click. The panel will be cut if the *Return* or *Enter* key is pressed. If the *Esc* key is pressed, then the panel cut is cancelled.

- ◆ **Separate folder**: This is where we choose how the new panel is stored.
  - ❑ **Duplicate Layer**: This will duplicate the frame border layer, including all child layers it contains.
  - ❑ **Create Empty Folder**: This will make the new panel empty.
  - ❑ **Not Change**: This will not change a thing. It should have been "No Change", but it is what it is.

- ◆ **Horizontal and Vertical space**: This is how we set the gutter width. In some manga and western comics, the horizontal and vertical spaces are different. Since we're keeping things (relatively) simple, we'll make both the same. The amount is in millimeters. Since we would like our gutters to be about an eighth of an inch (0.125 inches), a value of 3.2 (which is in millimeters) will give us a width that's close to what we want. To change the number, click on the numbers, select them, and type in the value. Otherwise, we can click on the up or down triangles to adjust the value. Experiment around with the number value until you get a gutter width you like best.

 Any of these settings can be changed for each new panel we cut.

Time for action – cutting frames out of the frame folder layer

Now we're going to cut the frame into panels. We can perform **Save As** and save a copy with `flat frame folder` appended to the file's name.

Depending on how your page is broken down, you may want to start cutting vertical slices. For our example, there's a clear horizontal cut we can do between panel one (which serves as a smallish splash or title panel) and the rest of the panels. Be mindful about the second and fourth panels (see the screenshot of the page earlier in this chapter) because the third and fifth panels are a single panel. This is how things roll in comics.

1. With the cutting frame tool active, set **Shape of curve** to **Linear** and **Separate folder** to **Not change**.

2. On the canvas, with the **Frame folder** as the current layer, click where you want the middle of the gutter to be, hold down the *Shift* key so the gutter will be parallel to the top and bottom, and drag the mouse horizontally until you see black lines that should be where we want the horizontal gutter to be.

3. Release the mouse or cursor; we should have something that looks like the following screenshot:

4. A quick look at the layer palette should show us that both panels are on the same layer. If we draw a line from top to bottom, it would be in both panels and be interrupted only by the gutter and the outer framing mask.

5. To do the next panels, we'll change the **Shape of curve** setting to **Polyline**. This setting will end one line segment, where we click and begin another. In our example, we want to click where we want the line to begin, click where we want it to end, and move our cursor holding down the *Shift* key, so we get a nice horizontal bottom line of the panel. This is the source of a possible problem. We want the bottoms of panels two and four to be on the same horizontal line. Unlike other tools, the frame cutter doesn't snap to anything. So we've got to observe it. The quickest way to do this is to make our canvas grid visible and make the grid lines match up where we want the bottom horizontal lines of those panels to be.

6. Go to the **View** menu and select the **Grid** menu item. We lucked out, there is a grid line that lines up pretty well. The following screenshot shows the grid along with where we have to click to create our next panel:

7. To perform perfectly horizontal and vertical cuts, hold down the *Shift* key. On the screenshot, click where you see the diamonds and drag where there's a white arrow. Press the *Enter* or *Return* key when done. You should have a page that looks like the following screenshot:

8. Follow the same sequence for the fourth panel (where the dude's jumping off the cliff). Now this page is all paneled.

What just happened?

With careful selection of settings, we were able to cut panels into the larger frame border folder. This gives us a flat page, with all the panels being cut into the same mask. This is fine, but having each panel in its own frame border layer can give us more flexibility when drawing, inking, and adding special effects.

Setting up panels in separate folders

The only difference between making panels on a single layer and making panels in multiple frame folders is changing the separate layer setting of the **Frame cutting** tool from **Not change** to **Duplicate Layer** or **Create empty layer** setting.

Before we begin going all gonzo with making panels, we need to think things out a bit.

The main purpose of creating multiple folders for panels is to have a separate layer within the folder for our pencils, inks, and colors. So, whenever we create a frame layer folder, we'll have to create those layers within it. I could swear there's something we can do to automate that.

This series of things is just the purpose that **Auto actions** was made to fulfill. **Auto actions** performs repetitious things we need to have so we can focus on what we want to get done.

We need to be clear about what we want this action to do:

- Create a new frame folder
- **Background pencils**: A raster greyscale layer with a layer color of green and a draft setting (so we can choose not to have this layer print or be exported out)
- **Foreground pencils**: A raster greyscale layer with normal (blue) layer color and a draft setting
- **Inks**: A vector layer with a purple layer color and no draft setting

This is a bit complicated but totally worth it in the time it'll save us. The beauty of this is that it'll work for a single layer with multiple panels as well as a page with multiple layers for panels. Remember that the cut frame tool can duplicate layers, including any child layers within the parent folder layer. Cool, huh?

Before we start recording actions, a few things to keep in mind are:

- The action will record all text that we enter into dialog boxes along with any choices we make in them.
- The actions will record what we do in the order we do them. We can always reorder, copy, and delete the individual sub actions when we're done with the action recording.
- It's always good to look at the action palette when recording. When a step's completed, it's added to the action.
- Even though it may take a bit more time to complete, use menu commands and not keyboard shortcuts. This helps us build up some muscle memory about what's inside some menus.

◆ If a large series of commands is making your action not work in the way you think it should, then break down the big action into little actions. This can be of immense help in figuring out why something doesn't work. Don't forget that we can duplicate and move subactions around; so we can build a large action from the smaller ones.

We can create this new action in the file we have open or we can make a new comic page document and name it "action tester", or some such name. Actions are (mostly) file agnostic, which means that they'll do the same thing on any document of any size or dimension. The thing to be concerned about is if the action requires a specific size to do its thing. A good naming convention is to put a brief description of requirement in parenthesis at the end of the name of the action.

Since we want to keep an eye on the action palette and be doing quite a bit with the layer palette, we need to see both at the same time. We need to make the **Action** palette a floating palette. Click on the tab with the **Action** palette's name, and drag it over the canvas area. When the whole palette becomes visible and tinted red, release the stylus, and we have our action palette floating above all the canvas. We can move it back when we're done with our action recording.

Let's do it. Note the time when starting this.

Time for action – creating an action to create a frame folder layer

This is a bit involved and each step must be done in order. It would be best to read through these steps once or twice before trying them out. Actions are pretty sturdy things and they cannot break your computer or install Manga Studio (I've tried). When we're done, we'll have an action that'll make a full page frame folder complete with layers for pencils and inks.

1. With a document open, go to the **Action** palette, and from the palette menu, choose the **Add new auto action** menu item.

2. Name this new action `Panel Set-up`.

3. Click the red-colored begin recording button.

4. In the **Layer** palette, go to the layer palette menu, choose **New layer**, and select **Frame folder...** from the hierarchical menu.

5. In the dialog box, give this **Frame folder** a name, such as `Panel 1`. Adjust the line width to suit your needs. 15 pixels is what we used last time.

6. Click on **OK** and see whether the action was recorded.

7. Now, **Frame folder** should be selected in the **Layers** palette. When we add new layers, they will be made within **Frame folder**. That's exactly what we want.

8. Go to the **Layer** palette menu and navigate to **New layer | Raster layer**.

9. Name the layer `Pencils BG` and set the expression color to **Grey**.

10. Click on **OK**.

11. In the palette menu, go to **Layer settings | Set layer as draft**.

12. In the **Layer Properties** palette, click on the layer **Color** button on the **Layer Properties** palette.

13. Click on the color swatch (it defaults to blue) and change the color to green.

14. Make another new layer like we just did. Name this layer `Pencils`. Change **Expression color** to **Gray**, go to **Set as Draft Layer**, click on the **Layer color** button on the **Layer Properties** palette, and leave **Layer color** as default blue.

15. Two layers down, one to go. In the **Layer** palette menu, navigate to **New layer | Vector layer...**.

16. Name this layer `Inks`.

17. Set **Expression color** to **Monotone** or **Gray**.

18. In the **Layer Properties** palette, click on the **Layer color** button and change the color to purple.

19. Click on the square (stop recording) button.

What just happened?

Now check the time. Subtract a minute or two because of reading these instructions while creating the action. Let's say it took you three minutes to do all of this. I'm not a rocket scientist, but all this set up over a 22-page story adds up to an hour. With it now being an action, it's done in an instant. Now, that hour of time can be used to draw.

The idea of using two layers for pencils is that we have one for backgrounds and another to add any perspective rulers or such. By separating foreground from background, we can move either around to get a better composition and avoid tangents. We'll get into tangents when we start penciling our page.

A vector layer was created for our inks, as that's my process. As we use vector layers, we can decide if they work well for us or not. The big advantage of using vector layers is that we can adjust the vectors like we do in an illustrator or a vector editing app. With Raster, we just have to erase and re-ink. And when we get to coloring, we'll learn that Manga Studio can be set to allow us to always color inside the lines. The coolness just doesn't stop, does it?

Now, on a new document (or one that's open and doesn't have any frame folders in it), test out your new action. If things don't happen the way you think they should, open the disclosure triangle and look at each of the subactions to make sure they got recorded properly. Sometimes it's better to just start over, and since we're learning about Manga Studio, that's not a bad thing to have to do.

Have a go hero – creating an action to create a frame folder layer

Each layer can have its palette color changed from the default color to any color from the pop-up menu near the top left of the **Layer** palette. If you want, add a new subaction where the pencils have a palette background color that reflects the layer color. We've covered many ways to add new actions to an existing action, so go have a go at it.

We can also add new commands to an existing action. If we click on the disclosure triangle next to the name of the action, we can see all the commands it contains. If we select the last action and click on the red dot, or go into the **Auto action** palette menu and choose begin recording auto action, we can add what we do next to that **Auto action**. What would happen if we create a new color raster layer and name it Colors?

Making panels separate frame folders

This is where all that set-up work we did in creating this action pays off big time. We have our page with its rough layers and panel breakdowns on layers. Now, with our fancy pants action, we can create a new frame folder layer with layers inside it. But that's just a single panel that takes up the entire page.

What we want to do now is to create new panels, have each panel be its own frame folder, and have copies of the layers that the original frame folder has. See where we're going on this? (Remember, at this time only the original layers we drew on have any art in them; the layers mentioned in this part are empty.)

 In *Time for action – creating an action to create a frame folder layer*, we made a single layer with multiple panels. Now, we're creating individual folder layers for each panel The benefit of this method is that our pencils, inks, and colors are all on their own layer and we can delete or fill that layer without messing up other panels.

Perform the following steps to get things set up:

1. Make the **Frame folder** layer active by clicking on it.
2. Now click on the **Cut frame border** button in the **Layer properties** palette.
3. In the **Tool properties** palette, set **Shape of curve** to **Polyline** and **Separate folder** to **Duplicate Layer**. **Horizontal space** should be at the setting it was when we last used this tool. Leave it as it is or adjust it to your needs.

This will make it so that any new layer folders that are created will be a copy of the original frame folder (and that means children are copied for free).

Now, we can create new panels like we did a lifetime ago, or just a few pages back. The big change is that each panel is now its own frame folder, and this change means we have to be more mindful of how we cut out new panels.

Time for action – making new frame folders using the cut frame border tool

The first few times you cut a frame folder, it's going to seem strange. But it will begin to make sense. It may be good to read through this section once before beginning this exercise.

The following screenshot shows what we're going to do with the frame folder cutting tool. We'll be referring to numbers that's on it, so keep it bookmarked for the time being.

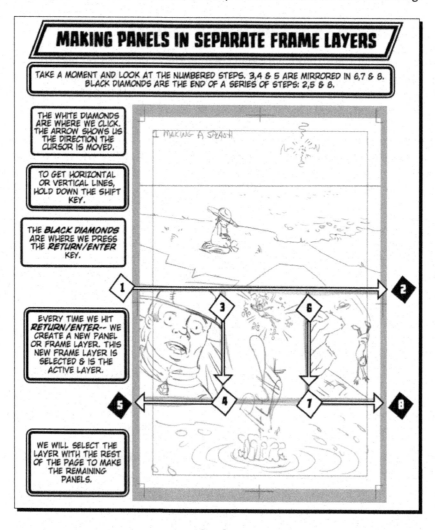

1. With our example page open, make our first cut from where the white diamond **1** is, hold down the *Shift* key so the cut will be at a horizontal level, move the cursor to where the black diamond **2** is, and press the *Return* or *Enter* key on the keyboard.

2. Faster than a speeding pixel, we now have two frame folders. The original one should still be named `Panel 1` and the new one should have a name like `Frame 1`.

3. The new frame folder and the active layer are selected. We don't need to do any work on them. So, we look down the list in the **Layer** palette and click on the **Panel 1** layer.

4. As mentioned in the previous screenshot, this is how Manga Studio does frame cutting. The new frame is selected and put on top of the old frame. We just need to click on **Frame folder** that has the rest of the page we want to cut and carry on.

5. For the second panel, we want to click once where diamond **3** is, hold down *Shift* key so the line is a true vertical, and click where diamond **4** is.

6. Still holding down the *Shift* key, we move our cursor to the location of diamond **5** and press the *Enter* key to make our newest panel.

7. In the **Layer** palette list, this new layer is called **Frame 2**.

8. Click on the **Panel 1** layer to finish with the last panel.

9. Click where diamond **6** is, hold down the *Shift* key, and click on diamond **7**.

10. Continue holding down the *Shift* key and move the cursor to where diamond **8** is, and click on *return*.

11. This makes our final panel of this page.

I've found that no matter what I name the original layer, the new frame layers will always be named **Frame X** (where X is a number starting with 1 or 2 and increases towards the total number of panels on the page).

Since I like things nice and neat in my layer palette, layers will have to be moved and renamed.

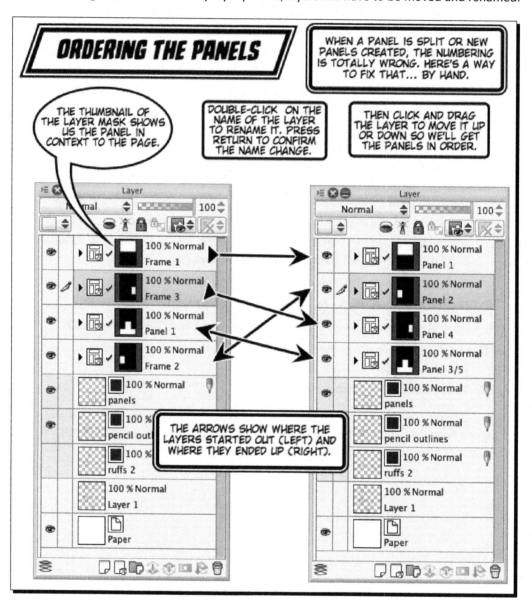

To change the layers, perform the following steps:

1. Click on the disclosure triangle to close the layers. We want to work just on the naming and order of the frame layers. We don't need to see or work with the child layers.

2. Using the thumbnails of the **Layer** masks, we can see where the panels are in context of the page.

3. Double-click on the name **Frame 1**, and the name's selected.

4. Type in `Panel 1` and press *Enter* to commit to the change.

5. Do the same for **Frame 3**, rename it to `Panel 4`.

6. **Frame 1** is renamed to `Panel 3/5`.

7. **Frame 2** is renamed to `Panel 2`.

8. Now, drag the frame layers around so they are in order; `Panel 1` on top and `Panel 2` below it, and so on.

9. The one issue we'll have in this example is the upside-down "T" panel that's been renamed to `Panel 3/5`. Where should it go?

10. `Panel 3/5` could be placed after `Panel 2`, but it felt like it belonged at the end of the panels because the area for `Panel 5` is larger than the area for `Panel 3`. This is just an arbitrary choice. If you feel better putting it elsewhere, it's your page to work on.

11. For practice, click on various layers and see what happens to the appearance of the page in the canvas. Only the current frame layer escapes the blue mask.

What just happened?

We have taken our page filled with rough sketches and panel lines and refined the roughs into simple line drawings. Then, we figured and used the frame layer and cut frame tool to make our layers. Along this winding path, we also made a few actions that will save us a good chunk of time as we continue to make comics. We thus ended up with a page that has its panels all nice and neat. Each panel has layers for us to draw our backgrounds and foregrounds on, and to ink when the pencils are done.

What if we want our panels to go to the edges of the page, like for a full-bleed page? Read on.

Time for action – bleeding out to the ends of the page

Although the panels end at the active area of the page, we can make them go to the edges for a full-bleed effect. Go to a panel that has at least one side on the basic frame, also known as **Active area**.

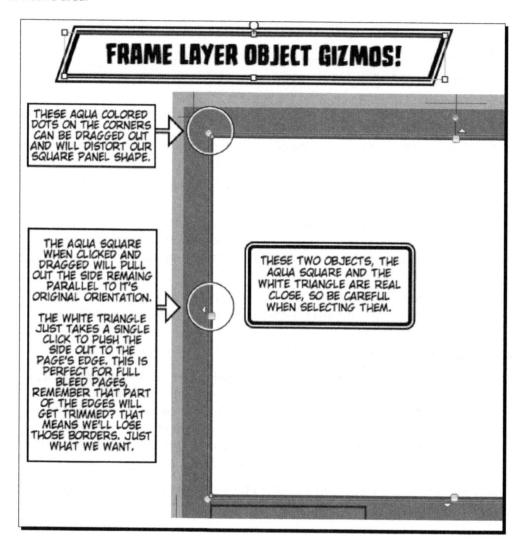

1. With the **Mask visibility** option turned on in the **Mask status** menu, go to the **Layer properties** palette and click on the **Object** tool.

2. Look at the canvas. Notice the aqua-colored dots and squares. The previous screenshot describes what they do.

3. A single click on the white triangle moves the line to the edge of the page. Since we allowed bleed, this border will be cut off when the page is trimmed.

4. If we want to break up the squareness of the panel, we can click-and-drag on the round aqua dots.

Now, just go from panel to panel and look through them until you get the exact panel arrangement you want.

Pop quiz

Q1. What's the equivalent of panels in comics in Manga Studio?

1. Art containment objects
2. Frame borders
3. Binding border areas

Q2. Masks allow us to define areas that are hidden.

1. True
2. False

Q3. **Auto actions** can't be changed once recorded.

1. True
2. False

Q4. When cutting a large panel into smaller ones, can we make a copy of the layers within the panel folder at the same time?

1. True
2. False

Q5. Which of the following can have a mask?

1. Raster layer
2. Vector layer
3. Text layer
4. Folder layer
5. Cake layer
6. All but (5)
7. All but (3) and (5)

8. All of the above

9. None of the above

Summary

Whew! This was a major chapter. We've gone from roughs to panels. Along the way we also learned a bit more about how Manga Studio does things and how we can make it work for us. We made actions that performed routine tasks for us, possibly saving us from hours of boredom. We also made individual panels all nice and neat on their own layers.

Life is good. Unfortunately, text will vex us in the next chapter.

5

Putting Words in My Mouth

Lettering, in comics, is how we give our characters a voice and our narration a tone. Unlike hand-lettering, computer text is always legible. The downside is that sometimes it looks too mechanical, especially with fonts not designed with comics in mind. In this chapter, we'll learn what we can do with text in Manga Studio, and more importantly, what we cannot do. Along the way, we'll learn about some quirks that comic lettering has and some basic proofreading tips and hints.

In this chapter, we will cover the following topics:

- Introducing comic fonts
- Type of lettering in comics
- Creating a script
- Using Manga Studio's lettering tool
- Working with text areas and avoiding some common problems

The soundtrack of comics

Since the dawn of comics, words have been a partner in telling stories. What would a drawing of Superman flying be without the phrase "Up, up, and away!" or Charlie Brown be without his trademarked "Good Grief!"? Without "!?!" in comics, they would be a typo. Sure, there's been silent comics, but they are the exceptions.

Unlike the printed (or pixelated) words in books or e-books, the words in comics are much more than just dead letters; when placed in a word balloon or caption box, these collection of words become an integral part of the artwork itself. Text in comics is where we can establish our character's voice and set a mood for our stories.

Now, with computerized lettering, good lettering is available to all of us. As one who had done hand-lettering, this is a good thing. There are hundreds of comic lettering fonts out there, waiting to be downloaded and used. It's our job as comic creators to use them well.

Got to get them all

When it comes to comic fonts, there's (in my humble opinion) just two main places to get them.

Comicraft is one place where we can get many different kinds of comic lettering fonts. The URL for this site is `http://www.comicbookfonts.com`.

The prices are a bit steep, but the quality is there. Since there's just us here, let me tell you a secret. If you visit Comicraft's website on New Year's eve, the fonts are on a never-to-be-repeated sale. Last year, 2013, each of the fonts were on sale for 20.14 dollars! The next New Year's eve/day, the price per font will be 20.15 dollars. I registered on the site and made a wish list; I usually begin saving up for this sale a few months before the year ends.

On the other hand, Blambot (`http://www.blambot.com`) avoids all this sale stuff by just pricing their fonts at a lower price all the time. Check out the variety on Blambot's site and download some of the free fonts that are offered to indie comic artists. Don't forget to look at Blambot's home page and see whether there's a code for a 10 percent off on your font purchase.

Be sure to print out or archive your e-mail receipt for your fonts that you've bought from Blambot. First of all, they are your proof of purchase, so that if there are fixes for fonts you've bought, all you have to do is provide the transaction code and you'll get your fixed font files e-mailed to you without any hassle.

With Comicraft, make sure you register at the website. They'll keep track of your purchases (although it's always a good thing to keep the e-mail invoices). These are business purchases, and could be tax deductable, depending on your local laws and regulations.

Font formats

When purchasing or downloading fonts, we have our choice of a few different formats:

1. Postscript
2. TrueType
3. OpenType

Postscript is the oldest type of printable font. What Postscript fonts started was the ability to scale fonts to any size without any jaggies (stair stepping and aliasing like in a bitmap raster drawing where we've zoomed in too far).

TrueType fonts were the first real alternative to Postscript fonts. What made them so great was that they could be sized to any point size and still look great on the computer screen and print out well. Unlike Postscript fonts, we no longer had to use a bitmapped version of the font.

OpenType's been around for about ten years now and it is what I'm slowly converting all my fonts to. One thing that makes OpenType so great is its auto-ligatures. Ligatures are when there are two letters, such as a double "L" or "O", or a "TH", and an OpenType aware app can substitute the regular text for a special symbol that combines the two letters. This is sweet because it makes the text look more unique and less computer generated. Here's a comparison of Blambot's Monsterific OpenType font used in an app that utilizes OpenType and Manga Studio:

Notice how different the letters "T", "I", "R", and "L" are in this example. Any program that can use the special features that OpenType gives us can really make things pop.

Spoiler warning: Manga Studio 5 doesn't make use of OpenType features. If you do use OpenType fonts, be sure to rasterize the text before printing or exporting, as Manga Studio is pretty unreliable when it comes to most things that relate to fonts. In fact, rasterize all text once it's finished. If you don't foresee making any changes, it is a good practice for Manga Studio. One time I had to reletter an eight-page story because Manga Studio changed the font to a plain sans serif, instead of the comic dialog font I had used. What was supposed to be a quick export of a short story, became an exercise in resetting all text. We'll touch on rasterizing text towards the end of this chapter.

The main selling point of OpenType fonts is that it helps to prevent our lettering from looking too computer-generated and sterile. There may be ways to complete that with plain old TrueType or Postscript fonts, but they take some time and effort to do well, and OpenType does it for us for free.

Comic lettering font conventions

If we look at the font samples on the vendor's websites and from most comic books, we'll notice one thing about comic fonts; it's that most of them are all uppercase fonts. This has to do with legibility, since uppercase letters are more easily read at smaller sizes than mixed-case letters are at the same size. The fact that hand-lettering all uppercase letters is a faster process makes it the standard for comic text; not to mention that the printing presses of the 1930s were very crude compared to our present-day home printers.

Uppercase and lowercase letters referred to the time when text was cold set. This means that each letter was an individual block (like a rubber stamp, only made out of metal), and the person doing the typesetting, the typographer, had to put each letter in one-by-one into the plate that would be put into the printing press. The old-school typographer had two drawers, each filled with lots of letters. Those drawers were called cases. What's right?, the drawer on the top was all capitals, and the lower drawer was all little (non-capital) letters. That's where this uppercase and lowercase terminology (and more, as we'll discover) came from.

Comic lettering fonts are usually sans serif, which means that there's no little feet on the bottoms of letters like "F", "M", and so on, except for one very, very special case: the personal pronoun "I". It's a convention in comics for the "I" to have serifs. In most comic lettering fonts, we can get the pronoun "I" by holding down the *Shift* key and clicking the *I* key, just as if we're typing in a capital "I". If a comic lettering font doesn't do that, sorry to say, it's not a true comic lettering font, except for some comic lettering fonts that contain both upper and lowercase letters.

Although it comes with most computer installations, the last font we should ever use is the dreaded comic sans font. Nothing screams amateur louder than using that font. There are dozens of better and free fonts that can be used for comic lettering so much more elegantly. Do yourself (and your readers) a favor, go to www.blambot.com and download one of the free fonts there. You will not regret it.

Categories of comic fonts

Take a few seconds and think about the kinds of text we see in comics. There's the text inside word balloons, captions, sound effects, titles, and the "to be continued" box at the end of the issue. It stands to reason that there's going to be specific categories of comic lettering fonts for each of these, right?

- **Balloon text or dialog fonts**: These are what we use for most of our dialog and caption boxes. This category is very legible at small sizes.

- **Sound effects fonts**: These will put the boom in the dynamite, the swoosh in the plane landing, and the splash for that rock that was thrown in the pond.

- **Display or design fonts**: These can be used for titles, credits, and other instances where text needs some oomph.

- **Dingbat or symbol fonts**: These are for those times where there's a wizard muttering arcane incantations or an alien asking to be taken to our leader, and also for some good old language.

Within these categories, there may be other flavors of fonts, such as fantasy, Sci-Fi, and so on. If all this is new to you, take a bit of time and look around the sites that were mentioned. Do an Internet search on comic lettering. Comic lettering is a direct descendent from the art of calligraphy. Both these disciplines have a rich history, and we should be aware of it even if the only ink we use is pixel-based. Many techniques and methods used in analog calligraphy are transferable to the digital realm, just saying.

But this is a book on Manga Studio, so let's do some lettering in it.

Lettering in Manga Studio 5

In most aspects of creating comics, Manga Studio is like seeing a super-wide full screen 3D movie that doesn't give you headaches. Then when it's time to letter, that screen becomes a grainy weak UHF signal on a little 12-inch black-and-white screen.

I've been using Manga Studio since Version 3, and to be brutally honest, its lettering abilities have been very lacking in the past versions up to the present version (I would almost say they've been getting worse). If our demands on lettering are low, Manga Studio can do a fair job. If we really want to do involved lettering, then it comes up quite short—to the extent that it's more work than it would be to get better results in another program and import the rasterized lettering into Manga Studio (which is what I usually do). In this section, we'll letter a sample page with Manga Studio and see where the shortcomings are and how to work around them.

Preparing our page for lettering

If we all have been following along, we should have a few things already done. A page or more is already at the line-drawn stage. Now, it's time to work on the script. Manga Studio is best used when there isn't going to be much editing.

First off, let's make sure that our script is all formatted so we can copy and paste our text. There really isn't a set format for comic book scripts. Usually, some conventions from screen and stage plays are used.

Here's a short sample of what kind of formatting our script can have:

```
Page 1. A six panel page. It takes place on a tropical island. Our
main characters, Mary and Max are sitting on lounge chairs watching
an UFO land in the water.

Panel 1. Establishing shot of the island.

Caption: An undisclosed location in the Pacific Ocean.

Max: What's on our itinerary for today, sweetie?

Mary: Rest, relaxation and --

Panel 2. The UFO appears. All kinds of light and energy blasts
surround it. Mary and Max stand up, spilling their tropical drinks on
the sand.

SFX: TRAAA-AAKA-THOOOOM!

Panel 3. Close Up of Mary.
Mary (excited): --Figuring out what brought that flying saucer here!
```

There's nothing special about this formatting. It can be typed out using a basic text editor, as what comes with either Macintosh (TextEdit) or Windows (Notepad) operating systems. This example was typed using TextEdit and pasted to this page.

Each new comic page could start on a new page of the script, followed by a double-line space between the end of the page description and the `Panel 1` description. Another double-space is needed for the character name, caption, sound effect (shortened to SFX), any parenthetical information, a colon (:), a space followed by what the character is saying, and the contents of the caption box.

For the rest of this chapter, we'll consider options for us as a sole artist/writer and the artist's part of an artist-writer team. When we're part of a team, we don't make changes to the text unless we have permission to do so from the writer. As the artist part of the team, words aren't our job. We can, however, add line breaks and spaces to the text so it will fit within balloons and captions better.

We'll be working on a sample page called the dialog page. There's a Manga Studio LIP file and a TXT file in the exercises folder that you can open up and follow along, if you wish. Just to keep us on our toes, the artwork for this dialog page has mistakes in it that we'll find as we progress with our lettering work.

Time for action – writing the script

If you want, here's an exercise to help you write your own script. The only requirement is a basic text editor (Notepad or TextEdit) and some imagination:

1. Finish up the script for your story, if you haven't already. There can either be a script for the entire story or just one page.

2. Follow the formatting as shown. Character name, type of caption, sound effects, and the dialog or contents of the caption/sound effect should be on the same line(s).

3. Read the dialog out loud. This is a great way to make sure that the dialog rings true and emphaszes the words right. In comics, we'll emphasize words by formatting them in bold and italics. Since we'll be copying the text to Manga Studio from our word processor, it's best to leave the file as a plain text file. If we don't, Manga Studio will use the font that we used in the text.

4. As we'll learn later, Manga Studio's the text objects doesn't have word wrap (when a new line is created automatically). Therefore, in long passages of text (dialog or captions), break the text into multiple lines. Look at the penciled page to get an idea of how many words a caption or dialog balloon can have. It's not going to be exact, but it will allow us to have a text object we can move around easily before fine-tuning the text.

5. If you can, print out the script. Looking at the script in various ways (monitor, tablet, or hard-copy) can enable us to find that one, single typo that has avoided detection.

What just happened?

We went through a process of creating our own comic scripts. Some of the steps (such as reading the dialog out loud) may seem odd, but it's quite good in practice and can lead to some good results. As for projects, it's sometimes a good idea to let our scripts cool off overnight, as mistakes and such can be more evident once we're looking at our script with fresh eyes. Now, we have a script that we can copy text from to paste in Manga Studio.

Even if we don't intend on writing our own stories, it's something that is good to do at least once, so we'll have an idea of what it's like writing a script. Knowing how the "other half" lives is always good knowledge.

 Watch out for errors like using "it's" when you mean a possessive pronoun like "its". "It's" is a contraction for "it is". The same goes for "your" and "you're". One is a pronoun, "your job...", the other is a contraction for "you are" like "you're on the job roster..." These are little errors that the reader will notice and break the spell of storytelling that we've spent so much effort weaving.

It's time to have a look at our rough penciled page. Here's the example page we'll be working on in the following examples. If you want, work on your own page.

Notice that the pencils are rough in this example. The perspective is all done by eye. Any shading that's done is real basic, serving more to give a foreground-background distinction than anything else. Don't get too detailed at this stage. The reason for this is if we compare the rough page with the script, there's a lot of dialog in some panels that are small to begin with, so putting in the text will be a challenge.

One thing to note is that this page was done with the page template we created earlier. The innermost thin rectangle is where all text must be within. We can't go over that boundary. If we do, some text will either be cut off or be very difficult to read if the book is a trade paperback or hard-cover book.

Before we can start lettering this page, we really need to look at the text tool in Manga Studio.

The text tool

If there's an area in Manga Studio that shows the app was created in Japan and translated into English, the text tool waves that flag loud and proud. Unfortunately, a lot on that flag is just superfluous and useless to us, unless we're doing our comics in Japanese or another Asian language.

Let's explore this tool, shall we?

Time for action – using the text tool

Start up Manga Studio 5, if it's not already running, and then perform the following steps:

1. Create a new document. Use the comic page template if you want.

2. Click on the text tool; it's the one with the uppercase "**A**" on it. If it's not on the toolbar, then it may be that the word balloon tool was used last. Click on the icon that looks like a word balloon.

Usually, the text tool will be in the last section of tools (just above the color swatches). If you move your mouse slowly and hover over each tool, you'll see a tool tip. Unlike the icons, which always show the last tool used, the tool tips will always show the name of the tool. In this case, the fourth down is the text tool.

3. Then, go to the **Sub tool** palette and find the text tool there. If it's not selected, then click on it to select it. The icon will have an uppercase **A** on it.

4. With the text tool selected, go to the **Tool properties** palette and click on the wrench icon to bring up **Tool Settings**. Although the **Tool properties** palette has some of the settings that the text tool has, **Tool Settings** has all of the categories and options for text that we'll be looking at.

5. There are four categories of text tool:

   ❑ **Font**: We choose the font, size, and other font-specific settings here.

   ❑ **Text**: We can change how the text is aligned (here it's called justify), the leading between lines of text (here it's called line space), and how the text is colored.

   ❑ **Reading**: This is supposed to be a way of having some kind of text above other text, or some such thing. This has never worked for me and won't be covered in this chapter. This may have some utility for Asian Manga, but for western comics, it's just so much wasted space.

   ❑ **Edit settings**: Here, we can establish essential things if our text is on a horizontal or vertical direction. Some of them are: how the text is rendered on the page, whether a new text layer is created for every text object, and whether to show the resize handles on the text objects.

6. Make sure that the font category is selected. Choose a comic font that was (hopefully) downloaded and installed earlier. Check your operating system for instructions on how to install fonts if you're uncertain about how to do it.

7. Set the font size to a size around 24 points. This is just an exercise, so the exact size is up to you. You can type in any text you like, or you can use a line that's on Blambot's page, "The lazy penciler eats salt and vinegar chips and blows another deadline."

8. Notice that the text will just keep on going. The only way to create a new line for text is to hit the *Return* key. Manga Studio has no word warp.

9. The text area is bound by a box with aqua-colored dots and boxes. The dots, when clicked-and-dragged, will increase the text size. The boxes will scale the text wider (on the horizontal sides) or taller (on the vertical sides). While this may be useful in sound effects, we don't usually want our text to be distorted. Be careful when moving the text block.

10. Unlike most modern text editors/processors, Manga Studio has no spell checking. That's why it's so important to spell check before copying and pasting from a text editor to Manga Studio.

11. After typing, move your cursor around the bounding box that contains the text. The cursor will change from an "I" beam into a diagonal, horizontal, or vertical double-arrow when moved over the aqua dots or boxes. When the text object itself can be moved, the cursor changes into a four-direction set of arrows.

What just happened?

That was fun, wasn't it? The major takeaways from this are:

- The only way to create new lines for text is to hit the *Return* key and continue typing

- The controllers (the aqua dots and boxes) just resize the text

- Once text is in Manga Studio, there's no way to spell check, except manually by using our (or somebody else's) eyes

There are a few things that were discovered by trial and many errors:

- Unlike most other apps, if something goes askew with fonts, and they have to be reinstalled, Manga Studio will not recognize them anymore. Manga Studio will treat them as new and any page that uses that font will now open and display a generic sans serif font. So that means every single word, balloon, caption box, or sound effect in the text has to be manually selected and the intended font has to be rechosen. If we're working on a 20-page story, that's a good chunk of a morning or afternoon!

- Because of the lack of any word wrap, hard returns have to be deleted and redone if text is added or deleted. Again, for a 20-page story, this is not a simple task. This is another reason to work from a typed script. It's already been edited and revised, so we won't have to do this after creating the lettering in Manga Studio.

- The Bold icon in the **Text properties** palette will only work if Manga Studio recognizes a font style as being bold. So, bold-italics won't show up unless we choose that style from the font drop-down menu.

- In cases where the letters go past the top or bottom margin (as defined by Manga Studio), the parts that are outside will get cut off. The only solution is to add a hard return before and/or after the text.

- Sometimes, the last letter will get partially cut off in a line. The only way around it is to add a space at the end of the line. Depending on the alignment (like center or right), a space will have to be added to the beginning of every line in the text object so the text will balance out.

◆ The text area box, the bluish lines with the aqua squares and dots, scales the text. Mostly, every other app that has text selection areas (where a block of text is selected as an object) has ways of resizing the area the text fits into rather than resizing the text itself. This could be caused by the fact that Manga Studio doesn't have word wrap. Again, it's a flat screen HD TV compared to a black and white cathode ray tube.

Text tool settings

There are four categories of settings for text in the **Tool Settings** palette. There's one we won't be covering and that's the reading category; that's because I've yet to find any use or purpose for it in western comics.

Font category

The two options that are used most frequently are the **Font** drop-down menu and the **Size** setting. The rest are of no use other than window dressing.

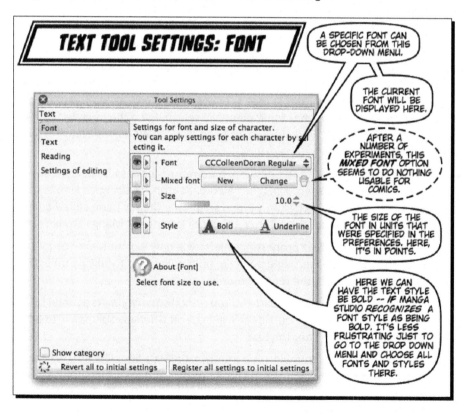

Text category

If we want to change how the text is aligned or the color of the text, this is where we do it. Line space is very limited, as we can't get the lines of text as close together as we can in any other app.

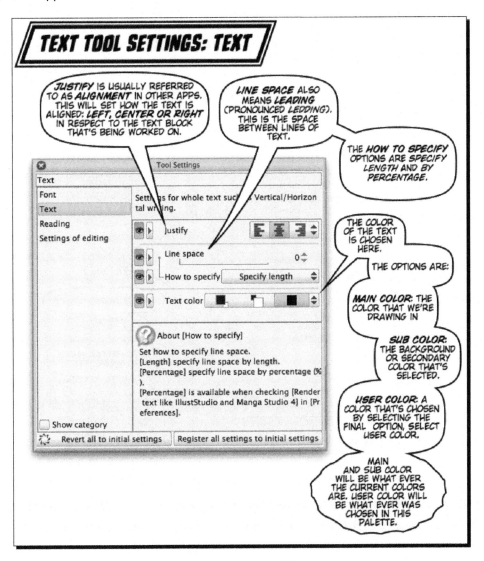

Settings of editing category

Usually, we'll want to use the text direction of left to right. There may be times where we'll want to have letters in a vertical arrangement, such as in a marquee. Choosing vertical gives spectacularly useless results.

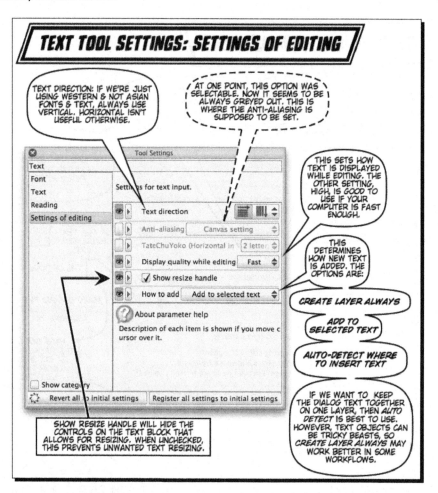

Time for action – creating a text tool for dialogs and captions

Unlike most word processors and modern graphic apps such as illustrators, there's no way to create paragraph styles in Manga Studio. However, we can create a custom sub tool that will serve as a poor substitute. If you haven't installed a comic book font, do so now. This process is pretty much the same as the other times we've created new sub tools, so let's do it!

1. Select the text tool from the tool bar.

2. In the **Sub tool** palette, go to the palette menu and choose **Create custom sub tool**. You should see a dialog box similar to the following screenshot:

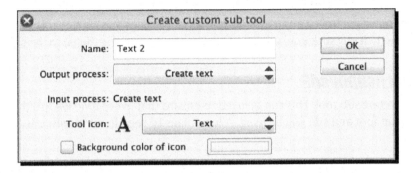

3. In the **Name** textbox, type in `Text Dialog`.

4. The **Output process** option should be **Create text** by default.

5. The **Tool icon** option should read **Text**; it looks like an uppercase "**A**".

6. We can change the option against **Background color of icon** to a color of our choice; this way we can easily distinguish our text tool from the others.

7. Click on **OK**.

8. In the **Tool properties** palette, click on the wrench icon to bring up the **Tool Settings** palette.

9. In the **Font** category of the **Tool properties** palette, choose your dialog font from the drop-down menu. In the example, "BlamBot Casual" is chosen. Choose a font of your choice.

10. Font size is set at **9** points. If that seems too large, we can go as small as **6.35**. Usually, **9** points should be fine for most cases.

11. Click on the **Text** category and click on the eye-con icon, so that it is displayed in the **Tool properties** palette. Set it for center alignment.

12. On the **Text** category, set the line space to zero. Click on the eye-con icon, so that it appears in the **Tool properties** palette. Sometimes, it's good to be able to adjust the space between lines quickly.

13. In the **Edit settings** category, click on the eye-con icon to make this appear in the properties palette. Set it to **Create layer always**. Even though this will create many different layers, they can be moved around using the layer move tool, which is a bit easier and less prone to accidental text scaling than using the text tool to move them. As we get more experience with text and Manga Studio, we can change this to **Auto detect where to insert text**.

14. Once all the settings are satisfactory, go to the **Tool properties** palette menu (click on the upper-left corner of the palette, the button looks like a stylized menu, and choose **Register all to initial settings** from the pop-up menu.

15. There we go. Now we can use this tool for our dialogs and captions. Any changes we make to it will stick until we revert (go back to the initial settings) to the saved settings.

What just happened?

We created a text sub tool. This can be used to ensure that every time we use this particular tool, the same font and size will be used. A few things to keep in mind with this new sub tool are:

1. If for some reason we have to remove/reinstall the font, Manga Studio will probably not recognize the reinstalled font. So, this sub tool would have to be modified to use the "new" old font.

2. This is not a style as used within other, more modern, text handling apps. If this sub tool gets changed, the changes will be applied to new text, and the old text has to be manually changed to reflect the new text settings.

3. If there's any change that we want to make to the text, such as color or size, we need to select the text that we want to make the changes to. This means if we want to change the entire text object, we have to first select all the text and then make the changes.

Putting down text on the page

Okay, we're all set to begin lettering in Manga Studio. We should have our script written, pages roughed in, and our text sub tool created, and we are familiar with the settings and shortcomings of using text within Manga Studio, so let's get going!

Time for action – lettering our first page

We can work on our own stories, or we can follow along using the dialog page Manga Studio file and the script file.

1. Manga Studio should be running; start it up if it's not open.

2. Open the page we want to letter. For this example, it's `dialog page.lip`. In the *Time for action – lettering our first page* section, instructions will be specific for that example.

3. Open the panel folder named `Panel 1`. Inside that folder is the layers that we created via the action we created in *Chapter 4, Roughing It.*

4. Click on the **Pencil** layer to make it the active layer. In the **Properties** palette, click on the **Layer color** button in the **Effects** section. This will ensure that the pencils will be displayed in blue and the text we'll be creating will be easier to read because of the blue pencil color.

5. At the bottom of the layer palette, click on the **New layer folder** button. Name the new layer folder "`text-dialog`". This will be handy if we want to work on the entire page without having lettering get in our way; we'll just hide the layer folder.

6. Open the script in a text-editing program of your choice. Select the first line of dialog and copy it as it is.

7. Back in Manga Studio, click with the text tool on the canvas roughly where we want the text to be.

8. When the cursor appears, paste the copied text. In most cases, the text should be pasted and the font that we chose in Manga Studio should be the font used. If the font of the document you copied from is in the Manga Studio text, then select all the text and choose the desired font from the font drop-down menu.

9. We now have a single line of dialog.

10. All we have to do is figure out where to put the line breaks in, so we'll have a few lines instead of one.

We interrupt our scheduled *Time for action* for a bit of info on how to break dialogs into lines. In our dialogs and captions, we want to avoid islands and rivers. Islands are when there's a one or two letter word all on its own at the beginning or ending of a line of text. A river is when spaces between words form a stream of white space from the first line of text to the next several. The following screenshot is an illustration of that. The grey dashed line shows where the rivers are.

THIS IS AN EXAMPLE HOW RIVERS LOOK LIKE IN TEXT. THESE RIVERS MAKE SOME PARTS OF THE TEXT SEEM TO STAND APART AND JUST PLAIN LOOKS BAD.

In this example, the rivers make a pair of islands on both sides of the text (rivers are shown as dotted lines). Preventing rivers and islands in Manga Studio can be challenging, but it can be done, and should be done because good solid blocks of text without rivers or islands look more professional and read better.

There are some tricks to avoiding these issues:

Firstly, add a space or two at the beginning or ending of a line. Sure this is cheating, but it works and won't get us thrown out of professional sports.

Secondly, change the alignment of text. Sometimes, left or right alignment looks better if the dialog/caption box is at the edge of a panel. Usually, the text is centered in dialog, but that's not a hard rule.

Thirdly, make the line of text longer or shorter by ending a line sooner. This means that some work will have to be done to even out the line length, but that's what happens when there's no word wrap.

Sometimes, it can't be helped, so we just learn to live with islands and rivers in Manga Studio text.

We now return to the regularly scheduled *Time for action – lettering our first page*.

11. When the text is finished, drag the text layer into the `Dialog-captions` folder. Now, when we create new text objects/layers, they will be within the `Dialog-captions` folder if we make the latest text layer the active layer.

12. The first bit of dialog was broken down as shown in the following screenshot:

13. There was a river on the last two lines of text—between "great two" and "steps back"—it was eliminated by adding a space between the exclamation point and the "k" in "back" and adding a space before the "g" in "great" in the line above. Even though it looks like it was right-aligned, that's just the way it turned out. That's something we can live with better than dealing with a river.

14. Now just repeat for each word balloon and caption for the rest of the page. While doing this, keep in mind the following points:

    ❑   Most times, dialog is center-aligned. When the balloon is cut off at the left or right sides, we can have different alignments if we want. The next screenshot shows that the top text is left-aligned and the lower text is right-aligned. Small panels usually need some special attention.

    ❑   Try not to have a single word on a line by itself. In typography, that's called an orphan. If the word by itself is important, as in the previous example, then the word "Right", said by Rhojo, is to indicate a pause and would be a good use by an orphan.

    ❑   Captions can be right- or left-aligned, depending on which side of the panel/page it's touching or nearest to. Because captions are usually in a rectangular container, center-aligned can look odd in some instances.

❑ Unless you're writing the script, do not make changes (aside from adding returns and extra spaces when we need to) from what the writer sent you unless they give permission to do so. We wouldn't want writers to make changes on what we drew, do we? Put the entire text on the page, even if it covers up coveted parts of our art. It's our job to make the art work with the text.

❑ In the previous example, the first caption box goes on forever. It cuts into the drawing of the spaceship. That's why, in this digital workflow of ours, we did minimal penciling. This way, we can resize the art in the panel to better fit with the amount of text, to establish a better balance of art and words. When we finish the pencils, they will match the new size much better. As much as it may pain us artists, comics are a balance between art and words all in service to the story.

15. Sometimes, making two passes at lettering a page is good. The first pass is like a rough draft, get the dialog and captions close to where we want them. The second pass is refining the location, adding bold-italics to emphasize words and checking for rivers and correcting them. We should keep our proofreading eyes on during this. Typos have the oddest habit of revealing themselves when we least except it, mostly after the comic is published.

What just happened?

We went through the page and methodically lettered it. We dealt with rivers and islands of text. When encountering too much text for the space, we made a note to ourselves to redo the pencils when needed so that the words and pictures could work together.

We can open up `dialogPage lettered.lip` and see what the final lettered page looks like.

Adding dialog balloons and caption boxes

Although they belong together, balloons and caption boxes are not created at the same time as text in Manga Studio. However, they can be created or added to the same layer as the text. One thing to know is that balloons usually take quite a bit of time to get right where we want them. In the *Time for action – making a custom dialog balloon sub tool* section, there will be times where we'll have some actions that consist of "tweaking." This is just the way things are in Manga Studio currently.

One thing about dialog balloons and thought balloons is that while some may call them thought bubbles or text bubbles, we'll refer to them as balloons. That's what most comic artists call them now and historically too.

A number of attributes for the dialog balloons and caption boxes are the same as for brushes and other tools. We'll focus on the basic attributes needed for plain dialog and caption containers. As we learn more about the various settings, we can revisit these settings for balloons and boxes and make adjustments on our own. Feel free to experiment if you want. It can be fun and the root of focused play, as we've learned.

All dialog balloons and caption boxes are vector-based since they are created on a text layer. Although we can adjust each control point in the vectors, our job here is to get the basic balloon where we want it in relation to the dialog text. What we want to do now is to create our own dialog balloon sub tool with custom settings.

Time for action – making a custom dialog balloon subtool

Much like how we worked on the pencils, we'll do the same here. First, create a duplicate tool. Then, make adjustments to the copy. We'll step through making a custom tool, and then use it to make our dialog balloon.

1. With the lettered dialog page open (or use the `DialogPage Lettered.lip` file), click on the text tool. In the basic installation of Manga Studio, it should be the second tool from the bottom, just before the color swatches.

2. In the **Sub tool** palette, click on the **Ellipse balloon** sub tool.

3. In the **Sub tool properties** palette, click on the palette menu (the icon is in the upper-left of the palette), and choose **Duplicate sub tool** from the contextual menu.

4. Name the duplicate tool `MS4B dialog balloon`, and select a teal icon color from the icon background color menu. The specific color isn't important to this exercise; it's chosen to separate our custom tools from the Manga Studio's default tools.

5. We want to keep all the settings from the original tool, except for the brush size.

    ❏ With the new `MS4B dialog balloon` selected, look at the **Properties** palette. If there isn't a brush size attribute listed, click on the wrench icon, and in the **Tool Settings** palette, go to the brush size category. We may want to click on the eye-con icon (the box that leads the category entry), so the eye appears. This will make this category visible in the **Tool properties** palette.

    ❏ Set the **Brush size** to **8**. We can go back and change it later if it appears too thin or thick on our page.

    ❏ If the **Tool Setting** palette is open, close it.

    ❏ In the **Tool properties** palette, click on the palette menu and choose **Register all to initial settings** from the contextual menu to save our new settings.

6. Now we're ready to make some balloons.

What just happened?

We just duplicated a tool, made some adjustments in it, and saved the changes as the initial settings. This is a common thing we'll be doing for a while as we make custom sub tools in Manga Studio. Once we get a good set of custom sub tools created for the tools we use most, this whole thing of making a duplicate will be something we'll do less often. Right now, we're in the process of "breaking in" Manga Studio, so there's a lot of customization that we'll be doing.

Making dialog balloons on the page

We have our custom sub tool for dialog balloons made and ready to be used, so let's letter a panel. It'll be an interesting experience!

Time for action – ballooning our dialog

A word of warning before we start. It's tricky, sometimes, to select the word balloon. It's an acquired ability that only comes with some practice. So take time on this exercise. Do things slowly and don't hesitate to use undo as much as required. The instructions in this exercise are as complete as they can be. But some things just have to be done to understand the process. Patience is our friend here. You may come up with a better method that works best for you. That's great. It's also okay if you don't. Let's do this!

1. With the page that's been lettered, select our new `MS4B dialog balloon` tool.

2. Look at the text in the upper-left corner.

 Please note that I changed the font used for the dialog. This is to keep us focused on the process and not on the fonts used. That's my story and I'm sticking to it.

3. On your screen, the text is up against the red border (this is on the active border layer in this file, created to help with showing what's the active/live area of the page; if you're working on your own page, this border will be the color set in preferences) of the live area of the page. That's the space that text needs to be within. If there's any text outside that area, it may be cropped or not printed correctly.

4. Now visualize, not world peace, but a rectangular area that encloses the text. Since the balloon tool draws from one corner of the oval to the opposite corner, click on one corner and drag it to the opposite one.

5. You may notice that the beginning of the oval may overlap the text. That's okay, we'll just make the balloon a bit bigger to offset that. We can move the balloon when we're done.

6. As shown in the screenshot, we got the balloon close to where we want it to be. Now we'll just use the object selection tool to move it. Try pressing the letter *O* key and see what happens.

7. If the shortcut settings were not altered, the object selection key should've been chosen and the balloon selected.

8. If the *O* key doesn't do that, just press the icon in the toolbar (it's the third from the top).

9. Try moving the balloon now. It moves both the balloon and the text.

10. The preceding screenshot shows the difference between having just the balloon selected and the text object selected. We just need to click on the block of space the text occupies.

11. Now, with the text object selected, we can move the text so it's centered within the balloon. We can do this by clicking-and-dragging the text object. Or a more accurate way is to just use the keyboard cursor arrows.

12. We should end up with something like the following screenshot:

13. If the balloon doesn't hold the text, we can select the balloon and click on the mid-cubes (the squares mid-way on each side) and resize the balloon. The text object will adjust to the new size of the balloon. Just be careful not to accidentally select the text object, as that will scale the text and not the balloon.

14. Now we have to create the tail for the balloon. The following screenshot, **The Science of Tail Placement**, has a few pointers for us to keep in mind:

The curved line between the balloon and the speaker's mouth is because most times we'll want a curved tail for a dialog (or speech) balloon. If the speaker was a robot, TV, or alien, we may want to use a straight line. And yes, a jagged line (like for a robot) can be based from a straight or curved visualized line.

15. If we're having some problems with visualizing this curved line for the tail, create a new layer and draw the curve on that layer to make things easier for us. We can also delete that layer when we're done with it. Just be sure to go back to our text layer after drawing the tail curve "guide."

16. To create a tail, we need to choose our balloon tool from the toolbar.

17. In the **Sub tool** palette, notice that there are two tail sub tools:

    ❑ **Balloon tail**: This is what we'll be using for our word balloon

    ❑ **Balloon rounded tail**: This will give us the bubble tail for thought balloons

18. Choose the **Balloon tail** sub tool.

19. In the **Properties** palette, we'll want the settings to be:

    ❑ Type of balloon tail: **Normal**

    ❑ How to bend: **Spline**

    ❑ Width of tail: **100**

    ❑ **Make corners pointed** should be checked

20. If we don't see all of these options, click on the wrench icon, and in the **Tool Settings** palette, find these settings and adjust them as above.

21. Before we start clicking away, we need to realize that what the **Balloon tail** is actually doing is drawing a long triangle. The base of the triangle (the widest part) is where we'll click first, the next click is at the middle of the tail where we want the most of the bend to be. We'll then position the cursor where we want the tail to end and press *Enter* to finish the tail.

22. With the **Balloon tail** sub tool active, click about where the "E" is in "STEPS"; this is going to be the widest part of the tail. It should be well within the balloon, so it doesn't have a corner of the base pointing outside of the balloon.

23. Notice that when we move our cursor/stylus, we see a ghost of a triangle. This is helpful as we can see where the tail will be. We'll click next is for the apex of the curve. The exact placement is something that we'll have to find by eye, experience, and error. Undo is our friend here.

24. Once we've clicked for the apex of the tail's curve, move the cursor to where we want the tail to end; usually, this is about a third of the way between the balloon and the speaker's mouth. When the cursor is where we want it to be, press the *Enter* or *Return* key. We don't want to click, as that'll add another curve and can make editing the tail difficult.

25. Now our balloon looks similar to the following screenshot (which shows where we clicked while constructing the tail):

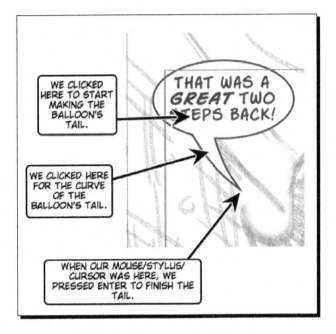

26. Now, look at what our hard work has done. While this Time for action had several steps, after performing them a few times, it will be rather easy and much quicker.

27. We can choose the object tool, and by clicking on the tail itself, select just the tail. Then we can move, rotate, and resize the tail to our tastes.

What just happened?

We learned that making a dialog balloon has a few steps to it: first we create the basic balloon shape, and then we make the tail. The object selection tool will select the entire balloon, and when moved, will also move the text and tail along with it. We can then click on the text object or tail, and move these parts of the balloon separately.

Have a go hero – ballooning our dialog

Caption boxes are usually square, with sharp or rounded corners. Sometimes they have a fill color (such as light yellow or blue). They don't have tails. Since we're all experienced at making custom sub tools, let's create a custom caption box sub tool with a light blue fill. Make the brush size thicker than the dialog balloons. Panel 5 is an all-caption panel, and if you listen closely, it's daring you to make caption boxes for it. You can do it.

One thing about making the balloon tail that wasn't mentioned, but you may have noticed, is that there was no brush size option/category for this sub tool. Yet, when we drew out the tail and pressed *Enter*, it had the correct stroke around it. That's because when a balloon is made, it sets the stroke for all objects (except text) on that layer. If we'd look at the layer icon before and after making a balloon, we would have noticed that the layer icon changed from having an "A" in it to having a balloon shape in it. If we would selected the dialog layer we're been working on, choose the balloon sub tool and draw out a second balloon, overlapping the first, what would it look like?

It appears to be merged with the first balloon. But, it's still a separate object. And if we move the second balloon away from the first, and move the tail so it begins in one balloon and ends in the other, what does that look like? Hmm, we can do multiple text objects on a single layer, and now we find out we can create multiple balloons on that same layer. Why could we do separate balloons with text in them and use a tail to connect them? This could help out in `Panel 6` of the dialog page. Look at the file `DialogPageLetteredFinished.lip` and see how the objects are arranged in `Panel 6`. Now do it on your own.

As good as the text and ballooning tools are in Manga Studio, they are still somewhat clunky and a real speed-bump in our comic production.

It sure would be nice if we could just create a dialog balloon with text in just one simple step. There is a way, which is covered in the comic life downloadable online chapters.

Pop quiz

Q1. Which of the following are treated as special when lettering comics?

1. The number 1
2. The pronoun I
3. The word at

Q2. What is the graphic representation of a character thinking called?

1. A thought bubble
2. A thinking cap
3. A thought balloon

Q3. Most commonly, the font style used for comic lettering is...

1. Upper and lowercase

2. Sans serif

3. Comic sans

4. Script

Q4. A comic script can be written using just a plain old text editor.

1. True

2. False

Q5. Manga Studio's text has word wrap and automatic spelling correction.

1. True

2. False

Summary

Lettering comics with Manga Studio is basic, at best. It's possible, but it's time-consuming and gives us bare-boned results. There's no simple way to make sweeping changes, like if we find a font that fits our uses better. For better and more professional results, we'll need to resort to another app for lettering. Do check out the comic life supplementary chapter for a quick (and inexpensive) way to get good-looking lettered pages with much less hassle than with Manga Studio.

Now that we have our page all lettered, we just need to work on the pencils. This is a major part of Manga Studio's strength and, therefore, the most complex. A lot of what we'll be learning will apply to the rest of our work, inking a coloring, especially in Manga Studio.

Get your stylus or drawing device of choice ready, here comes pencil mechanics.

6
Pencil Mechanics

Pencils are an area where Manga Studio just shines. Best pencils ever. We'll look at the different attributes a pencil has and create our own custom pencils. As comic artists, that's just the beginning to penciling a page. There's perspective to consider along with drawing curves when we need to. It's not practical to put vanishing points or a French curve on our tablet, so we'll explore how to use many of Manga Studio's rulers and put them to our use and reuse. Then there's references. Sure we can Google all day long, but what good are all those images if we have to launch another app to see them. As with many other aspects of comic crafting, Manga Studio has an answer: the sub view palette, where we can have our images and see them all without having to open a second application. We've barely cracked open the door to what Manga Studio can do here, we'll swing that door wide open and see what's inside!

In this chapter, we'll cover the following topics:

- Creating new pencils for detailed work
- Using selection tools
- Basic use of rulers
- Using perspective rulers
- Introduction to masks
- The sub view palette

It needs to be mentioned that this chapter can be considered a foundation chapter. Many of the techniques and settings we use here will be used in all the aspects of Manga Studio. Because of the depth that these topics have, a deeper examination can be found in the *Chapter 12, Along for the Ride*, which is an online chapter.

The hidden hand of comics

That's what penciling has been in the past. The usual bullpen procedure was that the penciller drew the pages (either using the trusty graphite pencil or a non-photo blue pencil) and then handed them off to the letterer. In our new digital workflow, we did line (or form) drawings that we then lettered over. We did this for one important reason: so that we can adjust our drawings to fit within the panel and give space to the word balloons and captions. Even if we're working with others (a writer and inker), this method may seem to take a few extra steps, but in the long run, it saves much more time than not. For example, let's say we've put in a lot of effort drawing a set of stairs, with people on it in various poses. It really sets up a mood in our mind. Then comes the writer who covers up all that work with a word balloon or caption. Now we have to either have a truncated panel or redraw it from scratch so that it'll look good to us. Or we just let it go and let hours of work get covered up. Wouldn't it be better to know about that text before we spent all that time? That's why we did the form drawing and then lettered the page. Now comes the refinement of the drawings and tying everything together into a nice harmonious whole.

We can't refine the pencils until we get a good pencil that we can add the detail with.

As usual, let's figure out what we're looking for in a basic detailing pencil. This is just the starting point; we'll cover a number of aspects of the pencil we can use in the following *Time for action – preparing our workspace* section:

- A fine point that will be responsive to pressure, for both the darkness of the line and the size of it. The size should be good for basic figure drawing and backgrounds with perspective. Something like a .5 mm mechanical pencil with HB lead.

- A line that could have some tooth; that means it simulates paper texture. Or maybe just a smooth flat tone.

- The pencil needs to be good for showing crosshatching, so it will be clear to the inker what's required when inking.

- It would be good to have several sizes of the pencil that we can switch to at a click of a button.

The size of the pencils we'll be creating is based on a 600 dpi document; so, if we're working on a smaller resolution (say 300 or 150 dpi) document, then divide the numbers in the exercise by half for 300 dpi documents, or a quarter for 150 dpi documents. In other words, adjust the settings given here to suit your needs.

In the process of creating our detailing pencils, we'll explore some ways to create a method to create new pencils (and eventually other tools) in a way that we will save the good ones and have a back up that we can then experiment with to create new pencils.

Time for action – preparing our workspace

Before we begin creating all kinds of new pencils, let's prepare our sub tool palette so that our experiments will be in their own location. It's hard to find the right pencil if we have dozens of them in one group. So, let's create a new duplicate pencil from one that already exists and make a group for it to be in. This way, we can make all the adjustments we want and leave our golden pencils untouched. So, open Manga Studio if it's not already running and let's get started!

1. Create a new document. This'll be like scratch paper. We can save it as `Scratch paper.lip` so that we have a document that we can open up and use for making new tools. Save it in your MS4B folder. Make this document the same DPI/resolution as that of the pages you'll be working in. In this example, we'll be using 600 dpi for a document that's 7 x 10.5 inches.

2. In the sub tool palette, choose a pencil like the rough sketch pencil we created a few chapters ago. This will be our base pencil that we'll be changing attributes of.

3. It's important, at this point, to save this sub tool so that we leave our rough sketching pencil as it is. It's frustrating to spend time on a new pencil and save it only to realize that we changed a pencil and don't remember its original settings.

4. In the dialog box that pops up, name this new tool `BasePencil MS4B` and give the icon any color that you'd like, so it will pop out at us as a kind of template pencil we can mess with and delete if we need to. It's just there so that we don't change our source pencil tool.

5. Since we want to be able to have separate shelves for our pencils, let's create a new tab for our detailing pencils. Drag our new BasePencil MS4B tool to the tabs until we see a horizontal line between tabs.

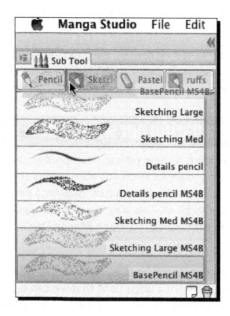

6. Now we should have a new tab named **BasePencil MS4B** (remember that **MS4B** stands for **Manga Studio for Beginners** in all our examples) in our sub tool palette. Right-click on that tab and choose **Settings** of **Sub Tool Group** (it's the only item in the contextual menu).

7. In the dialog box, rename this group **MS4B Pencils**. Hit the **OK** button.

8. Now, when this group is the currently active one, any new pencils we create will be put into this group. And any copies of pencils we make elsewhere can be dragged onto this group's tab and moved into this group. When dragging a pencil onto a group, make sure the tab is outlined in a red rectangle, not a vertical line.

9. If we look at the tabs, chances are that we will only see MS4B for the name. It's important to not only give our tools and groups good meaningful names, but for the tool groups, especially, the first word or 5 spaces or so, will be visible; so like the newspaper editors of old, don't bury our lede. Have the first word be the most important/descriptive one. Here, it's MS4B, named after this book we are working through. Other names could be *ruffs* for Rough Sketching or *pastels* for pastels, chalk, and charcoal type pencils.

What just happened?

We just learned how to make a new pencil based on an existing one and how to make a new tool group for it to live in. This is a good practice to get in the habit of doing. While we won't do this a lot when we've been using Manga Studio for a while, it is the type of thing we will be doing a lot to set up Manga Studio for us to be able to work with in a way that's logical and quick for us to use.

Making a basic detailing pencil

What we need for good penciling is a group of pencils that can do detail well and a pencil that we can use for solid shading and crosshatching to indicate grey areas and some kinds of shadows. Let's make a fine detailing pencil and work up from there.

The *Time for action – configuring the pencil size and pressure settings* section includes a long set of instructions, so take your time and don't hesitate to put this book aside for a moment or two and just experiment with the various settings we'll be using. Just experimenting with different settings can give us one of those great Ah-Ha! moments that puts a lot of things into place and increases our understanding more than just reading alone can do. If things get really out of control though, we can always hit the **Revert all to initial settings** button at the bottom of the **Tool Settings** palette and then change them to match the images in this section. So, there's no excuse for not seeing what any tool category can do for us. Manga Studio's great for this kind of experimentation. Let's do this!

Basic pencil settings

In these next few *Time for action* sections, we'll be making a new pencil tool based on the basepencil sub tool we've made earlier. Each one of the sections will be a piece of the process for creating a new marking tool.

Time for action – configuring the pencil size and pressure settings

When creating any new tool, we need to begin with establishing the basic settings. First we need to think about the basic size of the tool and how it interacts with the pressure settings from our stylus. We'll be working with the `BasePencil MS4B` that we just created. Eventually, we'll be saving this pencil under its own name, so do not save the settings or revert to initial settings unless you get lost. In case you happen to get lost, just start all over again:

1. Make sure that the `BasePencil MS4B` is still the active pencil tool by clicking on the tool name in the **Sub Tool** palette.

2. In the **Tool Property** palette, click on the **wrench** to bring up the **Tool Settings** palette. Take some time to look at the palette. Click on the various categories (the list on the left of the palette) and see what they reveal.

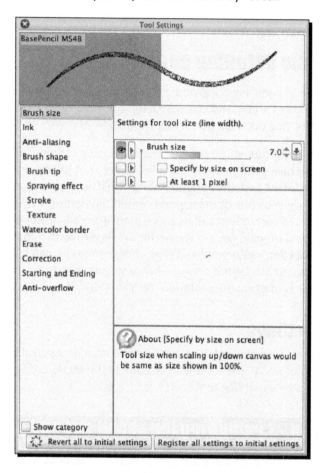

3. The first category we want to work with is the brush size. For my style, I like a rather fine point, so I set it at `7.0`. But we can take our time and try out different sizes. Zoom in to our Scratch paper document to 50 percent and make some scribbles and doodles. Draw some triangles, pyramids, cubes, and faces. Try a larger size, like 10 or 15. See how it feels and looks (don't forget to select **Zoom to Fit** to see how things look in context). Keep in mind that we want a good basic pencil that we can refine our rough sketches and form drawings with.

4. One method is to go for something really large and then really small until we get the size we like.

5. Next, we need to adjust the pressure sensitivity. To get to the pressure dialog, we need to click on the icon button on the right-hand side of where the brush size is chosen.

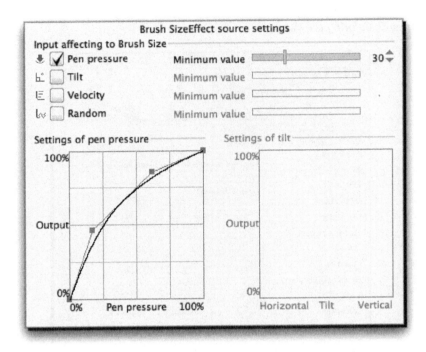

6. The setting shown in the previous screenshot is what we can call an up-curve. This will start out with light pressure giving us a thin line. Then, as the pressure increases, the line will get thicker as we press on our stylus harder. Finally, it tops out at 100 percent.

7. Set the minimum value to zero or one. this will tell Manga Studio when to begin to take pressure on the stylus into account while drawing. The higher the setting, the less the pressure will be that will affect our line.

What just happened?

We made the first of many adjustments to a pencil tool. We experimented a bit and settled on a good size to use. Then, we adjusted the pressure settings to get the best feel for our pencil. Now, let's set how the pencil will make the marks by adjusting the ink and anti-aliasing settings.

Time for action – configuring ink and anti-aliasing settings

Here's where we begin to set the pencil's look. While we'll be adjusting a few of the ink settings, the rest of the settings will come into use when we begin coloring our art, as we'll see in *Chapter 8, Coloring the World*:

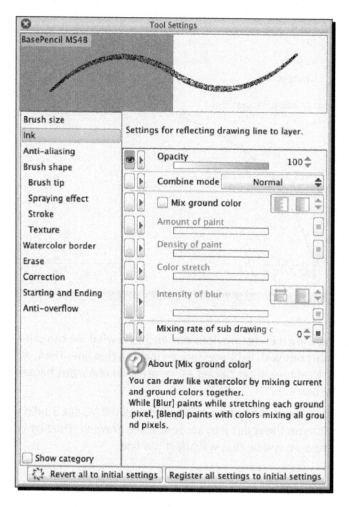

1. Click on the **Ink** category. **Opacity** is set at **100%**. We'll adjust the darkness of the line in the next few categories.

2. **Combine mode** is set at **Normal**. We can try out different modes; the **darken** and **multiply** modes are good ones for pencils. Find a setting that feels right. We'll be using this pencil a lot so we might as well be comfortable with it. The combine mode uses modes that are commonly used in other painting and drawing apps, so we aren't going to go into the details of these attributes here.

3. Click on the **Anti-aliasing** category.

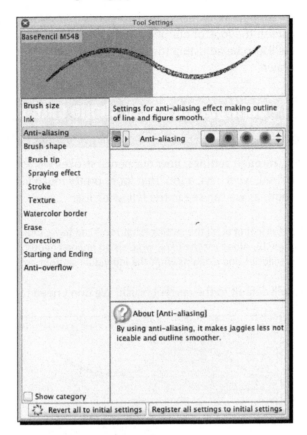

4. The **Anti-aliasing** category is set to **Little** (second from the left). This category is good for setting how the marking tool will fuzz out the edges of the mark. Overall, the anti-alias setting can be set differently for different tools; for example, **Little** or **Moderate** is excellent for sketching pencils, **None** is best for inking, and **Strong** can be used when painting in a color that needs to be blended. Don't hesitate to experiment with these settings and find the one that works best for you.

What just happened?

By adjusting the **Ink** and **Anti-aliasing** settings, we were able to make sure that the opacity of our ink was 100. Furthermore, we set the **Anti-aliasing** setting to **Little** so that the edges of the line are slightly fuzzy. A lot of the functionality of the **Ink** category is unused in pencils, but when we want to begin blending colors, this category becomes very important. If we can't wait to see what the options in **Ink** can do, click on the checkbox for **Mix ground color** and adjust the setting below **Mix ground color**. We'll be going into these settings in *Chapter 8, Coloring the World*.

Establishing a look for the pencil tool

In the *Time for action – configuring brush shape categories and settings* section, we'll be looking at ways to establish the look of our pencil; whether it'll be a smooth or textured pencil, for instance. We'll also be adjusting the degree, if any, as the tool will smooth out the line as it's being drawn.

Time for action – configuring brush shape categories and settings

Here, we'll be creating, through settings, how our pencil strokes will look when drawn. If all the steps are followed, we'll have a tool that looks pretty much like a pencil drawing on paper with some tooth as we can see in the following list:

 For a full listing of all the settings that tools can have, look inside the *Chapter 12, Along for the Ride*, which is an online chapter, which lists all 13 categories and explains what the individual settings are.

1. **Brush shape** will default to the current brush. We don't need to adjust anything here.

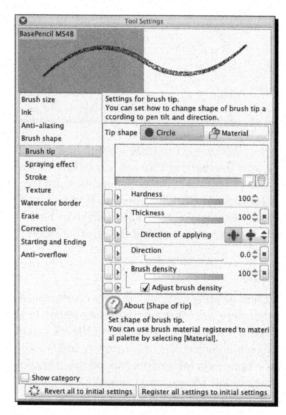

2. **Brush tip** is a category that has a number of settings. We want a simple tip, so **hardness** and **thickness** are at **100**. The **direction of applying the settings** is set to **Horizontal** (the item on the left of the menu). The **Direction** is at **0.0**. The **Brush Density** is at **100**.

In any attribute in the **Tool Settings** palette, we can hold our cursor over an item, and in the **About** section at the bottom will be a brief description of what that attribute will do. Sometimes it's hard to read, because words will be broken across lines, like "materi" and "al" are in the previous screenshot. As we've experienced from the previous chapter, Manga Studio has many issues with western text.

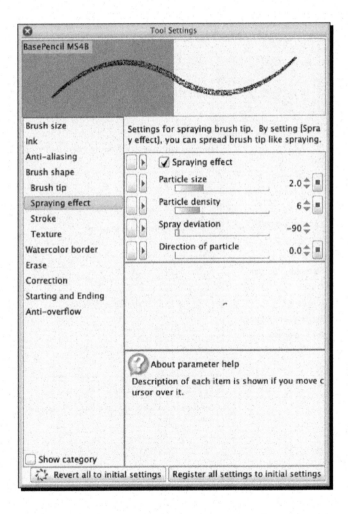

3. The **Spraying Effect** category is where we really set this pencil to look like a pencil. The following values for each of the attributes can be looked on as a starting point. They do interact with one another. A larger **Particle size** with a higher **Particle density** will look different than a smaller **Particle size** with the same density. Experiment with different values and find a set that you like. And when you do, be sure to click on the **Register Settings** button at the bottom of the palette to save your settings. Click on the **Spraying Effect** checkbox:

   ❑ Set **Particle size** to **2**

   ❑ Set **Particle Density** to **6**

   ❑ Set **Spray deviation** to **-90**

   ❑ Set **Direction of particle** to **zero**

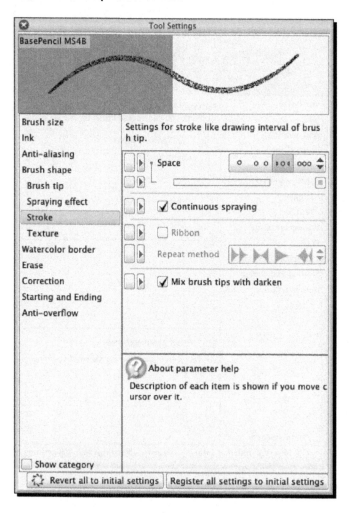

A big note of thanks goes to Eric Merced (`http://ericmerced.com`) for introducing me to the wonders of the Spraying Effect category. He's a good guy and a great cartoonist!

4. In the **Stroke** category, **Space** should be set to **Normal**. **Continuous Spraying** should be checked. This is set so that we get a good even spray of our texture:

    ❑ **Ribbon** should be unchecked. This is a good feature for inking (which will be covered in *Chapter 7, Ink Slingers*), but not so much for most penciling tasks.

    ❑ The **Mix Brush tips with darken** field should be checked if we want overlapping strokes to darken where they overlap. Sometimes, when using a sketchy-style for penciling, this is a good setting to have on because the lines we go over will be darker than the ones that aren't. Just like an analog pencil.

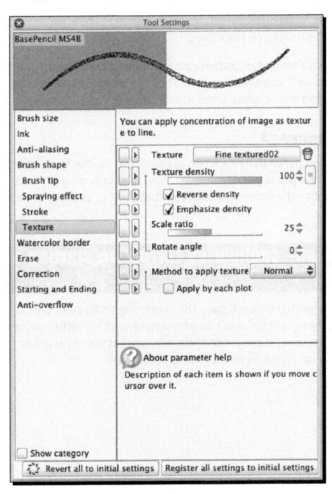

5. The **Texture** category is a big help in giving our pencil line some more texture. The top attribute, **Texture**, is a drop-down menu that lists all the textures that Manga Studio currently has in its `materials` folder. The list has a large thumbnail of the texture itself. The trash can icon to the right of the menu will not delete the texture from the materials, just from the pencil using a texture. In our example, we're using the **Fine Textured 02** texture. Try some of the other ones out and see what difference it makes:

   ❏ Set **Texture Density** to **100**.

   ❏ **Reverse Density** and **Emphasize Density** should be checked.

   ❏ **Scale ratio** should be set to **25**.

   ❏ **Rotate angle** should be set to **zero**.

   ❏ **Method to apply texture** should be **Normal**.

   ❏ **Apply to each plot** should be unchecked. This would have an obvious effect on larger sized pencils (and other tools) in how this attribute will overlap the texture on thick lines.

6. The next two attributes, **Watercolor border** and **Erase**, aren't really useful for pencils, so we'll skip them for now. They will be important in the up coming chapters and we'll explore them at that point.

What just happened?

Here we set how the pencil behaves when drawing. We set the spray effect, so the pencil will make marks like a pencil would on paper. Turn the spray off and make some marks with the pencil tool. Notice the difference between these marks and the marks made with the spray effect on.

Time for action – configuring correction, starting, and ending settings

We're almost done with our pencil now. The remaining three categories are all that remain. Some of these settings won't be of use to us until we either ink or color our art. It's important to get some exposure to them now so that when we get to them they will be somewhat familiar, as shown in the following screenshot:

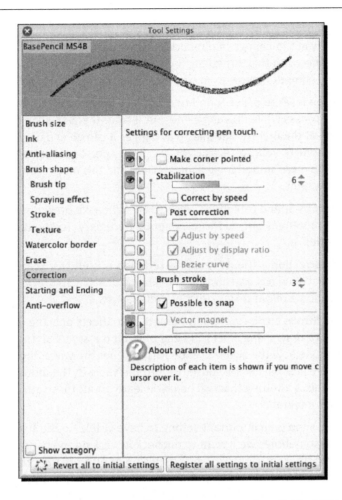

1. This category, **Correction**, is one that leaves many artists divided. This is mostly because it allows Manga Studio to alter the line we draw. The settings we choose here really depend on what we want from our pencil lines. Do we want to have Manga Studio capture each and every wiggle of our line or do we want to have Manga Studio smooth out our lines? This is a personal choice and will vary depending on our style and preferences.

2. The **Make corner pointed** category will make angled lines, such as a **V** or **L** shape, more pointy at the change of direction. This is checked off in our pencil. Try drawing angled shapes with this turned on. If you don't notice any difference, then turn it off. Why waste computing power on something that we don't notice?

3. **Stabilization** is set to **6**. I've found this to be a good setting that captures a lot of my natural *shakiness* while drawing a line, but it smoothens the line out enough that it looks good at the first try. Set this up as high as it can go and draw some shaky lines. Adjust this one to your taste, as it really is a very personal choice. The higher the number, the more smoothing will be applied, and this may result in some lag time on some systems.

4. The **Correct by Speed** category is unchecked. When we draw faster, our line naturally smoothens out, so this may not be necessary. Try it out and see if that's your experience.

5. The **Post correction** attribute is unchecked. This is useful for some perspective and architectural drawings as it corrects the line after it's been drawn. We'll use this setting for some of our inking brushes and markers.

6. The **Brush Stroke** attribute is oddly named, as it affects only the ending of a stroke; like when we draw a line and at the end of it, lift our stylus off the tablet. This setting will determine how the stroke is ended. The higher the value, the more tapered and long the line will be. The closer to zero the value is, the more the line will just end. This is a setting that will help you learn about these attributes through some experimentation.

7. **Possible to snap** is an important setting to have visible on the **Tool Properties** palette, as sometimes we'll want to uncheck it. Click on the left rectangle button so the **Eye-con** appears. Now we can turn this on or off from the properties palette. This setting determines whether the tool will snap to rulers, guides, or perspective vanishing points. If we're drawing a scene using perspective rulers and want to draw an arch, then being able to turn off snapping would be very helpful.

8. Since we're working on a raster layer, the previous setting, **Vector Magnet**, is greyed out and uncheckable. If we were working on **Vector Layer**, then this would give our lines the ability to be attracted to other, nearby vector lines.

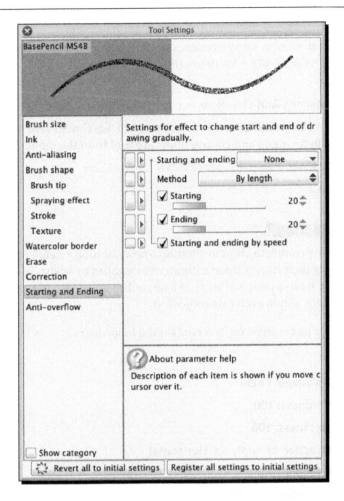

9. **Starting and Ending** can be used for all marking tools except for markers because markers are intended to have uniform size throughout their stroke.

10. The first attribute controls the starting and ending. We can choose among **Brush size**, **density**, and many others. For our pencil, we'll set it to **none**.

11. The **Method** attribute, or how the starting and ending is done, is set to **By Length**. Other choices are **By Percentage** and **Fade**.

12. **Starting** and **Ending** are both set to **20**. This sets the amount of the stroke that will be tapered down or up according to the **Method** set in the area above.

13. The **Starting and Ending by Speed** attribute is checked. This will factor in the speed the stroke is drawn in determining how the stroke is begun and ended.

[For those of us without tablets, the **Starting** and **Ending** settings can do a lot for simulating a line drawn with pressure sensitivity.]

14. The last category, **Anti-Overflow**, is best used either for solid fills or painting.

15. Once we're all set with our new detailing pencil, we should save it. Go to the **SubTool** palette menu and choose **duplicate tool** from the menu.

16. In the dialog box, name this pencil MS4B Detailing.

17. Click on **OK**.

What just happened?

We went through the complete steps in creating a new subtool, a detail pencil in this case. Most of the marking tools have a baker's dozen of categories to adjust. In all future subtool creation, we'll treat it like a recipe of sorts. It'll be broken down into the category with the value of the attributes within each category listed.

Brush Tip, which we just worked on, will contain the following:

- **Brush Tip**
    - **Tip Shape: Circle**
    - **Hardness: 100**
    - **Thickness: 100**
    - **Direction of Applying: Horizontal**
    - **Direction: 0.0.**
    - **Brush Density: 100**
    - **Adjust Brush Density**: checked.

Since we're familiar with creating new tools, we'll forego any images of the specific category, unless there's compelling reason to include it.

Have a go hero – the selection tools

Look at the **Tool Settings** palette. Select the **Brush Size** category. Immediately to the right of the **Eye-con** in the attributes is a tall triangle button pointing to the right. Clicking on it will give us a drop-down menu with a number of options. Near the bottom is a menu item named **Settings of indicators**. This is a new (as of Manga Studio 5.0.2) feature. An indicator is a series of five blocks that can be individually set for any attribute that uses a slider.

If we select the **Settings of indicators** option, we're presented with a dialog box with five boxes in which we can enter numbers. If we enter in a small number in the first box and increase the value as we move towards the right, we're creating "steps" that we can easily choose to make one pencil work like five. We can still use the *[* key (open bracket) to decrease and *]* key (close bracket) to increase the tool size by one. However, it's a real time saver to have set amounts that we can just click on to restore our pencil to a known value. What other attributes of marking tools can this indicator be useful for? We can always switch back by clicking on the triangle button and choosing **Show Slider** from the menu. And Manga Studio will remember the indicator settings if we should return to the indicator for that attribute.

The settings within the **Settings of indicators** attribute are universal, which means that once set, these will be the settings whenever the indicators are used. So, if we use "5, 10, 15, 20, 25" in the **Settings of Indicators** dialog box, those will be the values used whenever the indicators are used even if the settings are in percentages or units.

Now that we have a pencil, the drawing of our page can be started. Since this isn't a how to draw book, it's assumed that we all know how to draw, so we'll look at making selections, using the selection launcher, and creating keyboard shortcuts to make our drawing a bit easier.

Making selections and working with them

We all need to work with selections at one time or another. It's part of why working digitally is different from analog. Instead of redrawing something, we just select it and resize or move a selection of our art and deselect. It's done. No erasing or redrawing required. No tracing or using a light table. Manga Studio makes working with selections very easy. Once we get to know our way around them, we'll find that the selection work in Manga Studio is far superior to most other graphics apps, as we can see in the following screenshot:

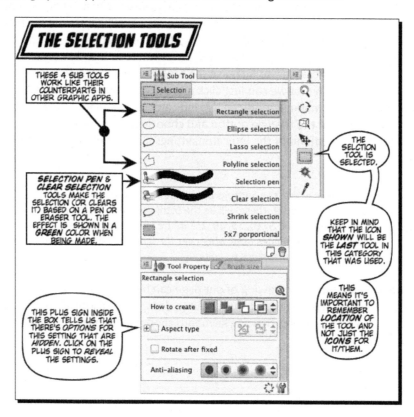

In the preceding screenshot, the **Selection** tool is selected. The top-left area is the **Sub Tool** tab. Here we can choose between **Rectangular selection**, **Ellipse selection**, **Regular selection**, **Polyline selection**, and **Lasso selection**. Like the screenshot reads, these are just like their counterparts in other graphics apps. However, there are selection tools that we haven't seen elsewhere: **Selection pen** and the **Clear Selection** eraser. These two tools work like their marking tool counterparts, except the **Selection pen** tool creates and adds to a selection in the fashion that a pen would. We can make the thickness of the pen dependent on the pressure we apply to the stylus. And the selection eraser is just like an eraser, only it clears the selection like an eraser. Take five and play around with these selection tools on a scratch paper doc (or any new document) and get a feel of how they work and can be adjusted.

The next tool is **Shrink Selection**. Depending on the options selected, this will shrink the selection to select only pixels with content. That is, only nontransparent pixels will be selected.

If there are any tools after **Shrink Selection**, chances are they're custom tools or subtools that have been added in an update after this book was written. Custom selection tools are made exactly like we made custom pencils earlier.

Below the **Sub Tool** palette is the **Tool Property** palette. The attributes shown there are explained as follows:

- How to create. The available choices are:
    - **New**: This will create a new selection. If one already exists, this will clear the old one when the new selection is created.
    - **Add**: This adds to the selection. So, if we have a rectangular selection and then switch over to a lasso and make a free-hand selection, that selection is added to the rectangle one.
    - **Subtract**: Manga Studio calls it "deselect partially." So, if we have a square selection and then make this attribute active and draw out a circular selection inside the square, the circle area will be deselected. This is handy when we want to have specific areas deselected and not the whole area.
    - **Common Selection**: This is called select the selected one, which isn't the most meaningful of names. If we picture two overlapping shapes, what gets selected is what the two have in common.

- **Aspect type** has two options: percentage and fixed amount. This allows us to create selections that are either the same size (always 100 x 100 pixels) or proportional (always a ratio of, for example, 1 to 1.5).

- **Rotate After Fixed** allows us to rotate (from the ellipse's center point) the selection after drawing it out. It is very handy for making tricky perspective oval selections.

- **Anti-aliasing** is the same value as we saw in the custom pencil section. Currently, it's set to **None**. But we could set it for **weak, moderate,** or **strong**. The stronger the anti-aliasing, the more the selected area will be *fuzzy* around the edges. This is good for when we're moving around colored or inked areas. Anti-aliasing helps to blend in the new location of the selection with its surroundings. With penciling, we don't have to worry about having moved as selections blend in perfectly.

 One thing to remember is the modifier keys: Option/*Alt* will subtract and *Shift* will add to a selection no matter what mode is selected for the subtool.

Resizing panel artwork and the selection launcher

In *Chapter 5, Putting Words in My Mouth*, we noticed that in panel 2 of the `dialog page.lip` file, the art could be reduced a bit to make the text fit better. We'll do that here. Since just reducing a selection is a basic operation, let's take this opportunity to dig deeper and learn a bit about what we can do with selections in Manga Studio. It'll be a while before we actually get to reducing the selection, but like in life, it's the journey that's the most fun, not necessarily the destination.

To prepare for the next few *Time for action* sections, let's get some housekeeping out of the way:

1. Start up Manga Studio (if it's not already running) and open either your dialog page or `dialog page.lip` that's in the downloaded files that we got from the Packt Publishing site. All instructions are based on the `dialog page.lip` file, so make adjustments if working from your own page.

2. Click on the panel folder named **Panel 2** or the panel that has art that needs to be reduced on your dialog file.

3. Show the contents of the panel folder, if it's not already showing, by clicking on the disclosure triangle before the panel folder icon.

4. Click once on the layer that contains the art we want to transform.

Now that we have everything set up, let's think what it is we want to do. Simple. In the specific case of the `dialog page.lip` file, we want to reduce the art in **Panel 2** so that the dialog text will fit better in it. In the course of this action, we'll learn about the Selection Launcher, how to modify it, and about the Transform selection command. Each one of these will be a separate *Time for action* section. We're ready to do this!

Time for action – adding a button to the selection launcher

First off, we'll add a button to the **Selection Launcher** to toggle the visibility of the dashed-line marquee of the selection. In computer graphics, this is called *marching ants*. While it makes seeing selections easy, sometimes it's more of a distraction; especially when we're drawing inside a selection. So here we go...

1. Choose the **Rectangular Selection** tool.

2. Select an area that's slightly larger than the panel. We want to do this just to have a bit of extra pixels selected. Better to do it when we don't need to than to not do it when we need to. Even though the masking on panels hides whatever we draw that's beyond the panels, it's still there. So by selecting a bit outside the panels, we're selecting hidden parts of our drawing. Now we have a bit of extra area to play around with.

3. Looking at the bottom of the selection, there's a horizontal button bar. That's the **Selection Launcher**.

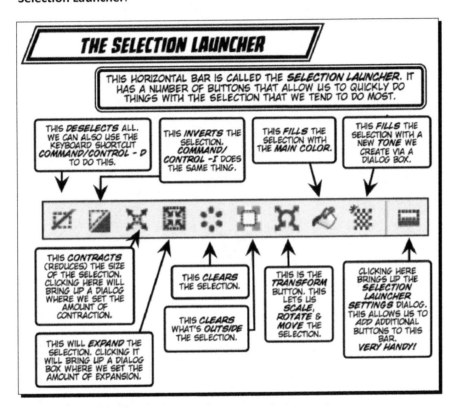

4. The button that's a circle with the open bottom area and the four outward pointing arrows (the fifth from the right) is the **Transform** button (called **Scale Up/Scale Down/Rotate** in the tooltip). We'll be clicking on that one later. Right now, we're interested in the button on the far left: **Selection Launcher Settings**.

5. The rest of the steps are for adding a new button to the **Selection Launcher** settings button.

6. Click on the **Selection Launcher** settings button. This brings up the **Selection Launcher settings** dialog box.

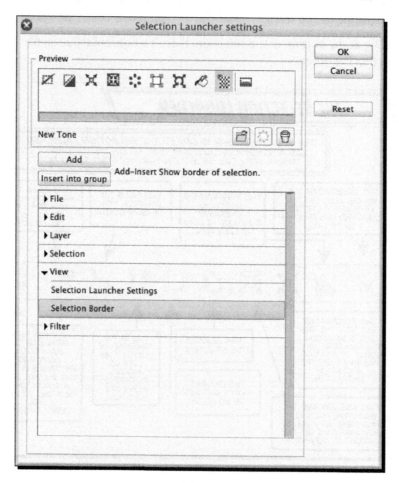

7. This dialog box can be considered to have three distinct areas:

    ❑   **Preview area** is where we can see not only what icons our launcher has, but we can select an icon and any new buttons or groups that are made will be in a relationship with the selected button. At the bottom of this area is *tip text* that identifies the selected tool and a series of buttons, open (an open folder icon), clear (the familiar whirlpool icon), and delete (the ubiquitous trash can icon).

❑ We can call the middle (unlabeled) area the **How to Add** area. There are two buttons here: the **Add** and **Insert into Group** buttons; both of these are add buttons, but they do it differently as their name implies.

❑ The bottom area, also unmarked, is the **Menu Item** area. Here's a list of menus that we can open up by clicking on the disclosure triangle. Then, we can select the menu item we want to be made into a button for our launcher.

8. In the **Menu Item** area, click on the triangle in the **View** menu. The dialog should now look like the following screenshot. In the opened menu, click on **Selection Border**.

9. Moving our attention to the **Preview** area, click on the **Tone Fill** icon. Now that it's selected, it becomes the focus for our adding to the launcher.

10. In the **How to add** area, we need to figure out how we want to add the new button. The following screenshot should clarify the difference between the choices we have:

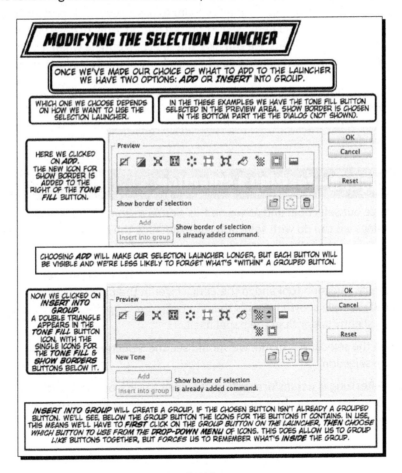

11. When there are a lot of different selected areas, and all we're doing is just filling or painting things into them, the marching ants can be a distraction. That's why adding this button here can be such a time (and sanity) saver. And this is a toggle button, that is, when it's active, it will have a dark grey background and clicking it will make the selection border visible if it's hidden, and the reverse if the border is hidden.

12. Since this button needs to be visible all the time, we click on **Add** and not **Insert into group**.

13. Click on **OK**.

14. Now click on the new button in the launcher. Nice to make the marching ants go away, isn't it? The presence of the launcher is a visual cue that there's still a selection because it only appears when there is a selection.

What just happened?

We learned about one of the best things about selections in Manga Studio: the **Selection Launcher**. Now instead of reaching for the keyboard to press keyboard shortcuts or going up to the menus and selecting a menu item, we just press a button. Now that we've put in a button to hide or show the marching ants, we can hide the selection outline when it's distracting, but know that we still have a selection because of the visibility of the **Selection Launcher**.

Thankfully, we only have to create a button once. So, the next T4A will be what we wanted to do in the first place: resize a selection. It's good to think of resizing, or most any time we want to change the contents of a selection, as a transform action. This will make a lot of sense when we do it.

Time for action – resizing a selection

Now we'll resize our selection, and as we do this simple action, we'll take some time and see what other things we can do with selections by examining the options that Manga Studio gives us, as shown in the following steps:

1. If the selection that we made in the previous T4A isn't still selected, go to the rectangle selection tool and in the Pencil layer in the panel we want to change (in the example shown here it's the dialogpage.lip file, **Panel 2**), select an area that's slightly larger than the panel itself.

2. When the selection is made, we should see the **Selection Launcher** at the bottom of the selection.

3. Since **Resizing** is a transform action, we want to click on the **Transform** button on the launcher. (It's the fifth from the right, looks like a circle with no bottom and has arrows coming out of it.)

4. After the **Transform** button is clicked, we lose the selection launcher because we're now working with the selection's contents.

5. As the previous screenshot shows, if we look at the **Tool Properties** palette, we see that it's totally changed with new options that weren't there before.

6. In the following screenshot, it has the settings we'll be using to change our current selection. Your values may be different depending on your needs.

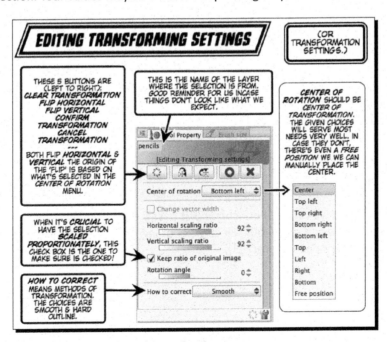

7. If you don't see all the settings attributes, click on the wrench icon, and in the **Tool Settings** palette, click on the **Eye-con** button to make them appear in the **Sub Tool Properties** palette.

8. The set of five buttons near the top of the **Tool Property** palette are a good assortment of things that we may sometimes need:

    ❑ The first one uses an icon that's used all over Manga Studio's interface. Let's call it the whirlpool icon, because just like a whirlpool in any sink or bathtub, it clears things out. In this case, clicking on this button will clear out any changes we made to the selection. It'll still keep the area selected. This can save our sanity if we totally mess up a transform action and need to get back to our starting point.

    ❑ The next two buttons, **flip Horizontal** and **flip Vertical**, will use the center of rotation setting and flip the selection accordingly. This is useful if we've drawn a reflection in a mirror and forgot to flip it while drawing, or if we want to create a reflection of what we've drawn. If we have the center of rotation anywhere other than the center, the flipped selection may be off the canvas or outside the panel, so it will have to be dragged back to where we want it to be. Just click in the selected area and drag the selection around.

    ❑ The last two buttons, the **O** and **X** icons, will confirm the transformation or cancel it. We can also hit the keyboard's *Enter* key to confirm and the *Esc* button to cancel.

9. Similar to what was written in the screenshot, **Center of Rotation** should've been labeled Center of Transform. There are a number of presets here. Clicking on the button drops a menu as shown to the right of the palette in the previous screenshot. They are pretty self-explanatory. The center is shown as a black + so it's usually good to turn on the layer color attribute before making selections, as we did at the beginning of this chapter, because it'll make seeing the center cross easier on blue pencils than on black ones. For the options of **Top**, **Left**, **Right**, and **Bottom**, the transform center is centered on those sides.

10. The **Vertical** and **Horizontal** scaling ratio makes more sense if we think of them as scaling percentages. The checkbox below them, **Keep ratio of original image**, is good to check if we want to keep the proportions of our drawing intact while scaling it.

11. Even though we can hold our cursor just past the selection and get a two-headed curved arrow and rotate our selection by dragging, using **Rotation Angle** allows us to rotate our selection precisely.

12. Our last option is the **How to correct** setting. We have the following two options:

- ❑ The **Smooth** option will scale and/or rotate the selection and blend it with the surrounding pixels to make for a better blend and help eliminate some jagged edges.

- ❑ The **Hard Outline** option will do its best to preserve the outlines. This may result in some fringing (light/dark pixels at the edge of the selection) and some harsh, jagged, pixelated lines.

13. So, for our little resizing exercise, we want the values as they are in the image:

- ❑ **Center of rotation: Bottom left**

- ❑ **Horizontal Scaling Ratio: 92**

- ❑ **Vertical Scaling Ratio: 92**

- ❑ Keep **Ratio of original image** as checked

- ❑ **How to correct: Smooth**

14. Once the settings are what you want them to be, hit the **O** button (confirm transformation) or your keyboard *Enter* key. The transform is applied and we are back to our normal selection mode, as we now have the selection launcher back.

What just happened?

By going in depth into the selection transform abilities of Manga Studio, we learned that we can use selection transform to create reflections as well as resizing and rotating the selected area. We now have a set of steps we can follow when making selections:

1. Before we make a selection, we decide what we want to do.

2. Make the selection. In cases of selecting an entire panel, make the selection a bit larger than the panel, so in cases where we're reducing the panel's contents, we have a bit of room for positioning.

3. Look at the selection center cross. This is where all our transformations will have as their origin point. We can click on it and drag it manually to where we want it to be.

4. Perform our action; if it's drawing within the selection, we can hide the selection marquee (marching ants) from view. If we're transforming the selection, take our time and look at the **Tool Property** palette and see the options it has to make our work easier.

5. Know that the whirlpool icon will reset (clear) the transformation if we need to do it. The *Esc* key will cancel a transform, while the *Enter* key will commit to it.

Take a break. We deserve it after covering all this ground. In the upcoming section, we'll leave selections and go into rulers and learn that they are much nicer in Manga Studio than *Game of Thrones*.

Rulers and curves

In this section, we'll see how rulers measure up and apply them to a few panels in our sample dialog page. We'll want to keep our scratch page open, because we'll need a blank slate to put our rulers to work.

What good are rulers?

Unlike Joffrey, rulers in Manga Studio are great helpers and assist us in drawing curves and straight lines. Just like we would use french curve, ellipse, and other templates in analog drawing, rulers in Manga Studio do the same thing. There's one crucial difference: we create these rulers ourselves and make them fit the job at hand. So, instead of moving a template around to get just the right curve, we just go ahead and make a curve that fits our needs. So, what Manga Studio calls rulers would be guides in another app.

Once a ruler is created, we can set our pencil (and later our pen and brush tools) to snap to the ruler and we can automagically trace the curve.

The knowledge we may have acquired in using a vector drawing app will be handy, but not essential, in this section. In some cases, knowing little to nothing about vector drawing may be better than knowing a lot.

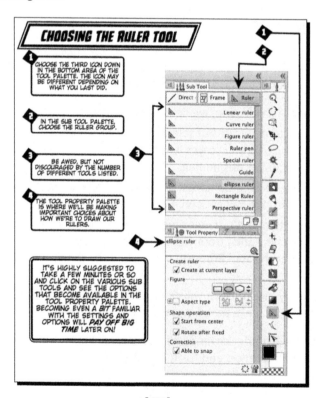

As shown in the preceding screenshot, we need to select the ruler tool. With the way Manga Studio has grouped its tools, we may have to select a tool that doesn't look like what we're after. The ruler tool shares space with the **Direct Draw** and **Frame** tools. As shown in the screenshot, click on the third tool down from the last section before the color swatches.

Then, in the **Sub Tool** palette, click on the **Ruler** tab to view the contents of the ruler group. Even though there are a whole lot of subtools, we'll only be focusing on a few:

+ The **Linear ruler** subtool is where we go to create straight lines or curved lines. This tool only allows us to initially create a single line with a start point and an end point.

+ The **Curve ruler** subtool is used to create all kinds of curves or straight lines. Waves and spirals are easy to make with this tool once we start making curves. It may help us to think of this tool as being able to create a line (straight or curved) with many line segments, which are created by control points.

+ The **Figure ruler** subtool is used to create a Hexagonal selection tool along with creating ovals and rectangles.

Rulers in Manga Studio

As far as Manga Studio's concerned, rulers are vector objects. They can be on their own layer or added to a layer that has artwork on it. Think of the ruler as being on a sublayer that co-exists with the raster art. Let's look at some definitions first, so we're all using the the same terms:

+ **Raster is all bitmap**. It's at a set resolution and any enlargement will result in either *jaggies* or *fuzziness*. Any reduction will result in losing pixels. Once a raster image's been reduced, that data (pixels) is gone... forever.

+ **A vector uses math to figure out where points are** on a 2D plane and how the points are connected. Vectors can be enlarged or reduced and will look good in either case. Each vector point may contain information on the curve (if any) that that specific point has.

Unlike other apps that use vectors (such as Photoshop), Manga Studio's vector is its own thing. When we export a vector drawing done in Manga Studio, it's always as a raster image; all the vector information is lost in the conversion to raster. It's still a vector within Manga Studio as a LIP file, but not as a PNG, TIFF, or PSD.

All of this is also true for rulers, except that they won't be seen in an export unless we use a marking tool (pencil, pen, brush, and so on) that has snap enabled so we can draw over the curve and keep on the ruler's line.

Before we start with creating a ruler to aid in our drawing, let's explore the different kinds of lines we can create using rulers.

Creating an abstract design ruler

This is an involved, multiple-part *Time for action*. So, we may want to read it through once before actually performing the steps listed. We'll be covering a lot, and most of this can be applied to general vector drawing in Manga Studio.

Time for action – setting up our document and tools

In this section, we'll be setting things up so we can trace the rough pencil sketch using rulers. What's nice about rulers in Manga Studio is that the ones we create by hand (excluding perspective, parallel lines, and so on) can be copied and pasted into other pages. We can even save them in our material palette for reuse whenever we need them.

1. The previous image is the shape we want to create as a ruler. It's an element that will appear in several places in our art, so we'll create it as a ruler and move the ruler around to where it needs to be. We will resize it as required.

2. This image is in the `CurveRuler.lip` file in the MS4B download.

3. Because this image was created to be an indication of what's needed, no special effort was put into making the squares or circles perfect. The outer sides should have 90 degree corners. The curves leading into the spiral are basically what they should be.

4. Select the ruler tool, and in the `sub tool` folder, select the figure ruler. We'll be making a copy of this subtool for our squares and rectangles.

5. Go to the **Sub Tool Palette** menu and choose **Duplicate tool** from the menu.

6. Name the tool `MS4B Rectangle Ruler` and give the icon a teal color. If you're using a different icon color to indicate tools that are created for the examples in this book, choose that color. We can be flexible.

7. Adjust the **Tool Property** settings as shown in the following screenshot. If you don't see the attributes shown, click on the wrench icon to bring up the **Tool Settings** palette and find the attributes there. Click on the **Eye con** to make them appear in the properties palette. We can close the settings palette when we're done.

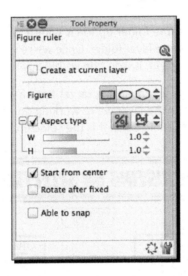

8. Here are the default initial settings for our rectangle ruler maker. For this exercise, let's make some temporary changes.

9. Uncheck **Create at current layer**. We want to put the rulers on their own layer so we can hide it when we need to. Besides, we don't want the rulers on the same layer as our rough drawing. We may need to hide the rough drawing to see how our ruler is looking. This also allows us to use the same rulers when we're doing our final penciling and inking without any extra hassle.

10. Uncheck **Start from center**. This way, we'll create the square from the corner and drag it down to the opposite corner.

11. Now let's draw out a square ruler.

12. Click on one corner of the rough square.

13. With the stylus still on the tablet, drag to the opposite corner and lift the stylus from the tablet.

14. Notice that a few things happened; when we released the stylus, the ruler on the canvas turned purple. A new layer named ruler was created. It has a snazzy ruler icon on it and there's a new drop-down in the layer palette.

15. The new menu on the layer palette is for how the ruler layer is visible (and can work as a guide). Click on it and you can see the three options it has:

  ❏ The **Always Visible** option is where the ruler is visible no matter what other layer we are working on.

  ❏ The **Show in same folder** option is where the ruler is visible for all other layers in the same layer folder. Once we're working on a layer outside the folder the ruler's in, it won't be visible any more.

  ❏ The **Show only when editing target** option is used when we just want to make a ruler on the layer we're working on. When this option is selected, it will only be visible when it is the selected layer.

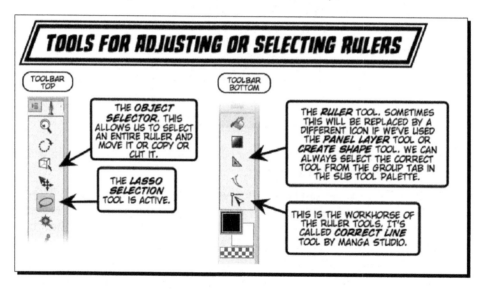

16. The previous screenshot is the tool palette with callouts to tools we'll be using often in this exercise.

17. Instead of drawing out another square ruler, let's copy and paste this one.

18. In the tool palette, choose **Object selector**.

19. Click on the square ruler we just created. Use the **Command Bar** buttons, **Edit** menu, or the command *Ctrl + C* and copy the selected ruler.

20. Paste the ruler onto the current layer.

21. With the ruler still selected, move it to the bottom-right corner of the rough sketch. Since we're working from a rough sketch, don't stress over getting it perfect.

22. Now we'll create a new ruler subtool.

23. Following the same instructions from the beginning of this exercise, create a duplicate of this rectangle ruler subtool; name it `Ellipse Ruler`.

24. Open up the **Tool Settings** for the new tool.

25. In the **Figure** category, select **Ellipse** from the **Figure** entry.

26. Repeat the same steps to make the ellipse a perfect circle.

27. Make the circles on the upper-right and lower-left the same way as we did with the square.

What just happened?

Not only did we get an introductory tour of the rulers, we also learned the advantages of creating them on their own layer and using copy and paste to duplicate selected rulers.

Creating lines and curves for the design

Previously, we created shapes. Now we'll create lines that we can use for intricate drawings. Again, although this example is simplistic, for more elaborate designs (especially ones that we'll reuse), the time spent in creating a ruler will pay off in a well rendered drawing. Let's look at the design and see what kind of lines we'll need:

♦ There are five straight lines

♦ An 'S' curve with a spiral at the end

We could try to do this as a single object, but we can join endpoints of the lines later on. So, we can just break it down to two rulers for now: the lines and the S-curve with the spirals.

Time for action – drawing the straight lines

In this section, we'll be drawing the outermost straight lines for our design. By adjusting the settings, we can do this quickly, as shown in the following screenshot:

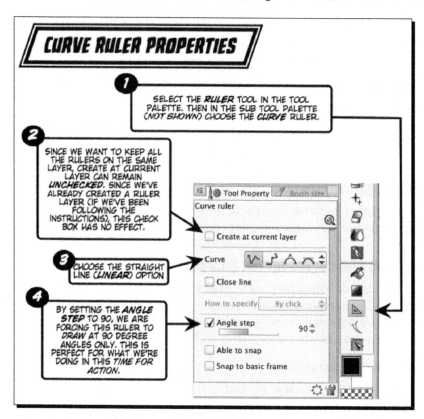

In the previous screenshot, there's a callouts to the attributes we'll be adjusting for creating the outer edges of our design.

We're using **Angle Step** to draw out our lines so they're 90 degrees to the edges of the window. We don't need to use the grid for this. Also notice that it's 90 degrees to the window, not to the canvas or to the grid. This means that if we rotate our canvas (space bar + *Shift* key) and draw out our right angled lines, they will be perpendicular to the edges of the window and not the canvas. This nuance of behavior can come in handy in other situations.

1. Make sure that the **Angle Step** is set at **90**.

2. **Able to snap** or **Snap to basic frame** should be unchecked.

3. Follow the numbers in the following screenshot to create the outer edges of our design. Make sure that you are working on the `CurveRuler.lip` file (or a copy of it) in order to follow along.

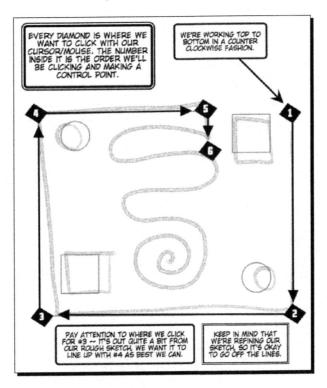

4. Now, just position our cursor at position #1, click and move the cursor to position #2, and click.

5. Although it's mentioned in the previous screenshot, the points between 3 and 4 are off from the sketch. So, be mindful of that when clicking for the corner at #3.

6. Follow the rest of the numbered positions and when we get to #6, click there and hit the *Enter* key.

7. We're done. If we want to, we can choose the **Object selector** tool from the tool palette and click on our rectangles and ovals and reposition them, as shown in the previous screenshot.

What just happened?

There's a lot that we can do with just drawing linear rulers. With judicious use of the **Angle Step**, option we can have the straight lines snap to specific angles.

Types of curves in Manga Studio

There are four types of curves that we can use with the curve subtool:

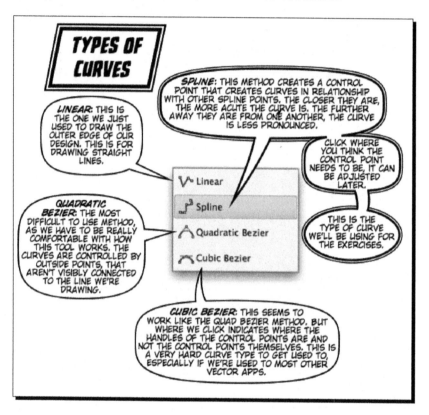

As stated in the previous screenshot, we'll be using the **Spline** method as it's the easiest and gives very good results. **Quadratic Bezier** and **Cubic Bezier** are hard to edit, as when we use the **Correct Line** tool, we only see the main control points and the outside control points for the **Quadratic Bezier** and the control point handles of the **Cubic Bezier** when we move our cursor over the line itself. And when we move our cursor over to the outside points or handles, the highlights on the points vanish until our cursor is directly over them. And that's a major pain in our art, for sure.

Time for action – making a curved ruler

Whenever we're making rulers (using straight, curved, or a combination of the two), we should always have a clear idea of what we want to create. This is why we're using a roughly drawn sketch of our abstract design. In a real-world example, we could be using a curved ruler for help in drawing a spiral staircase or curved wings on a starship:

1. Select the **Ruler** tool in the tool palette and the **Curve** subtool in the **Sub Tool** palette.

2. In the tool properties, choose the **Spline** method from the drop-down menu in the **Curve attributes** section.

3. Uncheck all the attributes that aren't greyed out.

4. Notice where the square dots are in the preceding image. That's where the cursor was clicked. (If you've downloaded the MS4B ZIP file, this screenshot is a color PNG file that shows the square dots are green with red outlines.)

5. The curves drawn using the spline method are additive, meaning that the points before and after a point affect the curve's shape.

6. Since we didn't check the **Close Shape** attribute, the beginning and ending points are hollow squares. These points can be snapped to other rulers on the same layer. This way, when we draw over them, the line is continuous.

7. Click and then move your mouse until the curve behind it approximately matches what's drawn.

8. When drawing a curve, imagine a compass circle. If we click on North, East, and South directions, we'll get a nice circular curve, like the second one from the top in the preceding screenshot.

9. Once we're done with creating a ruler for this shape, we can select the **Correct Line** tool from the tool palette and choose the **Control Point** tool in the **Sub Tool** palette.

10. Content of process controls what we can do when a control point is selected. The options we're concerned with are:

    ❑ Move control point

    ❑ Add control point

    ❑ Delete control point

11. Make sure the **Move control point** option is chosen.

12. With the **Spline** method we used, there are no handles or outside points to deal with. Just click on a point and move it around.

13. Don't expect to get this right away. It can be tricky to get the curve just right. Some good practices are:

    ❑ The **Add control point** subtool for the **Line correction** tool will add a point to a curve or allow us to move a point if the cursor is right over it. This is the best option to use when we're adjusting our curves as we just click on an empty line of our ruler to create a new control point.

    ❑ Don't add too many points, though. Too many will make modifying our curve harder than it needs to be.

    ❑ If a curve is too flat looking, that's the time to add a new control point or move some points on both ends of the arc closer together.

    ❑ Two points real close together is a good way to create a rounded corner.

14. When using the **Object Selector** tool, we can use our keyboard cursor (arrow) keys to move the selected object up, down, left, and right. As with most other graphic apps, if we hold down the *Shift* key and press the arrow keys, it'll move the selection more. And it's not obvious, but with nothing selected, press any arrow key and all ruler objects will move! Just make sure the ruler layer is selected.

15. The switch corner option in the process drop-down menu can make the point the opposite of what it currently is: either corner or curved.

16. Save the file.

What just happened?

We went through making an abstract shape using Manga Studio's ruler tools. We covered how to set up our document for rulers, the attributes we need to be mindful of, we created a ruler tool that'll draw perfect squares or circles and draw right angled lines, and we also worked with the spline curve tool. Good times!

Next up, we'll draw the shapes using the rulers we just made as a guide and see how it works in an example from the `dialogPage.lip` file.

Have a go hero – making a curved ruler

We now have the knowledge to create our own templates that we can use anywhere, any time!

Why not create a new document and make some curves that we may need to use over and over. If it's a superhero logo, or a repeated design, make one of your own. Start with a rough sketch. It can be very rough like our example, or a scan of something that is saved as a TIFF, JPG, or PNG format. Go to file, import the image to load it into the document. Make sure you save your file before and after importing. Use the layer color option for the layer to make the drawing blue, so it'll be easy to trace over. Now use the tools and whip up a few rulers of your own. We'll learn how we can store them in the **Materials** palette real soon.

Snapping our pencils in a good way

It's no good having the best rulers around if we can't snap at them; we'd be better off just drawing them by hand and avoid the ruler-making process entirely. Thankfully, for all the effort we put into making a ruler in the previous exercise, Manga Studio has very good snap-to features.

We'll be using just the snap-to ruler option. The other two we'll get to later. They all work pretty much the same:

- The snap-to ruler option will snap our marking tool to the ruler if it's visible.

- The snap-to special ruler option will snap our marking tool to perspective rulers, if visible.

- When the grid is visible, the snap-to grid option will snap our drawing tool to the grid.

Sometimes if the snap-to grid and snap-to rulers options are both active, snap-to grid may be off by a number of pixels in the first few lines. Sometimes it'll clear up but sometimes not. When that happens, turn the snap-to grid and snap-to ruler off and turn only one on.

When going over (tracing) a ruler, try to keep close to the ruler lines. If we stray too far away from the rulers, the line drawn by snapping will be quicker than expected. The line that's drawn in that case will be drawn at maximum darkness and pressure. If we trace the ruler carefully, it'll save us much time and annoyance.

Pressure does work with the snap-to options, which is another reason to take some care when going over the rulers.

Each line segment has to be drawn separately. This means, in the design we made, the outer edge will be drawn separately from the curves that lead into the spiral.

We're ready to begin to draw over our rulers now!

Time for action – snapping pencils to the rulers

When we set up our ruler tools, we unchecked the **Draw in Same Layer** option. What this did was to have Manga Studio create a ruler layer and make all the rulers within this layer. One reason we did this was to isolate the ruler. Click on the ruler layer in the `curveRuler. lip` file. There's the ruler options menu in the layers palette now as shown in the following screenshot:

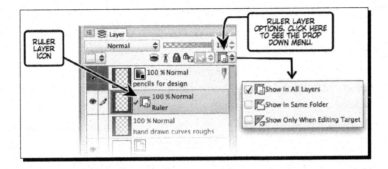

The selected option, **Show in All Layers**, is what we want. The **Show in Same Folder** option is pretty obvious; it will only show the ruler when we have a selected layer in the same folder as the ruler layer. The last option, **Show Only When Editing Target**, is for when we have a ruler within a drawing or inking layer. This will hide the rulers when we're working on another layer or a layer that's not a reference layer. I find it's easier and quicker just to have a dedicated ruler layer and not have to fuss about with sharing pencils or inks with rulers.

1. Select the MS4B base pencil from the MS4B pencils subtool palette group after clicking on the pencil tool in the tool palette. Make sure that the **Possible to Snap** attribute is checked in the **Tool Settings** palette (get that palette open by clicking on the wrench in the **Tool Properties** palette).

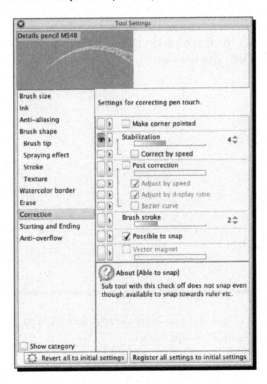

2. The **Possible to Snap** option is one of those settings that's good to have visible in the properties palette; so, click on the **Eye-con** button (it's at the extreme right of the row) to make that happen.

3. Glance at the command bar and make sure that snap to rulers is active (it'll have a darker grey background if it is). We don't need any other snap-to settings on for this exercise.

4. With the pencil tool, press your stylus like you're drawing and follow the ruler lines. Try to keep pretty much on the line of the ruler.

5. Each line has to be drawn separately. If the next line has a start point right on another ruler, go experiment with how far away we need to go to be able to draw that ruler, instead of the one we've already drawn on.

6. We can click on the visibility of the ruler layer and see how our lines look. If they look lifeless and cold, that's okay. This is the start of penciling; we can go over the lines freehand (with rulers off) and give the lines a bit of hand-drawn look that'll warm them up.

What just happened?

By using rulers, we were able to trace the design on a blank layer using a pencil that is able to snap to rulers. We learned that by having a separate layer for rulers, we're able to hide the visibility of the rulers and gauge our progress.

The next screenshot shows the first panel in the `dialogpage.lip` file with the rulers that traced the pencils on the left, and the plain rulers on the right.

All the perspective in that panel was eye-balled. We didn't have to, as Manga Studio has some excellent perspective tools, as we'll see.

Getting some perspective

If we spent any time searching on Google about perspective, we've seen things like perspective grids mentioned. And almost all of them are awkward to use as compared to what we can do with vanishing points, rulers, pencils, and paper.

It's expected that we all know the basics of perspective. If not, there are a number of excellent books that can expand one's knowledge of this important art at the back of this book. When using some esoteric aspects of perspective, those terms will be explained.

When I started using Manga Studio 3 and then 4, the perspective rulers were the biggest feature in my mind, only second to the brush and pen tools. They worked like their analog counterparts: vanishing points were easy to set up, and had a customizable grid that automagically created custom perspective grids. Life was good!

In Manga Studio 5.0.3, even though some of the customizable features from Version 4 were taken away, the perspective rulers are still among the best in any graphics app.

Let's see why they're so good.

Time for action – creating a perspective ruler

We'll cover how to create a one-point perspective ruler. We can also create two and three-point perspective rulers if we want. Let's just keep it simple for now as shown in the following steps:

1. With Manga Studio running, open up the `scratchpad.lip` document or create a new one.

2. Either go to **Main Menu | Layers** or **Layer Palette Menu**, select the **Ruler** menu item, and choose **Create Perspective Ruler** from the hierarchical menu.

3. Choose the **1 point perspective** option from the type section. Make sure **Create new layer** is checked.

4. Click on **OK**.

5. The perspective ruler is created in a new layer. The object selection tool is active. Don't click anything on the canvas.

6. Select the **Pencil** tool from the tool palette. Choose a fine point pencil from the subtool palette.

7. In **Command Bar**, make sure **Snap to special ruler** is on (it's the middle snap-to button) and that the pencil has snapping enabled.

8. Spend at least 5-10 minutes just getting the feel for drawing horizontal, vertical, and perspective lines. It's crucial to get a good feel for how your tablet works with the perspective ruler. The direction you first start when making a line will determine if the line is horizontal, vertical, or using the vanishing point as its origin.

What just happened?

We created and drew on a 1 point perspective ruler layer. We found that it takes some time to get used to how the snapping works.

If we still have our pencil tool active, draw one more line; and then, in **Command Bar**, click on the clear whirlpool to clear the layer of our test pencils.

Choose the **Object Selection** tool from the tool palette and click on a ruler line. Suddenly, we see all sorts of new symbols and colored dots and squares. The following screenshot should decode these new things for us:

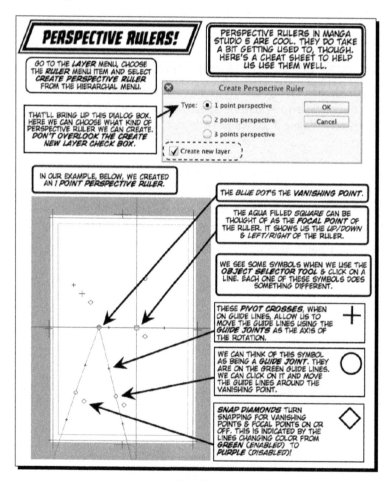

Even though our example focuses on 1 point perspective, this information applies to 2 and 3 point perspective rulers as well.

The aqua-filled square is our focal point of the ruler. It has two perpendicular lines running through it. The vertical green line shows us the angle our vertical lines will be in. The blue line is our eye-level or horizon line. 1 and 2 point perspective vanishing points (VP) are attached to this line. The little crosses on each side of the filled square on the horizon line tell us that the eye-level isn't fixed, so it can be rotated by clicking on these crosses. When it's rotated, the vertical green line also rotates. This is how we can create, as they call it in the movies, dutch angles. Don't forget that these two lines are what our horizontal and vertical drawn lines will be parallel to. Notice that there are two diamond shapes, one far above the filled square and the other a bit below the square. As the definition in the image says, these are what we can call **snap diamonds**, as they can turn snapping on or off for the line or object they are attached to. The upper snap diamond will toggle snapping for the vertical lines and the bottom will do so for horizontal lines.

These snap diamonds are a great feature, but beware! They don't change color or get filled when enabled or disabled! The only indication we have is that the perspective lines that they control change color from purple to green! If we're using a perspective ruler while drawing and we just can't get a snap to a vertical, horizontal, or perspective line, chances are we accidentally clicked on one of these snap diamonds without realizing it. The way to solve this all-too-common issue is to select the **Object Selector** tool and select the perspective ruler and click on the snap diamond that is causing the issue. We can only hope that in a future update, Manga Studio will give us better visual feedback whether a snap diamond is enabled or not.

The aqua-filled dot is our **Vanishing Point (VP)**. The two green lines radiating from it are guidelines. The circle is what we can call the Guide Joint. It can slide along the line and can move the guideline around. The crosses on either side of it can move the guideline using the joint as a fulcrum (that is, the guideline rotates around the joint and makes the Vanishing Point move). This is really helpful in fitting Vanishing Points to a hand-drawn rough sketch. This can also whack out our horizon line (eye level) and other Vanishing Points (when we have more than one). There's a snap diamond to the right and below the Guide Joint.

Alone in the upper-left is a set of two crosses and one more snap diamond. There's no line they're close to. They are for adjusting the entire ruler. The smaller cross, at the top, will allow us to move these three elements as a whole, so we can get them out of the way. This is helpful because it's really easy to get a ruler with many guides, and these three elements can really add to the clutter. The larger cross when clicked-and-dragged will move the entire ruler: focal area, horizon line, and Vanishing Points. The snap diamond will enable/disable snapping for the entire ruler. Another reason to move this assembly out of the way is because it's too darn easy to click on that diamond without realizing it and then spend, like, an hour trying to figure out why your ruler's not working. Note that I'm speaking from a sad, sad, experience, mind you!

The upcoming screenshot has some information on the contextual menu we get when we click on any ruler element (but not the snap diamonds!) with the **Object Selector** active:

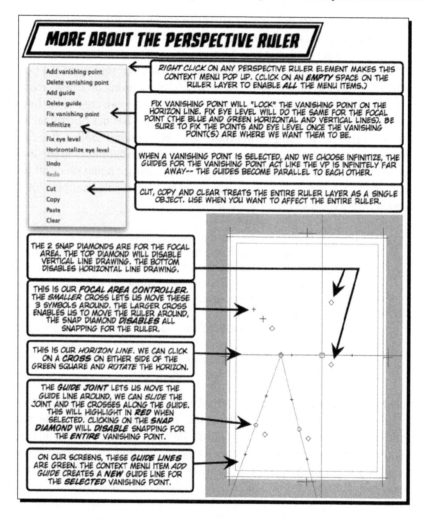

The following are the many choices the contextual menu gives us. The active choices depend on what specific element is selected when we right click. It's a good habit to first click on the element we want, then right-click on it. This builds up the association with the element and the options we have for that element.

- **Add Vanishing Point**: This is used when we realize that we need a 2 point perspective and not just a single Vanishing Point. The new Vanishing Point isn't bonded to the horizon line, so it can be freely moved without affecting it. However, if the new VP touches the horizon line, it will snap to it.

- ◆ **Delete Vanishing Point:** This will delete an offending Vanishing Point. For example, we have a 3 point perspective ruler and realize we only need a 2 point perspective.

- ◆ **Add Guide:** This is so very good to be able to do. In the previous screenshot, we can see that the Vanishing Point only has two "spokes" from it. We can select this menu item and make another guide. Why? We can create a guide just for the height of telephone poles going off in the distance.

- ◆ **Delete Guide:** This will delete the selected guide we right-clicked to bring up the menu.

- ◆ **Fix Vanishing Point:** This is good to select when we have a Vanishing Point just where we want it. We can still move the guides around, but the crosses will vanish when the Vanishing Point is fixed, so we can't rotate around the joint.

- ◆ **Fix Eye Level:** This is kind of tricky. It'll still allow us to rotate it by clicking on its crosses; however, when we click on the crosses on the guides and rotate the guide on the Joint, the Vanishing Point will slide along the horizon line. When unchecked, rotating the guide on the Joint will move the horizon line up or down.

- ◆ **Horizontalize eye level:** Whew, that's not even in my dictionary! What it'll do is make the eye level horizontal, no matter what angle it is. It will be horizontal to the document and not the angle of the canvas.

The rest of the menu items, undo, redo, cut, copy, paste and clear, do what we're used to these commands doing. Keep in mind that cut, copy, paste, and clear are for the entire ruler and not just whatever's selected.

One thing we haven't covered is the options in the tool property palette when we're editing the perspective ruler.

The options for **Select** are set up so we can select the rulers. It's fine as it is. Feel free to adjust the settings; just make a note of what they were so that they can be reset.

The perspective rulers **Snap** and **Fix eye level** can be set here also. They do apply to the entire ruler, though. It'll still be checked even if we've clicked the dreaded snap diamond on a guide.

The last section, **Grid**, is disappointing. It's very hard to get a good grid that's useful. The setting **Grid Size** affects all vanishing points and the ground plane equally. There are no real customizable features we can tweak to make it work for our workflow. But that doesn't mean they're useless. Turn them on by clicking on the various icons and see how they work for you. I find that they seem to just get in the way and clutter up the view of what I'm trying to draw. Especially when using a 3-point perspective, two of the grids are colored green. That makes its utility go down a few levels.

When we're used to doing all this perspective craziness, then do some work on the story pages we've been working on. Pick a few panels and add a perspective ruler to them. When a perspective ruler is made, it'll be at the bottom of the layer list, so it will have to be dragged up inside the panel folder it was made for. Then, set the visibility to be visible within the folder. This way, when we're working on other panels, we won't have to see all the other rulers for the other panels. We'll learn more about dealing with rulers in the upcoming section, but for now, work on some perspective. This book will still be here.

Managing perspective and other rulers

Over the years, there are some practices that have been found to be very helpful and save us frustration and time. Here's a screenshot to get us started:

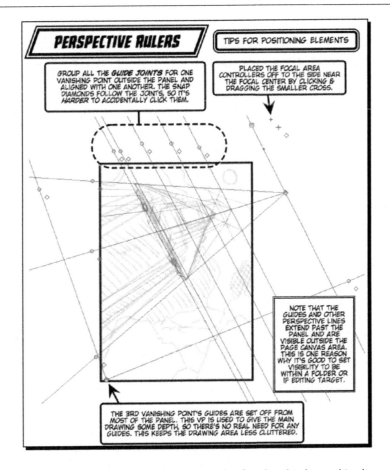

The preceding screenshot shows the perspective ruler for the third panel in the dialogPage.lip file. However, once we start drawing with a marking tool, the ruler's various elements (the snap diamonds, Guide Joints, and so on) are hidden; it's good practice to move them out of the panel once we're done with them. It makes working on aligning the guide much easier and it's clearer which joints belong to which guide.

When setting up the guides for something like a corner, place the joint at the corner of the object and use the crosses to rotate the guide on the joint. Don't be afraid to add more guides to Vanishing Points. Notice in the image that the ship has three guides going across its width and one extra guide along its center. As more work is being done on drawing the ship, more guides may be added; some may be moved or deleted depending on the needs of the drawing as it gets completed.

As with most drawing development, work big and then go into details. Work on just one Vanishing Point; lock its position. Move on to the next Vanishing Point. Working on all Vanishing Points (especially when the eye-level isn't fixed) at the same time is self-defeating, because as soon as we get one guide right, go to another Vanishing Point, and adjust one of its guides, the previous guide would have moved. Ping-pong is best played on a table with paddles and a ball, not with Vanishing Points. So, adjust one Vanishing Point, fix its position, and move to the next.

If there's need to have an extra Vanishing Point, like for roofs of buildings or angled stairs, a new perspective ruler layer can be made. We can toggle that new perspective ruler's visibility in the layer palette to make things better to draw. When a ruler of any kind is hidden, it can't be snapped to in any tool. Another good reason to put all rulers on separate layers instead of the drawing layer. We need to be mindful of any option that says create on the same layer or create on a new layer (or variations of that phrasing).

When we're done with drawing our object with the perspective rulers, one thing we could notice is how cold and precise the drawing looks. This is when we just turn off the rulers (by turning off snapping or turning off visibility of the ruler layer) and go over the lines freehand. Depending on the steadiness of our hand, we can preserve the accuracy of the lines, but the natural wobbliness of our line will give warmth to the drawing and make the object blend in with the rest of the drawing. Not drawing corners while the snap-to ruler is on is a way to add to this. Most things don't have perfect sharp corners, and by hand drawing them, we add more hand-drawn appeal to the drawing. It will make inking easier, as our muscle memory will kick in, and we can surprise ourselves by how nice the finished drawing looks.

If a perspective ruler is giving us massive trouble, delete it. Look at the rough sketch. Make a new layer with a different color effect and color. Hand draw the perspective guides and see where the Vanishing Points are. Most times, we'll see where we went wrong and the new perspective ruler we create and adjust will be easier than the first attempt.

Perspective is a skill; once the basics are part of our toolkit, we'll know how to do forced perspective and even curvilinear perspective. And that's way outside what we can cover in this book.

Interface tweaks to make penciling easier and faster

So far, in this chapter, there's been very little about actual penciling. That's because of the rulers and perspective aspects of Manga Studio we've had to cover. Again, the tools here may be analogous to the tools we would use on paper with pencil, but the tools here need a bit (okay, a lot) of explaining. While it's nice to be able to have a pencil snap to a ruler or perspective line, sometimes if we see where the guide is, we can just hand draw it without any snapping turned on. If we get too concerned with creating the perfect ruler or using snap-to when drawing things in perspective, our drawing can lose a bit of life. And this is different for each and every one of us. The best way to really make use of these rulers is just to practice with them and see what works best for you.

Now, with that being said, there's some more adjustments we can make to Manga Studio to allow us to draw our pencils better, easier, and quicker. We'll look at drawing with transparency, using layers, the mysteries of masking and modifying keyboard shortcuts, and the command bar to simplify operations that we do often.

Drawing with transparency and other digital benefits

This is an aspect of drawing in Manga Studio that hasn't been given enough attention. It may seem like nothing, but it can be quite the time saver.

On tablets, well at least the Wacom tablet I use, the eraser tool at the end of the stylus will use the eraser that was last used. If we hold our stylus eraser end down over the tablet, we can use the Bracket keys to make the eraser larger ([ ) or smaller ( ]). But if we want to, we can just select another eraser from the **Sub Tool** palette that'll suit our needs better.

Let's think about something: what if we could erase with the same tool we used to make the marks? And yes we can do that.

Time for action – drawing with transparency

There's an old method of creating art that uses paper that has color or colors painted on it and a layer of black ink or other coating applied to it. The artist then uses a tool to scratch away the black ink to create the drawing. We can do something like that in Manga Studio by using transparency as a color. Interested? Read on...

1. Open our poor abused `Scratchpad.lip` file, if it's not already open.

2. Create a new layer and hide all other layers.

3. Using a big dark pencil, fill in a good area.

4. Select a detail pencil.

5. In the tool palette, at the bottom of it, there are the color swatches. The swatch at the very bottom has the checkerboard pattern that indicates transparency. Click on that swatch.

6. Now draw on the previously drawn area.

7. It's like we're carving out areas from the pencil marks we did first.

8. Now switch back to the default black pencil color and draw a bit more.

9. Switch to transparency and make corrections. This method is great for adding gleams to pupils, metallic objects, or evil eyes staring at us from the darkness.

What just happened?

We just used our pencil like an eraser. Now it may not be as clean as a regular eraser, as our drawing pencil may have some texture in it. But it gets the job done pretty well and is much more accurate and faster than using an eraser to erase an area and then draw things back into it. This can also be used to soften edges. Think about drawing flames or explosions or billowing clouds of smoke with the addition of transparent pencil lines. Try turning off the spraying for the pencil and then see how it works as a transparency pencil.

Layering our pencils

While penciling, we can sometimes get frustrated because our foreground figures need adjustments and erasing. And if we're drawing them on the same layer as the background, well, it sometimes isn't too pretty.

Now we will create new layers for the different depths of our drawing. Way back in an earlier chapter, we covered actions. One of them was for creating new layers and changing the color of the color effect. Using that, we can create a system of color coding for layers that would contain special effects, background elements, and so on. This way, we can make sure our foreground figures are correct, even make alternate versions of them and not worry about messing up our backgrounds. The different colors (like green for background, maroon for special effects, and blue for foreground) will help us differentiate between layers, and allow us to draw through other elements so everything works together. We can merge these layers together when we're done and are ready for inking, if we want. It may make our file size larger, but since we're working with layers that are either greyscale or monochrome, they aren't as large as color layers.

We can then make new layers for our line drawing of the rough pencils, another new layer for adding shadows, and so on. We are working in a digital environment, so let's leverage what the digital realm can do for us.

Unmasking masks

One cover idea I had was for a hand gripping the double helix of DNA. It was a challenge, as the helix was difficult to draw and the hands... oh the hands... well, we all know how hard it is to draw hands, don't we?

The following diagram shows the pencils for the finished drawing:

I drew the Helix and the hand on separate layers. I used masks to give the appearance that it was all drawn on a single layer. Here's the unmasked helix layer to give us an idea of what masking can do:

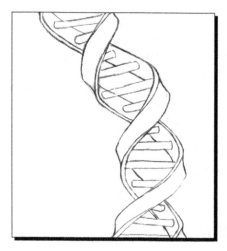

The biggest thing about masks is that they are non destructive. They don't alter what we've drawn, they just hide parts of the drawing. Masks in Manga Studio take just a bit of work to understand, and that bit of work will reward us in many ways in our endeavors. Even though we're using masks for penciling, they can be used in exactly the same way for inking or coloring.

Time for action – setting up our layer

Before we begin to use masks, let's set up our workspace so our work on masks will go smoothly. Masks aren't used too much at first, but after you get used to them, you'll find yourself wondering why it took so long to start using them:

1. From the **Downloaded** folder, open up the `MaskDemo.lip` file.
2. It has just two layers: FG ruffs and BG ruffs. They have color effects of blue and green, respectively. We'll want to mask out areas of the BG ruffs layer where the FG ruffs layer should be covering up the BG ruffs as shown in the following screenshot:

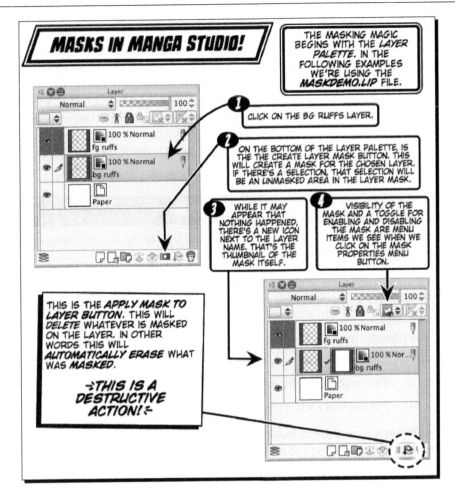

3. As shown in the previous screenshot, click on the BG ruffs layer. This is the layer we'll be working with.

4. Just for this exercise, make sure there are no selections.

5. On the bottom of the layer palette, as shown in the previous screenshot, click on the **Create Layer Mask** button.

What just happened?

Nothing happened! If we look at the BG ruffs layer, we see a new thumbnail image. This is our mask sublayer. The check mark between it and the regular layer thumbnail show that there's a link between the two. When we want to make a change in the mask, we need to first click on the mask thumbnail (as shown in the screenshot). This is crucial! If we want to work on the mask, we must make sure the mask thumbnail is active, otherwise we're just going to make marks on the artwork. Think of a mask as a cut-out that hovers above the artwork of a layer. We need to tell Manga Studio we want to work on the cut-out by clicking on the mask thumbnail.

Time for action – drawing on the mask

Drawing on a mask layer can be tricky, as we're seeing the results of our marks. Here are some steps to help us use masks effectively and easily:

1. A mask is a greyscale sublayer. But unlike any layer we've dealt with so far, this layer works with transparent pixels and filled pixels.

2. With our pencil tool, draw on the layer mask with black, white, and transparency. Only transparency has given us results.

3. We can consider the following points:

   ❑ Black, white, or any color doesn't seem to change the mask

   ❑ Transparency will hide (add to the mask) what it has drawn

4. So, in order to add to the mask, we draw with transparency; in order to subtract from the mask, we need to draw on it either with white or black.

5. We can click on the **Mask Properties Menu** button and see the two options it has:

   ❑ **Enable Mask**: This option will enable the mask, obviously. When it's unchecked, a red X will appear in the mask sublayer thumbnail to give us visual feedback that it's disabled.

   ❑ **Show Mask Area**: When selected (checked), this option will make the masked area appear in purple color. Select the **Marker** tool from the tool palette.

6. In the properties palette, make sure that the marker has no anti-aliasing.

7. Double-check whether the mask sublayer icon is selected (it'll have an outline around it) and with the marker tool, draw where the FG ruffs figure overlaps the background drawing.

8. When we're done with that, we can go to the FG ruffs layer and work on the pencils for the figure without worrying about messing up the background and not have the underdrawing clutter up what we're working on.

What just happened?

We learned how to draw on a mask layer to make things in the main layer invisible. We also found out how we can change how the mask works. Not that complicated, was it?

Time for action – applying the mask and merging layers

So far, all our work on masks has been nondestructive, which means that all of our work is still there, albeit invisible. Here's how we can apply our masks to our art. This is a destructive action; although we can perform an undo, be sure that this is what we want to do:

1. We're done with the penciling and now we want to apply the mask and begin to combine the layers so that we have a simplified document to deal with.

2. So far, our mask work has been nondestructive; our pencils are still there, just hidden by the mask, much like how Batman's cowl hides Bruce Wayne's face.

3. At the bottom of the layer palette, the button right next to the trash can icon is the **Apply Mask to Layer** button. Clicking on this button will erase what's masked. As the screenshot said in big warning letters, this is a destructive action. Once this button is clicked, we can undo and get the mask back. But if we save and close the document and then open it again, what was once masked is gone forever, or until we redraw it.

4. We can perform **Save As** and save this file as a copy of the original if we really want to be safe and have a backup copy. Or just make a copy of the layer and put it in a folder and click on **Eye con** to hide the folder from view.

5. Click on the **Apply Mask to Layer** button.

6. The only visible thing that happened is that we lost the mask sublayer icon. So, even though we don't see it, we used the mask to erase what it was masking and then delete itself.

7. Let's take this further. Now we want to combine both the FG and BG ruffs layers into one layer.

8. Unless we've made changes to the color effect, they should be on for both layers.

9. If we combine layers now, Manga Studio will combine them as one color layer. But we're hardcore and want them both to remain greyscale. That's how we roll.

10. Go to the **Layer Properties** tab and click on the color effect icon. This makes the drawing appear in greyscale. Do this for both layers.

11. Now with either layer selected, hold down the *Shift* key and click on the unselected layer.

12. Both layers are now selected. In the column immediately to the right of the **eye-con** column, we can see one layer with a pencil type icon and another with a check mark. This is Manga Studio telling us that we have multiple layers selected and the pencil icon is telling us which layer is the destination layer.

13. In the **Layer Palette** menu, select the **Combine Layers** menu item.

14. The two layers are combined. The layer has the name of the destination layer. Cool, isn't it?

15. If we didn't apply the mask, combining layers will automagically apply the mask to the layer and then combine that layer with the other layer or layers. That's cool times two.

16. Click on the **Color Effect** button in the layer properties palette. Notice that the color is now the standard non-photo blue color. We can change the color the color effect will display, but the layer's still greyscale.

What just happened?

We created a layer mask and learned how we can draw on it to mask out areas without erasing them. Then, we learned how to apply the layer mask, realizing that this is a destructive action. And we wrapped it up by combining both the FG and BG ruffs layers.

Before we go off and learn the advantages of keyboard shortcuts, here's a screenshot that explains what selections we need do when creating a layer mask:

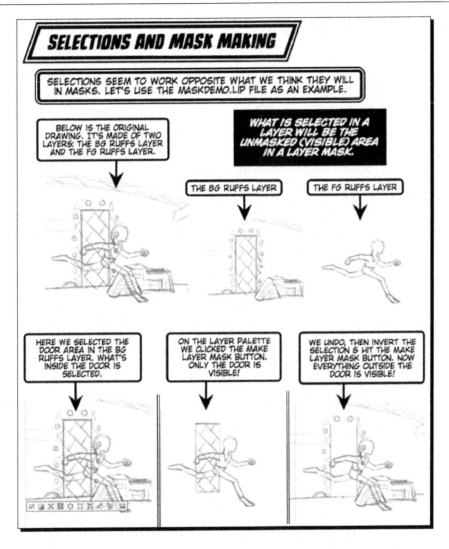

From the previous screenshot, we now know that when we make a selection for a layer mask, the selected area will be visible and what's unselected will be hidden.

Since we'll be masking what we want to be hidden so that another layer's content will be clearer, we need to be mindful that if we move that other layer, the mask on the masked layer has to be unlinked from the main layer. Right-click on the mask thumbnail icon, and from the menu, select unlink mask. Move the mask around with the move layer tool or with a section tool. Be sure to relink the mask with the layer when done.

Using reference images

One of the perks (or thorns, depending on our attitude at any given moment) of being a comic artist is that we're on call to draw anything at any time. We don't know if that conversation is taking place on a train or a zeppelin. Or if that climatic battle is taking place on the Moon or in a living room. We rise to this challenge by using one thing: reference!

Some artists, even in this day of Google and other search engines, have what's called Morgues. It's a collection of books and photos of things the artist is interested in and feels may be needed for a story assignment in the future.

Manga Studio has what's called the **Sub View Palette** (Manga Studio sure loves preceding every thing with sub, doesn't it?) palette. This is a very powerful tool to use for our reference drawings that we scanned into the computer, photos we took on our smart phones or digital cameras, and graphics we downloaded from the Internet.

What makes the **Sub View Palette** so great is that we can load up dozens of reference graphics and they are accessible every time we start up Manga Studio. We can trash specific images when we no longer need them (they'll still be on our hard drive, we just won't see them in the **Sub View Palette**). And these images don't add to our document file size or slow down Manga Studio. It's magic, I say, magic!

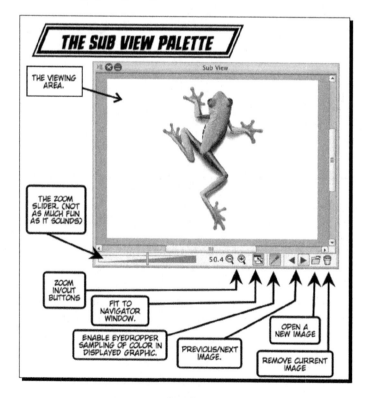

There's not a whole lot that this palette does. But, just being there is more than enough. We can zoom in and out of the displayed image so we can examine details.

If we want to have the image resized to fit in the palette viewing area (or Navigator window as Manga Studio calls it), **Fit to Navigator Window**, the little button with the two windows and an arrow can do it. In the screenshot, it has a grey background, so it's currently active.

The next button, the eyedropper, allows us to sample colors in the image displayed. This is great if we have a character sheet and want to match up the skin tone or clothes colors exactly. Or if we want to get the color of a tree frog's feet.

The buttons that look like a back and forward button allow us to go one image back or forward. There's no way to look at a list of images, so this is our only way to navigate what's stored in the sub view palette.

The folder icon will display an **Open file** dialog box. We can navigate to where the images we want to reference are located. We can open more than one file at a time as long as they're in the same folder by holding down *Shift* to select a range of images. Holding down *Command* (Mac OS X) or *Control* (Windows OS) will allow us to choose individual files (or in geek speak: noncontiguous selections).

That last icon, the trash can, may be scary, but it doesn't do anything to the files we've opened. Clicking on that button will just delete the image from the subview list. It's still on our storage medium. If we want to see it again, all we have to do is click on the open file button and go to where that image is on our hard drive, flash drive, or wherever it is.

It's good to have a folder that just contains images on a hard drive or flash drive. Those images can be organized further into folders or whatever system makes sense to you. I usually have character/story-specific images in a folder with the series name. Other images are filed in folders with a descriptive name. I have one for tree frogs, bats, and so on.

While it may sound great in marketing, and our operating system may allow it, you shouldn't use images that are stored on the cloud in the **Sub View Palette**. You may be working on a tight deadline and lose the Internet. And there goes our reference pictures! Same thing goes for using a flash drive. Make sure it's plugged in before starting up Manga Studio, else the images may not show up in the **Sub View Palette**. And, with the size of images, we could rack up bandwidth that may exceed the limits imposed on us by our Internet service provider. And that could be costly.

Pop quiz

Q1. The difference between Raster and Vector is that Vector...

1. Sounds more technical.
2. Is pixel-based.
3. Can be scaled up without getting blocky-looking.

Q2. The Spray category for pencils allows us to...

1. Create real-looking textures for our drawing tools.
2. Use our pencil like an air brush.
3. Have our pencil act like a fill bucket.

Q3. Masking is...

1. A destructive way to combine two layers.
2. A way of hiding parts of a layer.
3. A way of allowing the paper color to show through all layers.

Q4. Changing our pencil color is best done by changing the color mode of the layer.

1. True
2. False

Q5. Once sub tool properties are set, we cannot change them.

1. True
2. False

Summary

In this chapter, we went through the process of creating custom pencils and learning about the intricacies of the many settings available to us. Then we explored rulers that we can use to act as a guide for our drawing and perspective rulers that allow us to draw objects in perspective. As we progressed through this lengthy chapter, we discovered not only how useful masks can be, but how to create them and use them. We wound down this chapter by learning about the sub view palette, where we can keep reference images (photos or drawings) for quick viewing.

Now go out there and do some penciling! And once we have our pencils the way we want them, they'll need to be inked. Let's explore how to ink our pencil drawings by slinging some digital ink in the next chapter.

7
Ink Slingers

If Manga Studio pencils shine, Manga Studio inking pens and brushes are as smooth as polished white dwarf star matter. We'll look at our inked line's life and how varying the thickness helps it look more vibrant and work with our lighting. There'll be exercises to create a technical pen and an inking pen.

We'll learn how vector layers work in Manga Studio and some good benefits of using them to ink by learning how to adjust vector lines. We will gain flexibility in coloring our pages by separating our foreground from the background while inking. Masking will be revisited and used as a way to make our foreground and background distinct from each other.

We'll end this chapter by exploring a few special rulers and using tones for our inked drawings.

In this chapter, we'll be covering the following topics in depth:

- What is inking?
- Tools that Manga Studio provides to let us ink our artwork
- Using rulers and guides for inking
- Creating a customized brush for special effects
- How to use the Manga Studio default tones
- A walk-through inking example

The role of inking

Inking, sometimes called rendering or embellishment, was used to make the pencil sketches the artist drew easier to reproduce using photographic reproduction and presses that were used to make comics back in the 30s and 40s. This was because comics were printed using presses that could only print a limited amount of colors and couldn't print grayscale or full color.

Adding inks to a penciled page is the next step in creating what the reader will see in our comic. This is where we make our drawings vivid with clear lines and pools of shadows. By recreating the pencils with only solid black lines and fills, we end up with a page that is ready for toning or coloring.

One of the most important things that we should keep in mind while inking is if the inks aren't solid, clear, and understandable, we cannot expect to make it better with colors. Without good inks, we won't have a good page. We can fix some penciling errors with good inks; however, once we commit to our inks, we must be happy with them.

Another important thing to keep in mind while inking is that we're interpreting 3D objects using black lines. Any shading at this point is done by varying the thickness of lines, crosshatching, and feathering. If those terms sound unfamiliar, we'll get their definitions as we proceed with the exercises.

It's all about the lines

Before we examine the kinds of tools, we need to have an idea of the kinds of lines we need to create.

When we are penciling the page, we are interested in composition, lighting, perspective, and anatomy. When we're inking, we are interested in how the lines work in context to the rest of the drawing, as shown in the following figure:

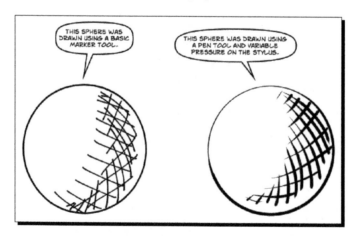

In the preceding figure, the right-hand side sphere was rendered using the default marker tool. It creates *dead-weight lines*. This means that the thickness of the line doesn't vary, unless we go back over the lines.

The sphere on the left was inked using the default G-Pen. With the pen tool, we can vary the pressure on the stylus to get lines of varying thickness. This results in a feathering effect, as shown in the following figure:

This looks simple and easy to do, but requires much practice. The example shown here took less than a minute to do. Feathering is a technique that we can do quickly and accurately once our hand becomes confident.

Crosshatching is another tool we can use while inking.

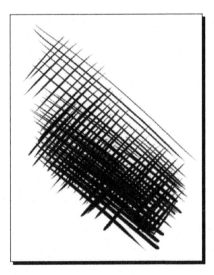

The preceding figure shows an example of crosshatching. Here, we can also provide an illusion of one color blending into another. Even though the example is made up of lines that are at a 90 degree angle from each other, we can alter the angle to give us different looks.

In each of these two examples, we can see how the thickness of the line and the spacing of the lines gives us a graphical illusion of shading.

For those of us who are wondering what we meant when we talked about *blending one color to another*, it's simple. Instead of only having the black ink, as in the analog work, we can use black, white, and even transparent colors in our digital inks. By using the color effects, we can give an inked layer, that is, a uniform color instead of black. Now, before we will get into more esoteric aspects of inking, we need to examine the tools we have at our disposal within Manga Studio.

Inking tools in Manga Studio

In the following **INKING TOOLS** diagram, there are explanations about the tools we'll be focusing on in this chapter:

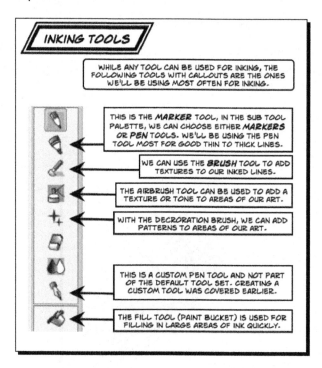

At this point in our learning about Manga Studio, we should know how to make the tool size larger or smaller and change to different subtools and main tools. We'll be creating some new subtools, so the topic that we covered in the previous chapter will be used here.

In the downloaded files, there's a file named `ch 07 inking tools.lip` that we'll use in the *Time for Action* exercises. If you want, use your own file. Just keep in mind that this is all practice; we will be deleting layers and experimenting with making different kinds of lines.

In the next part, we'll cover the various marking tools in Manga Studio and learn how to create new subtools of each kind. The new tools will be compared with other tools and the differences and similarities will be examined. After creating new tools, we'll render the objects in the `ch 07 inking tools.lip` file. First, we will outline the object and next we'll render in shading for the light source (from the upper-right side, just above our head).

As with the penciling chapter, it's assumed that you are familiar with the basics of the subject at hand. The bibliography for this chapter will have references that you can research to learn more about the art of inking.

Now let's get onto the tools!

Markers

We've all used these tools in real (analog) life. From sharpies to microns, these marvels of marking have aided artists in many ways, and hindered them too. For our purposes, markers have a uniform width. They do not get thicker or thinner no matter how hard we bear down on them with our stylus. We'll be using tools such as technical pen. These are the pens that have a metal barrel and are refilled with ink cartridges. In our digital world, the ink never needs to be refilled and the tip never dries out. Even though markers give us a dead-weight line, they do have the uses that are invaluable. Backgrounds, machines, and many other objects are best drawn first with a marker. We can go back and add shading, thicken the lines, or break the lines after we lay down the basic linework.

Time for action – making a technical pen subtool

In this section, we'll create a technical pen subtool that will be able to step though predetermined sizes and give us consistent widths quickly. Let's get started and perform the following steps:

1. Choose the **Marker** tool.
2. In the **Sub tool** palette menu, choose the **Marker** pen.
3. Go to the **Sub tool** palette menu.
4. Choose **Duplicate sub tool** and name it `Technical Pen` in the dialog box that pops up. Then click on **OK**.
5. Click on the Wrench icon to call up the **Tool Settings** palette.

6. Make the following settings in the categories that follow. If a category's not mentioned, it should remain as default.

- ❏ **Brush Size**: Set the brush size to 5
- ❏ **Ink**: Set the opacity to `100`, set the combine mode to normal
- ❏ **Anti-Aliasing**: Set this to None (the first or leftmost dot)
- ❏ **Brush tip**: Set the shape to circle
- ❏ **Hardness**, **Thickness**, and **Brush Density**: Set this to **100**
- ❏ **Direction**: Set this to zero
- ❏ **Correction**: **Make corner pointed** should be checked
- ❏ **Stabilization**: Set this to `6`, this is set according to the speed that is unchecked
- ❏ **Possible to snap**: Make sure that this is checked

7. We need to click on the eye-con button to show **Possible to snap** in the **Tool Property** palette. This way, we can turn off snapping for the tool and not for the entire document. Click on the **Register all Settings to Default** button present on the **Tool Settings** palette.

8. In the **Tool Settings** palette, click on the tall rectangular button.

9. Choose **Settings of Indicator...** from the pop-up menu.

10. We have five positions in which we can enter specific sizes. Let's start by entering the following in each of the indicator entry boxes from left to right: `5`, `10`, `20`, `30`, and `50` in the last box. Once that's done, click on the **OK** button. The slider will be replaced by the selection indicator. Each square contains the respective value we just entered. For example, the first square on the left will set our pen size to 5, the third one to 20, and the fifth one to 50. Notice that when we click on the squares to the right of the one we pressed last, the squares get filled with a darker gray color if they are further to the right.

What just happened?

We duplicated a marker pen, named it `Technical Pen`, and set it up with specific sizes, which we chose by clicking on a selection indicator. This pen will ignore pressure from the stylus so the line thickness will be consistent. We made sure that it had a stabilization setting to help smooth out some jitter that our hand can introduce.

It's nice to have the indicator for the technical pen; however, we must realize that this feature is tool-wide, which means that it's either on for all tools or off for all tools. The settings we entered are also for all tools. So, we must decide whether we want to have the indicators on for every tool or not. Once we're finished with the technical pen, we'll set the indicators back to our friend the slider.

Indicators, as implemented in this version (5.0.2) of Manga Studio, are a part of what I think of as feature. It is where a feature that would be great for a few tools affects all tools. The indicator values we entered in are used for all the tools when we choose indicators, a one-size fits all kind of thing. It's a bother to turn on and off because we have to right-click on each tool setting category that uses it and choose Show Slider on the contextual menu. It can't be set via a keyboard command or by an action. It's included here for those who may like it. I think that indicators are poorly thought out and need to be active and customized on a per-tool basis, maybe in a future update.

Now we're going to test out this new technical pen!

Time for action – inking basic shapes with the technical pen

With a new pen tool, let's see what we can do. Open a file to ink, create a new layer, and then begin inking by performing the following steps:

1. Open up the `ch 07 inking tools.lip` file.
2. We'll be working with a ruler layer, so make sure **Snap to rulers** is turned on.
3. On the **Layers** palette, choose the **Outlines** layer. This is the layer on which we will be creating our outlines. Shading will be done on the layer below it. This way, we can easily correct wayward lines without erasing our outlines.

 While you're working on the inks for a page, don't hesitate to use more than one layer. It may seem confusing at first, but once we get used to it, it will make our digital inking go much faster. For instance, we can have one layer for background inks and another for foreground inks. This makes cleaning up overlapping lines so much easier. When we're finished with our inks, we can combine the different layers into a single layer.

4. We will treat each of these four objects as foreground objects, so we'll want a thick outline on them. Choose the **30** or **50** size and outline each one. Be careful on the cube, it's made from two separate rulers and we don't want to have any interior lines inked in yet.

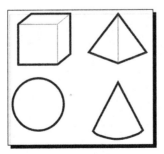

5. Keeping in mind that our light source is coming from the upper-left side, we want to have thinner interior lines for the edges on the top 2 objects: the cube and pyramid. We'll use the size 30 to outline the side of the cube that's farthest from the light and the size 20 for the horizontal edge and the edge of the pyramid.

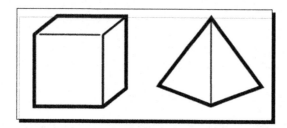

6. In the image for the finished outlines of the cube and pyramid, notice how sharp the corners are. That's because we turned on the **Make Corners Pointed** option in the **Correction** category of the **Tool Settings** palette.

7. We have a few choices for inking the cube. We could render in the shadowed areas by hand. That would be okay, but since this is a mechanical object, let's use a ruler to draw straight lines.

8. Select the Figure tool (it's the second tool below the paint bucket tool).

9. In the subtool palette, choose the **Special Ruler** subtool.

10. In the **Tool Property** palette, select the **Parallel Line Ruler** option from the top drop-down menu.

11. In the **Layer** palette, select the shading layer, as we're going to do our shading inks on that layer.

12. On the canvas, click-and-drag the ruler to adjust it to the angle of the top-right side of the cube (the edge that's going away from us).

13. Choose the technical pen tool. Make sure that **Snap to special ruler** is on in the command bar and snapping is on for the tool itself.

14. Now, lay down some of the horizontal receding lines. We can vary the distance between each line a bit.

15. Once we are happy with the horizontal receding lines, we can turn on the parallel ruler for the vertical lines. Choose the **Object Selection** tool and click on the ruler, as shown in the following figure:

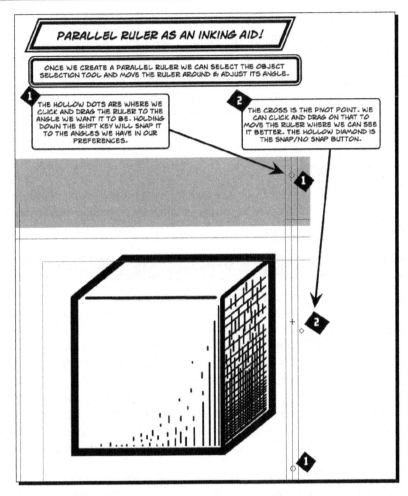

16. As shown in the preceding figure, we can now click-and-drag the object on a hollow dot to adjust the angle of the ruler. Holding down the *Shift* key while dragging will snap the ruler to the angles we've set up in the **Preferences** menu.

While adjusting the ruler, be careful that we don't accidentally click on the dreaded diamond! This diamond will toggle the snap of the ruler. The only indication of it being on or off is the lines turning from purple to green. So, if the marking tool has snapping on and if we have snapping on in the command bar but we aren't snapping to the ruler, then click once on the diamond with the object selection tool, switch back to the marking tool, and see if we're getting the snapping happiness we want. If the diamonds or the dots aren't visible, then zoom out and see if they are off the canvas area of the document. Use the **Object** tool to move the entire ruler so the dots are within the canvas area.

17. Now, we can lay down the lines at the sides and front of the cube.

18. Use the same ruler and ink for the pyramid and cone. The sphere will be done free hand, because straight lines will flatten out the sphere and make it look like a disc.

19. When inking, we should be aware that the mind of the eyes that gaze on our work are unconscious artists and will fill in the blanks. That's why the vertical lines in the figure are interrupted. This gives the impression of a vague reflection of the cube's environment, which adds interest to the final work.

What just happened?

We used rulers as an inking aid for the shape outlines and for the inking of interior shadowed areas. By using interrupted lines, we can make our shading look more random and interesting.

Have a go hero

Before we leave markers, there's an issue with the sphere. One thing that technical pens excel in is rendering mechanical objects. Unless our hand is supernaturally steady, our poor sphere may not look too good. There needs to be a way to create a curved ruler that would radiate from a single point. There is and it's from the same menu from where we got parallel rulers from the special rulers. It's named **Focus Curve**. We can select it from the **Special Ruler** menu. Then, in the shading layer, we click on the area where the sphere is highlighted (brightest area). We also click on a curve of the sphere. Usually two more clicks is enough to get a good curve. Press *Enter* to commit to the ruler. A focused type of special ruler will have a single point that will be the origin point for all the lines that are drawn. Now, we will use what we know about interrupted lines and cross-hatching to ink that puppy.

The difference between the focus curve ruler and the parallel line ruler is that on the focus curve ruler we can have curving lines coming from a point, while the parallel line ruler only allows straight lines.

Pens

These are the workhorses of inking. With a practiced (steady) hand, there's nothing we cannot ink with these tools. Unlike the metal and hair pens and brushes in the analog world, we don't have to worry about the sharpness of the points or ink clogging up the works. However, we need to learn to work with our graphic tablets and stylus pens.

There is something that we need to know while using our tablets and stylus. First, go to the maker of your tablet's website and make sure your drivers are current. Many times, an odd behavior can be attributed to an out-of-date driver. That being said, always have the previous installation file of the driver at hand. Sometimes, an update can cause more problems than it solves. Having the previous version at hand is a great insurance policy.

As for the stylus, I use a Wacom Intuos tablet and it's served me very well over the years. The biggest upgrade I did for it was to purchase a second stylus pen and extra nibs for it. While the solid plastic nibs that come with the tablets are fine to use, I purchased the felt nibs and the stroke nibs.

The felt nibs adds a bit of friction to the stylus without having to put a sheet of paper on the tablet itself. They tend to get blunt quickly, but they're still usable. I find these excellent to use with the marker tools. Because of the friction, they give a smoother line without adding extra correction to the pen in Manga Studio.

The stroke nibs have a pointed end and a spring in the middle of the nib. That spring adds a bit of resistance (almost feeling like a real dip pen nib) to pressure, and the smoothness allows for long strokes that can be very nice looking.

Both of these nibs don't seem to interfere with the pressure sensitivity of the stylus. All the stylus nibs will wear out eventually, so don't hesitate to replace them as you would replace a dip pen that doesn't have a sharp point. I bought a large quantity of nibs (the felt, stroke, and default plastic) a few years ago and that's been good, since I've had many 2 a.m. nib changes that helped save me a lot of waiting. If you've lost the nib changer that came with your tablet, a good pair of tweezers will suffice just as well. In fact, I like them better.

Our plan for the pens are two fold. First, we'll set up the basic settings for the pen in Manga Studio and then we'll adjust the pressure settings for the specific pen. As mentioned a few times earlier, pressure settings are very personal. Everyone's style and method of inking is unique. Consider the settings we'll be looking at here as a starting point. Never be afraid to change the pressure settings. If one doesn't work, just reset the pen to the initial state and try again. There is nothing wrong with experimenting with settings.

Once we create a pen, we'll ink in the four shapes using the pen tool. We'll experiment (there's that word again!) with using transparency to ink in solid blacks for a unique look.

Before we embark on our adventure in inking, take a moment to visit `http://smudgeguard.com`. I've used these for years and still have my initial two pairs. I use one for analog and the other for digital. They are fingerless gloves, except for the pinky and ring finger. For analog penciling and inking, they protect the paper from oils that's on our skin and from getting our hand all smudged up with the graphite from the pencil lead. If we are using one with the Wacom tablet or a display tablet, our hand won't stick to the plastic of the tablet's surface. My hand just glides across the tablet. They've made a big difference in my inking digitally. I didn't want to risk washing them in a machine so I hand wash them every couple of months or so, and they've held up amazingly well. In short, a bandana wrapped around the palm and the heel of the hand can work to avoid the heel of the palm from sticking to the plastic surface.

Time for action – creating an inking brush with custom pressure settings

The pen we want to create here is the one that'll have a good response at light pressure settings and get thicker somewhat quickly. We don't want the pen to correct our line too much, as happy accidents can be good.

1. Select the G-Pen from the pen subtool palette.

2. Make a duplicate of the pen via the **Tool Property** palette menu.

3. Name the duplicated pen `MS4B inking pen`.

4. Open up the **Tool Settings** palette.

5. We'll be making changes to the following categories; so if a category's not mentioned, set it to zero or make sure there's nothing checked in it.

   ❏ **Brush Size**: Set this to **11** (we'll get to adjust the pressure in the second part of this exercise)

   ❏ **Ink**: Set the opacity to **100%** and set combine mode to **Normal**

   ❏ **Anti-Aliasing**: Set this to **Little** (the second position from the left).

   ❏ **Brush Tip**: Set **Brush shape** to **Circle** (which should be set to already), set **Hardness** and **Thickness** to 100, set **Direction of Applying** to **Horizontal** (the setting on the left), set **Direction** to zero, set **Brush Density** to 100, and uncheck **Adjust Brush Density**

- ❑ **Correction**: Perform the following operations in this category:

  1. Uncheck corner pointed.

  2. Set **Stabilization** to 5.

  3. Uncheck **Correct by Speed**.

  4. Uncheck **Post Correction**.

  5. Set **Brush Stroke** to **6** (this helps to prevent the little "hooks" that appear at the end of a line).

  6. Uncheck **Possible to Snap**.

  7. For both **Possible to Snap** and **Vector magnet**, click on the eye-con button so that both of these settings will appear in the **Tool Settings** palette

- ❑ **Starting** and **Ending**: Perform the following steps for this category:

  1. Set the **Starting** and **Ending** options to **None**.

  2. Uncheck the **Starting**, **Ending**, and the **Starting and Ending by Speed** settings

6. Now, click on the **Register to initial settings** button present on the **Tool Settings** palette. Our new settings will be the default ones for this pen.

What just happened?

We did something that should be second nature to us now, creating a new tool and adjusting it to suit our needs. Our needs for this pen are simple and there are a number of categories that we didn't adjust or set. That's perfectly fine. Sometimes the best tools are the simplest ones.

Before we go into adjusting the pressure settings, take a moment and just doodle with your new pen tool. Get a feel for it. If you think the tip size could be increased, make it so. There's nothing to stop us from creating a multitude of pens. Just make sure you duplicate the pen and give it a meaningful name. Then, restore the original pen's settings and save the duplicate pen's settings.

Time for action – pressure settings

Pressure sensitivity is the reason why we use graphic tablets. It's also the most individual preference setting that is present. In this section, we'll set up a pressure curve and explore ways to customize it so that it'll work best for us. This can be done by performing the following steps:

1. In the **Tool Settings** palette (which is brought up by clicking on the Wrench icon in the **Tool Property** palette), to the right of the size indicator, there is a button that is clicked to bring up the **Brush sizeEffect source settings** window. It is shown in the following figure:

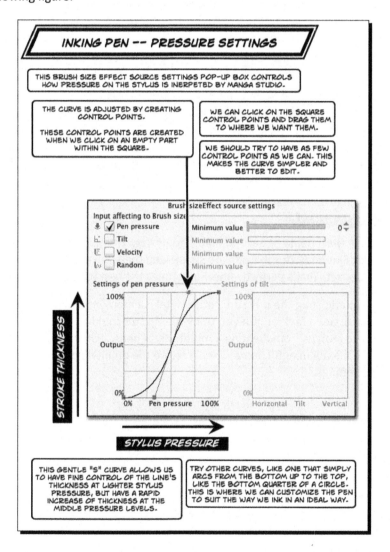

2. The stroke thickness is graphed from minimum width (that is, zero width) to maximum width. The minimum width being at the bottom, 0 percent, and the maximum thickness at the top, 100 percent. Pressure is mapped on the horizontal bar, on which left side is no pressure and right side is the maximum pressure. A default setting is a straight line from the bottom-left to the upper-right. In the **INKING PEN--PRESSURE SETTINGS** figure, the pressure setting has the form of an *S* curve. To get the curve, click on an empty part of the mapping square and a control point will appear. Without lifting the stylus, move the control point to the bottom as shown in the figure. Next, click on an empty part, create a control point, and drag it to the upper-left side as shown in the figure.

3. Now, test out how the pen works. Make a few doodles. Change pressure on the stylus quickly and slowly. Experiment with drawing faster and slower.

4. Save the settings as default by clicking on the **Register as default settings** button at the bottom of the **Tool Settings** palette.

5. As suggested in the figure, try other curves. Move around the two control points to get different shapes. Try a downward arc from the bottom-left side to the upper-right side. Test out each different setting on your canvas. Add new control points only to refine the shape. The more the control points, the more erratic the pen may behave.

What just happened?

Pressure sensitivity is the only setting that makes a pen "ours." By experimenting and trying out new curves, we can create a pen that'll work best for our own style. If your tablet and pen can utilize the tilt function, experiment with that also. Go to the extremes and back off slowly. Be sure to test out the changes on the canvas. We won't break Manga Studio. As long as we register our settings, we can adjust them as much as we'd like because we can always revert back to our initial settings if we need to.

Have a go hero – pressure settings

Make a copy of the pen we just made. Now, experiment with the **Random Velocity** and **Tilt** settings to get a pen that will make unique strokes every time. Go to the **Spraying Effect** category in the **Tool Settings** palette and see how adding a spray to the stroke can give us nice, pseudo-drybrush effects.

Speaking of brushes, the next section will focus on the brush tool. Although they really work best for color work, they can do really nice things for inking.

Brushes

Most of the brushes in Manga Studio 5 are best used for painting or coloring, the **India Ink** tab in the **Brush** subtool palette is good for inking. We'll look at one in particular as an example: the Bit Husky brush.

The Bit Husky brush is a fair digital approximation of a red sable brush that cartoonists sometimes use for inking. After opening a file (or by having a new layer created in the `ch 07 inking.lip` file), select that brush from the subtool palette, and make a few practice strokes to get a feel of the default settings of this brush. If you've made changes to this brush, make a duplicate of the Bit Husky brush with a meaningful name and revert to initial settings in the original Bit Husky brush.

In the default settings for this brush (at least in the version that I'm currently using), there isn't a good variation in line thickness. Let's fix that, shall we?

Time for action – using a Bit Husky brush for fine inking

Like we usually do, let's figure out what we want to do. We want to keep most of the quality of the brush intact, except for pressure sensitivity. We want to have this brush with thin lines and make it thicker according to pressure. In some circles, the line we want is called *Dagger Lines* because the line begins/ends really thin and ends/begins really thick, as shown in the following figure:

As we can see in the preceding figure, in the middle strokes, there are some light streaks. This is not a bad thing as it simulates the look of dry brush inking. Now that we've seen what we're after, let's do it by performing the following steps:

1. Make a duplicate copy of the Bit Husky brush. Name it `MS4B Bit Husky Inking`.

2. Open up the **Tool Settings** palette.

3. In the **Brush Size** category, set the brush size to **45**.

4. Adjust the pressure settings as shown in the following screenshot:

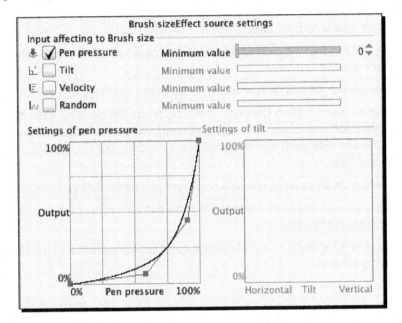

5. Notice the pressure curve. The angle at the beginning (the bottom of the curve) is where the sharp dagger-like lines come from.

6. Be sure to save changes as the initial settings.

What just happened?

All we did was adjust the size and the pressure curve of a tool to make an entirely new tool. Try out this tool on the canvas. Go through the categories and see how this brush is made. Notice that it has a custom brush tip. Creating custom brush shapes will be covered in the online supplementary chapters.

Airbrushes

If we've seen a van with a custom paint job, chances are that it was done with an airbrush. Although airbrushes are excellent if we want to color large areas of graduated colors, for inking work we can use **Tone Scraping, Spray**, and the **Droplet** subtools to add textures to surfaces or areas in shadow that we want to be dark but not totally black.

Time for action – using the airbrush for shading

We're going to use an out-of-the-box airbrush (so to speak) to shade in the sphere present in the inking demo page.

1. Open the `ch 07 inking.lip` file.

2. Create a new layer and name it `Outlines for shading`.

3. Using the pen tool we created a few sections ago, turn the **Snap to rulers** on for the pen and the canvas.

4. Make sure the ruler layer is visible. We can't snap to things that we can't see.

5. The light is coming from the upper-left side, so ink the circle to make it thinner at the upper-left side. If we want to get all fancy, we can make the line a bit thinner at the lower-right part, where the sphere is touching the floor, to the account for reflected light.

6. Below the **Outlines** layer, create a new layer and name it `Airbrush shading`.

7. The `Airbrush shading` subtool will spray out a texture and it can be darkened by going over the same area.

8. If the area is too dark, switch the active color to transparent and run the airbrush over the area.

Remember that since we're working in the digital world and using Manga Studio, transparency can be used as a color for our work. This may take a bit of getting used to but it's worth it—especially when we begin to tone or color our artwork. Recall *Chapter 2, Messing Around with Manga Studio 5*, and *Chapter 3, Formatting Your Stories*, where we explored grayscale layers, we can have black or white be transparent. Make sure that the layers we're working on has the combine mode (the drop-down menu in the upper-left side of the **Layers** palette) set to **Normal**. Then, look at the **Layer Properties** palette, see what kind of layer we're working on, and whether it's monotone or gray. There's a pair of boxes to the right of the layer type text. We can click on them to make the color button (either black or white) visible (will have a blue tint on the button) or transparent (will have a gray button background). Experiment with a monotone or gray layer that has both black and white lines by clicking on those buttons and see what happens.

9. For the reflected light at the bottom of the sphere, we can use transparency to create the highlight, as shown in the following figure:

10. Use the eraser to clean up any shading that's outside the inked outline. That's why we ink on one layer and add textures on the layer below, makes clean-up so much easier!

What just happened?

By using the unchanged default tone scraping airbrush subtool with black color and transparency, we were able to quickly shade in a pretty decent sphere.

Have a go hero

The real magic of the airbrush subtool we just used is in the **Spraying Effect** category in the **Tool Settings** palette. Take a look at the settings, make some changes, and see what happens. If you come across a setting that works for you, save it as a duplicate brush and don't forget to save it as the initial settings for the duplicate.

Decoration

This tool will create a *ribbon* kind of stroke based on the specific subtool. It can be used to add special effects to our inks. The major thing we need to know about this tool is that it needs to be used on a grayscale or color layer. The decoration tool works like a rubber stamp, only that it can have more than one *stamp* that it can put down at a time. The images it creates are black and white or full colored. The following is a sample created with the artificial scene group by using the rubble and crack subtools:

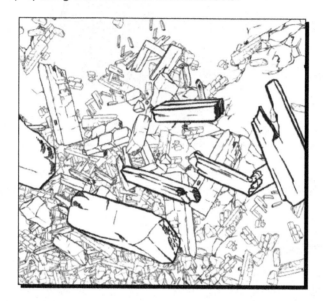

The real challenge in using the decoration tool is how well it blends in with our inked pages. There are things like lighting and rendering style to be considered. However, in the example shown here, the sense of depth was created by increasing the tool's size to obtain progressively larger hunks of rubble.

Making a Kirby Krackle tool

Kirby Krackle is not the rock group (which is a great band for us comic geeks), but the style used by the great Jack Kirby. The Krackle is a series of dots that use negative space as much as positive space to indicate energy, explosions, stellar nebulae, or smoke. If this term is not familiar, do an Internet search on it. The following is an example of it that is created by using the custom subtools in Manga Studio:

 While not scientific, one of the tests that I put all the graphic apps that I use to make comics is if I can create my own Kirby Krackle brush or pen or tool. Strangely enough, the apps that I can make a Krackle tool within are the apps I tend to use most often.

As we can see from this example, this tool can give our art work a definite look. We'll create a basic Krackle tool based on the airbrush tool. Then, we'll create some individual dots and allow the features built into the Manga Studio brush engine to use our created art. Let's get ready to Krackle!

Time for action – crafting a custom Kirby Krackle tool

What we're looking for in a Krackle tool is the random placement and size of the dots. Get Manga Studio 5 running and create a new 10.5 by 7 inch comic page document at 600 dpi. Make sure that the drawing layer is in grayscale or colored. If the document is set for a lower resolution, the brush size will have to be adjusted downwards. If the suggested size is way to large, reduce it dramatically by more than half or so and see if this gives us better results. We can craft a custom Kirby Krackle tool by performing the following steps:

1. Choose the airbrush tool.

2. In the **Sub Tool** palette, select the **Droplet** subtool.

3. Make a duplicate of the **Droplet** tool. Name it `MS4B Kirby Krackle` or any name that will remind you what this tool does.

4. Make sure that the new tool (we'll call it the Krackle tool) is selected.

5. Click on the **Register all settings to initial settings** button so that we all have the same brush to begin with.

6. Open the **Tool Settings** palette. We'll make changes to some of the categories. When a category's not mentioned (for example, the **Ink** category), we will accept the default. That's why we set the tool back to the initial settings.

   ❑ **Brush Size**: Set this to **700**. This tool is made of many smaller dots and it's not intended to create "fine" detail.

 The amount of dots that the Airbrush tool sprays is set in the **Spray** category. The brush size establishes the space the dots have to be in. The larger the brush size, the more space the dots have. The smaller the brush size, the dots appear denser as there's less space for them. In this case, the brush size controls the density of the spray. It is good to keep this in mind when we want to have a darker or a lighter Krackle area.

   ❑ **Anti-Aliasing**: Change this from **Moderate** to **Little**.

   ❑ **Brush Tip**: Set it to **Circle** from **Material**. The panel below will be grayed out. That's what we want.

   ❑ **Spraying Effect**: Set **Particle Size** to **100** and **Particle Density** to **3**.

   That's it.

7. Click on the **Register all settings to initial settings** button. Close the **Tool Settings** palette.

8. Test the new Krackle brush on the canvas. Experiment with shapes. The previous figure was a quick one. Try some figures of your own, clouds of smoke, nebulas, and energy blasts to get a feel of what this tool can do. Make changes to the **Spray** category's **Density** setting and see what happens. We can always click on the **Revert all to initial settings** button to get our original tool back.

What just happened?

Using a default airbrush tool, we made minor changes and created an unique tool. Part of what gives this tool its look is the random feature in the **Brush Size** category, as shown in the following figure:

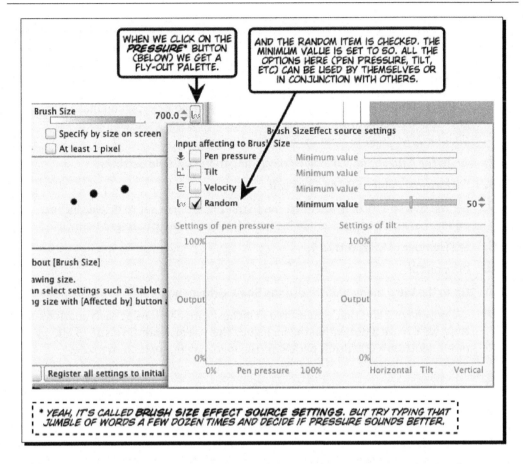

The only drawback to this tool is that the dots are identical. While the marks it makes are nice, it would be even better if the dots had some kind of randomness to it's shape. To do this, we'll have to add new shapes to the brush tip. We'll do just that right now by creating and adding new brush tips for a Krackle brush.

Although we'll be modifying an airbrush tool, the basic concepts can be applied to any marking tool that uses a **Brush Tip** category. We should save our work from the previous Manga Studio file. Then, create a new file, make sure it's 600 dpi, and name it `BrushWork.lip`. While the brush tips themselves will be saved as a material, it's always handy to have the source files for our brush tips around in case we want to refresh our memory or use the source file as the reference.

Time for action – creating the brush tips

In this section, we'll set up a document and create multiple brush tips by performing the following steps:

1. In the `BrushWork.lip` file, create a new layer, name it `Dots`, and make it a gray-scaled layer with white being transparent (this was covered in detail in *Chapter 2, Messing Around with Manga Studio 5*).

2. Go to the **Grid Settings** dialog by navigating to **View | Grid Settings**.

3. Set **Original Point of Grid** to **Top Left**.

4. Set the **Gap** to 1 inch. If you don't have your preferences set to display inches, either change it or approximate inches in the unit of measurement being used.

5. Set **Number of Divisions** to **4**.

6. Click on **OK**.

7. Go to the **View** menu and choose the **Show Grid** menu item.

8. We now have a grid that's measured in inches, with divisions at each quarter inch. Now, we'll make a dot within the inch grid. This will give our tip a size of 600 by 600 pixels. (600 dpi = 600 pixels per inch). The following figure is an example:

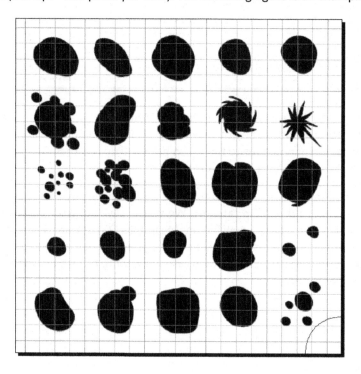

9. Like the example shown, create at least 25 different dots. We won't be using all of them, but this allows us to choose our favorites from what we created.

10. Use either a marker or a pen. We want nice crisp outlines with little to no aliasing.

11. Don't try to make perfect circles. Imperfect is what we want. Make the size different too.

12. Do these things quickly. Don't fuss over them. The example shown took less than a few minutes to do.

What just happened?

We created a new grayscale layer and named it Dots. Then, we adjusted our grid to give us a good size in which we can create our brush tips. This is important as the main divisions in the grid gives us the area within which we want to keep our tips.

Time for action – adding the brush tips to the materials

We can add the brush tips to the materials by performing the following steps:

1. Now that we have our dots all drawn, it's time to make them into materials.

2. Choose the selection tool. We want to use the **Rectangular Marquee** tool.

3. In the command bar, click on the **Snap to grid** button. This will ensure that our selections are of the same size and will snap to the grid. While not necessary, making all the tips of the same size will help with the size of the dots in the finished tool.

4. In the **Tool Property** palette, set **How to Create** to **New** (the first icon on the right-hand side, the single rectangle shape).

5. Set the **Anti-aliasing** option to **None**.

6. Making sure that we're on the layer with the dot artwork, select the first dot's square inch.

7. Go to the **Edit** menu. Choose **Register image as Material**. Since we have a selection, Manga Studio will register what's contained within the selection as shown in the following figure:

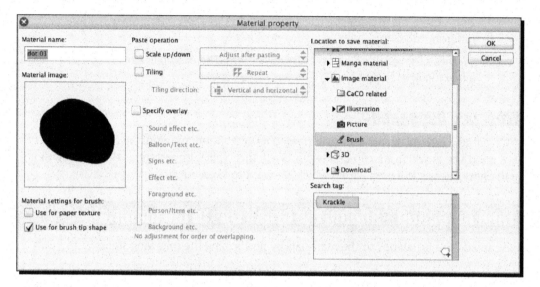

As the figure shows, we've named the dot dot 01.

8. The **Use for brush tip shape** option is checked. This will ensure that this shape will appear in a dialog when we add brush tips to our tool.

9. In the location panel, click on the disclosure triangle next to **Material**, click on the triangle next to **Image material**, and choose **Brush**.

10. In the **Search Tag** box, click on the tag icon at the lower left of the dialog box. Enter Krackle in the text entry area that appears. This is important. If we create a boat load of brushes, it becomes necessary to be able to separate them. Adding tags is a great way to do this. As we'll see in the next section, we'll make good use of the Krackle tag. We can also add a number of tags to each material. We'll stick to one tag for the time being. We can add more tags later if we want.

11. Click on **OK**.

12. Select the next square inch dot area.

13. Repeat this until there's at least 15 new materials of our dots. We need to have these many so that our dot pattern won't be obviously computer generated like our first Krackle tool.

14. We can use our knowledge of creating new shortcuts and/or adding buttons to the command bar to speed up the process by selecting the **Save image as Material** menu item.

15. When we're done, lock the layer with the brush shapes.

16. Lock that layer.

17. Create a new grayscale layer.

18. Now, we can craft a new brush and use the materials we just made.

What just happened?

This is, quite possibly, the most important aspect of this series of *Time for Action* sections. We created a brush tip, selected it, and placed it into the **Material** palette. This is something that we will revisit as we can use the **Material** palette to store such illustrations.

Time for action – adding the brush tips to the brush

We can add the brush tips to the brush by performing the following steps:

1. Select the airbrush tool.

2. If our Krackle tool isn't selected in the **Sub Tool** palette, choose it and make a duplicate. Name it **Krackle hand drawn** or some other meaningful name.

3. Click on the **Revert all to initial settings** button of the duplicate brush.

4. Open the **Tool Settings** Palette.

5. Choose the **Brush Tip** category. Where we had selected **Circle** before, select **Material**.

6. The following figure shows that our choice now becomes blackened, which means that we can now make changes to it:

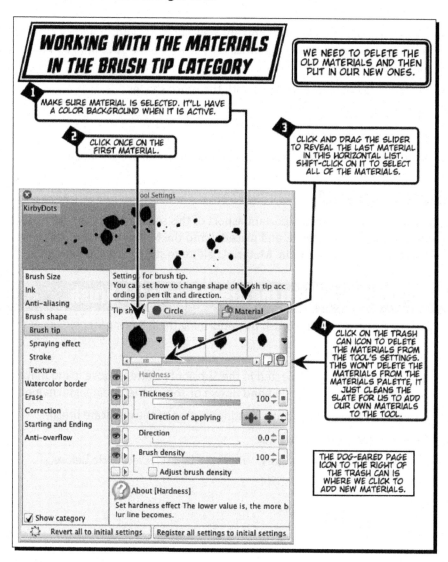

7. Now that we have a clean slate, let's add our new brush shapes to this tool.

8. In the material **Brush Tip** area, there's text that says **Click here to add tip shape**. Do what it says and you'll see a dialog box similar to the following one:

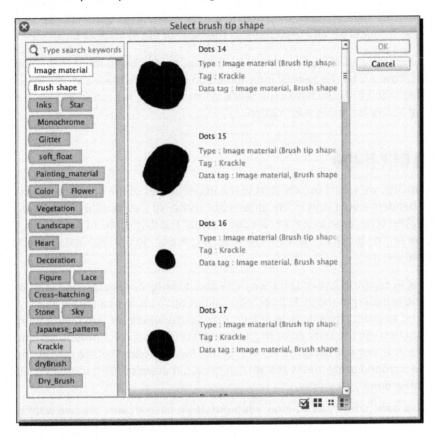

9. Notice that **Krackle** is selected. This makes only the brush tips that've been tagged **Krackle** visible. This is why we made sure that the `Krackle` tag was added when we created these brush tips a few steps ago.

10. Select the first Krackle tip shape and click on the **OK** button.

11. To add more than one brush tip shape, click on the dog-eared page icon to the right of the trashcan (delete) icon in the brush tip area of the **Brush Tip** category in the **Tool Settings** palette.

12. This will pop up the **Select Brush Tip** dialog box. Choose the next brush tip and click on **OK**.

13. Repeat this until we've got between 12-15 brush tips.

14. We can test out our tool's progress at any time.

15. When we're all done, save the brush settings to the initial settings.

What just happened?

We created a custom tool by using artwork we created for it. Instead of using dots, we could've used stars, squares, numbers, or letters for interesting effects. We saved our drawings as materials and used them as the basis of our Krackle airbrush.

Now that we have a good foundation of inking tools, we can begin to ink in our page. What will follow will be the general information on how to use Manga Studio for inking. It's assumed that we should have experience in inking. If not, we can search the Internet or our local library for inking information.

Inking our page

In analog inking, we would usually start in the upper corner of the opposite hand we draw with. Left handers would start in the upper-right corner of the panel/page and work down to the left. This is because as we ink, we don't smear the drying ink. In digital inks, that's not a worry, we're free to ink as we wish. The following are some tips and hints for us to think about while we ink:

- ◆ **Ink in separate layers**: Once we think about inking our background in its own layer and our foreground in its layer, possibilities open up. We can move our layers around a bit to avoid tangents (where lines meet/cross where we don't want them to). We can also use the layer color to give background inks a color other than black if we want. Inking our backgrounds in separate layers means that we can ink the entire background using masks and we can mask out areas of the background that the foreground obscures.

- ◆ **Use transparency as a better whiteout**: If we have an area that we want to be "clear" of inks, we can add this clear area by using transparency as our inking color. We can get some pretty nice textures by alternating between black and transparency for our inking color.

- ◆ **We can move the pencil layer above our inks for better accuracy**: To avoid accidentally inking on our pencil layer, make sure that the pencil layer has layer color turned on! This way, if our inks look blue, we know we're not on the correct inking layer.

There could be literally hundreds of pages written on these techniques, but the best way to learn them is, you guessed it, practice. Search the Internet for penciled pages that some artists put up for others to practice on inking. It's better to learn inking by practice than by reading about how to do it.

There are many sources for penciled pages to ink. A quick Internet search on penciled comic art pages should give us many examples to work on. Find a page that looks interesting. Then, decide to use only a technical pen to ink in it. Vary only the pen size. Ink the same page again with a brush tool. Make an effort to use thick to thin lines when outlining the foreground elements. Try another page and use only solid lines—no cross-hatching or feathering of line work, only use areas of black to indicate light and shadow. Try drawing a long continuous line with a single stroke. Try to ink and use only the eraser tool to delete lines, avoid using the Undo feature. Set a timer for 15 minutes and ink a panel in that amount of time. The work we're doing here isn't for anybody else but for us, so if we think it looks bad, well we don't have to show it to anyone.

Setting the tones

Before we leave inking, we need to explore using tones. Tones, in Manga Studio, are usually black and white, grey, or color patterns that we can use to add uniform or gradated textures to our inks. Unlike the analog world, we don't have to worry about running out of tones and buy more. We have an endless supply, so let's use some!

What's so great about tones?

Tones are a way to show solid or gradated grays using dots or solid gray colors. Before the digital age, tones were printed on clear plastic sheets with an adhesive on one side. They would have to be cut and then applied onto the artwork itself. It was very labor-intensive and could be quite expensive.

One of the best things about tones is that they can add depth and detail to artwork. A few long triangles in the background of a panel could indicate speed, lights, or environmental objects. Remember that the reader will fill in areas that we just hint at. That will engage the reader and provide a better experience for them, in most cases.

In Manga Studio, not only do we have tones of all kinds, but we also have patterns that can fill up an entire page. In this section, we'll see how we can choose a tone, ink, and prepare our artwork to use them. We'll then look at things we can do to tones once we've put them on our page. We'll wrap up by creating a tone layer for our art from scratch, just by using what's available in the **Layer Settings** palette.

In the following *Time for action* sections, we'll find the locations of the tones we can use. Although we'll be focusing on just the dot tones in the exercises, the process is the same for any tones in the **Material** palette. The `MS4B_toningExercise.lip` file is the file we'll be starting with. The other files have `-pencils`, `-inks`, and `-tones` appended after the title (but before the `.lip` extension) so that the progress can be seen and we'll have an example file to work with. Breaking with the format a bit, there will be a single *What just happened* section at the end of this series of exercises.

Just to make sure we're using the right terms, when tones are mentioned, we are referring to the materials that are used to add a layer of dots to the canvas of the document we're working on.

Time for action – locating tones in the Material palette

The tones in the **Material** palette are not the most intuitive aspects of Manga Studio. What we'll be doing in this exercise is that we will locate the `Dot` tone folder that's located within the `Monochromatic Pattern` folder inside the main `Material` folder. Along the way, we'll see what options can be used for tones before we apply them to our art.

Take a moment to look at the following image and see what the areas in the palette show:

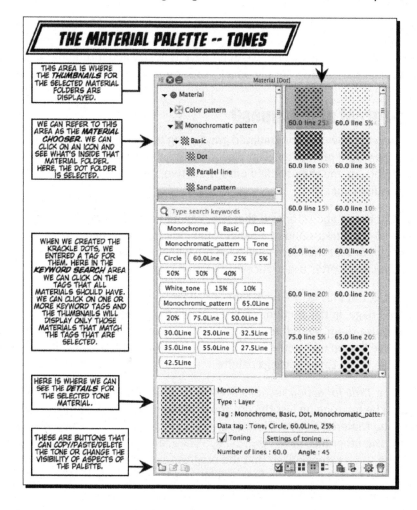

1. Open the **Material** palette and click on the disclosure triangle of the **Material** palette.

2. Find the Monochromatic pattern folder and open it.

3. Open the Dot folder.

4. We should have something like the previous image in our Material palette.

5. If we don't see all the areas in our palette as shown in the image, go to the bottom area of the palette where the icon buttons are present.

6. The first group of buttons on the left are for copying, pasting, and deleting the tags for the selected tone.

7. The following are the next group of buttons from left to right:

   ❑ Show/hide item: This will make a checkbox appear in the upper-left corner of the thumbnails. This is handy for making mass changes to many tones.

   ❑ Show/hide the details of the selected tone: It's active in the previous image and gives us the bottom area of the palette where we can see what type of tone is selected (**Layer**), it's tags, the **Toning** checkbox, and the **Settings of toning...** button along with the **Number of lines** (**60**) and **Angle** (**45**).

   ❑ The next three buttons change the way the thumbnails are displayed—small, large, and detailed.

   ❑ The next two buttons paste the current tone into the active document and replace the tone on the current layer with the tone that's selected, respectively.

   ❑ The gear-shaped icon brings up a large dialog box that lets us save a copy of the tone to an existing material folder.

   ❑ The last icon is a trash can button. It deletes the selected tone or tones if we have the item checkbox visible and multiple tones checked (selected).

8. The **Details** area has very useful information about the tone we've selected. If we want to use grayscale tones, we just need to uncheck the box labeled **Toning**. This is a toggle checkbox, it doesn't change the tone, it just changes its appearance. When we apply tones, we'll use this feature to add tones to the main figure in the illustration.

9. The **Settings of Toning...** button in the **Details** area pops up a dialog box that looks similar to the following screenshot:

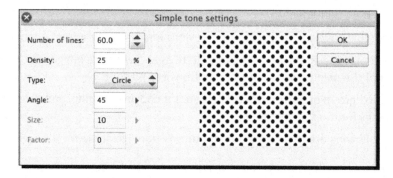

10. Be careful, any changes to this dialog will change the currently selected tone! We'll cover creating new tones in the last exercise. Just look at the setting and see what changes we can make and then click on the **Cancel** button to close the dialog box without committing any changes.

Time for action – preparing artwork for tones

When it comes to applying tones, we need to have that in mind before we start drawing our illustration or comic page. We need to have in mind that we are coloring our drawing. Albeit in tones, we must be mindful to leave areas that are to be toned and not shaded with brush lines. Look at the following figure:

1. This drawing started with a rough sketch on a draft layer. On that layer, the composition was finalized and the foreground, midground (figure), and background areas were detailed a bit.

2. In the sketch layer (not shown), tangents (where lines or corners of different objects overlap and can cause visual confusion) are eliminated. At this stage, the textures of the scene's objects become evident: the rocky protrusions and the sandy ground layer, the smooth space suit of the figure, and her transparent helmet.

3. When the rough sketch has enough details, two layers were created—one for the foreground and background and another one for the figure. In the previous image, the background and the foreground layers are shown in a lighter gray color.

4. Two layers were used so that the lines of the background mountains could be drawn through the figure. Having continuity of line makes a drawing look more logical to the viewer. Also, if we need to make changes, we just change the layer and we don't have to erase the line around the figure. This method makes the pencils very crisp and clear.

5. In the figure, the vertical lines remind that those areas are for tones. Since we're inking and toning our own work, we don't need to notate that.

6. In the background, BWS stands for "black with stars."

7. The pencils are detailed and complete. Notice how the light source is consistent for the entire drawing. The light was fixed to come from in front of the view on the upper right side. Having a defined light source helps to keep our artwork solid: we know what's in shadow and what's in light. This makes it simple to shade in areas and render with confidence. This confidence will make inking our art a smooth process.

Time for action – inking pencils with tones in mind

We have an illustration with clear, crisp pencils. Now it's time to ink it. Compare the pencils with the inks in the `toningExercise-inks.lip` file to see how the inker interpreted the pencils while inking.

We can ink pencils with tones in mind by performing the following steps:

1. The inks for this work were done on vector layers. Since vector layers should be used only for line work, a second layer was created for solid filled areas. However, that was the inker's choice and we can ink on a raster layer.

2. For more information on using a vector layer to ink on, refer to the supplementary online *Chapter 12, Along For the Ride*, which is devoted exclusively to vector layer inking.

3. Notice how little feathering and cross-hatching this inked work has. This is good, as the tones we'll be adding in later will give us the same effect as adding lots of line work.

4. It's important, especially when we're starting out, to have our inked drawing look as complete as possible. This inked illustration could be considered to be finished. It has a sense of depth (achieved by line width and areas of black) and the focal point, the woman space explorer, is rendered with smooth textures unlike those of the rock formations in the foreground and background.

5. Notice how the light source is kept in mind with the line thickness (thin where the light hits, thick in the shadowed areas) and placement of shadows (solid black areas).

6. The explorer's helmet only delineates the background with the contours of the mountains in the background. Shadows for the background mountains will be added with tones.

7. The stars in the background were created by modifying a copy of the Krackle airbrush we created earlier. The brush and particle size were reduced and the ink color was set to white. The outline for the nebula was done in a similar manner with black ink, adjusting the particle density in addition to the brush and particle size. Experiment with changing those settings and one brush can seem to look like a dozen different ones. Remember to save a copy of the original brush and change the copy. This way, if we really like the results we get, it'll be a simple click on the **Register all settings to initial settings** button to ensure we'll have this brush to use in the future.

8. When we're satisfied with our inks, we're ready to do some toning.

Time for action – applying tones to artwork

In the MS4B_toningExercise_tones.lip file, we can see a final result of toning. When toning, it was decided that a solid grayscale tone will be used for the figure and regular screened tones will be used for the setting. This can be done by performing the following steps:

1. Back in *Chapter 5, Putting Words in My Mouth*, there was a comment about the Ransom Note syndrome. When we're toning, it is important to keep that in mind. We don't want to use a dozen tones when a few will do. In this example, only five different tones were used. Three for the planet and two for the figure. Toggle the visibility of the tone layers (the ones with the checkerboard-type icon) and we can see where the tones were added.

2. Two light tones were chosen for the background and foreground medium shadows and a darker tone for shadowed areas.

3. In the **Material** palette, the tone can be chosen and dragged-and-dropped onto the canvas or the paste tone on canvas button clicked. In either case, a tone layer will be created above the currently active layer. It will have a default name that we can change to make it something that is related to its purpose in the artwork. In the example file, tones are called *bgLight* and *Shadow*.

4. The entire canvas is filled with the tone. We don't want that, so press the *Backspace/Delete* key to clear the tone.

5. Then, all we need to do is draw on the layer where we want tones to go. Black or white color will put tones down, transparent will erase tones. Just like how masks operate.

6. Try to put down solid areas of tone. Feathering and crosshatching is best when it's either black or a solid gray in most cases.

7. Tones can be layered on top of one another, which can give us a more pattern that may not print out well. Take some care when two tones are in contact with one another.

8. For the figure, we want solid gray tones. To do this, we just need to click on the checkbox in the toning details area of the **Materials** palette. Unchecking this box will make the tone solid grayscale colored. We can drag or click the paste button to put it onto the canvas as a layer.

9. If we placed the grayscale tone on the canvas, we'll notice that it's opaque. All we need to do is to change the **Combine** mode of the layer from **Normal** to **Multiply**.

10. To clear the tone, press the *Delete*/Backspace key as we did for the regular tone layer.

11. Now, we just paint with black or white to put down the grayscale tone. In the example file, a brush with no blending or aliasing was used. A marker tool could also be used.

12. Since the grayscale tone layer's **Combine** mode has been set to **Multiply**, we can layer our grayscale tones so that with only a light gray and a medium gray colors, we can get a darker gray color when the two tones overlap. Unlike the regular tones, this gives us a result that will print without any problem.

13. Notice that the nebula in the background sky isn't toned. That's because we'll be making our own tone for that.

Time for action – making our own tones

We have an endless supply so lets use some. All we need to do is to create a tone layer, adjust some settings, and we're good to go! This can be done by performing the following steps:

1. We need to create a tone layer. To do this, go to the **Layer** menu and choose the **New Layer** menu item. In the hierarchal menu, there are types of layers we can create. Choose the **Tone** menu item.

2. We'll be presented with a dialog box asking us for the tone settings. This dialog box shows us the setting of the last tone layer we worked with. Click on the **OK** button. We'll adjust the layer in the **Layer Properties** palette.

3. When the layer is created, delete the toned area from the canvas by pressing the *Delete*/backspace key.

4. In the `MS4B_toningExercise-toning.lip` file, notice how the layer named `Nebula 1` is below a number of other layers. That's because for the layer that has the stars using white, and we want the nebula toning to be below the stars, so we don't have to mess with going around each and every star. Stacking layers like this is a good way to achieve good looking effects with as little effort as possible. Sure we want our art to look good, but why work harder when we can just work smarter?

5. Now, we want to change the tone layer's settings. Hide the existing `Nebula 1` layer by clicking on the eye-con in the **Layer** palette. Now, click on the new tone layer we just created. Set the layer properties to the settings mentioned in the following screenshot:

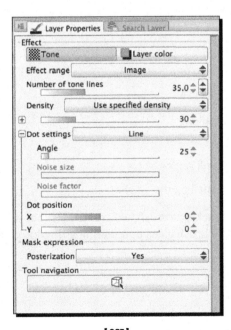

6. This gives us a parallel line tone that is different from the dot tones of the rocky surface and mountains of the planet our explorer's on. This is the sixth tone we've used in this work.

7. For fun, add 90 to the 25 in the angle setting (it'll be 115). Then make the `Nebula 1` layer visible. Neat, isn't it? In essence, we've made a copy of the original tone (nebula 1) and rotated the angle of the tone by 90 degrees. Change the angle of the new tone layer to other numbers and see what kind of effect it gives us.

8. If we want to create a grayscale tone, all we need to do is to click on the **Tone** button (underneath the **Effect** label) and change the **Layer Mode** option to **Multiply**.

What just happened?

We walked through the creation of an illustration from pencils to inks to tones. In the process, we considered the composition of the illustration and used layers in a way that makes the best use of tones. With multiple layers for our pencils, we will be able to make corrections without a great deal of involved erasing. Then, when we began inking, we made sure that we keep the light source in mind while laying down our lines. We thoughtfully inked objects with it's texture and lighting informing the way we render. As with penciling, we added new layers for the foreground and background elements. We added tones to finish our illustration. We saw that we didn't have to use that many tones to convey the look we wanted.

Pop quiz

Q1. The best way to get into an argument about inking is to say "It's just tracing."

1. True
2. False

Q2. A consistent light source is not...

1. Good for consistent inking
2. A waste of time
3. Something nobody will notice
4. Established when penciling the work

Q3. When we created the Krackle airbrush, we created a set of unique dots so that the result we get when using the brush gives us something that looks handmade.

1. True
2. False

Q4. Where are the tones located?

1. The Grayscale tone palette
2. The Sub view palette
3. The Effects Brush palette
4. The Materials Palette

Q5. A tone layer is like a mask layer.

1. True
2. False

Summary

In this chapter, we learned more about how pressure settings can help us to create lines that are responsive to stylus pressure and how to create new brush tips for airbrushes and other marking tools. In this process, we also learned how to add to the material palette. We began to realize how working digitally can be faster than analog and easier in many respects.

Much of what we learned here will serve us very well when we enter the world of coloring our comics using Manga Studio in the chapter coming up next.

8
Coloring the World

In this chapter, we'll take our inked drawings into the world of color. Using Manga Studio 5's color tools, we'll add hues to our art to create a world that's just a step closer to reality. We'll learn how to sample colors from the subview palette and create our own custom palettes. We'll explore how to use the intensity and the color wheel to make our colors grab attention without looking like a rainbow had an accident. Using the anti-overflow settings of our tools, we'll make the colors within the lines look so good that we'll wish we had Manga Studio for our coloring books. We'll take an inked drawing from flats to finished colors. Coloring comics can be a challenge to do well, but the tools in Manga Studio ease the work and make exploring what we can do with them much easier. The chapter will wrap up with how we can use selections and masks to work with our colors. Let's open this virtual paintbox and see what's inside.

In this chapter, we'll cover the following topics:

◆ Reviewing the color theory and how it works within the digital realm

◆ A brief history of color comics

◆ Most of the color tools that we have in Manga Studio and how to use them

◆ Creating color flats that we can use as a starting point to color our art

◆ Creating a color palette and brushes, and using the subview palette for color sampling

Using the color theory for digital works

This isn't going to be one of those passages where we'll talk about wavelengths, chroma, or monitor calibrations. These subjects are for other books; we just want to get down to what we need to know about using color.

Let's get some of the following definitions out of the way first so that we can understand the meanings of the terms we'll be using for this chapter:

◆ **Color**: This is everything we see, gray, blue, and the splotches we see when we close our eyes too tightly.

◆ **Primary colors**: Apart from monitors and RGB colors, we will consider red, yellow, and blue as primary colors. Most modern computer painting programs will act as if they're analog canvases, and Manga Studio is no exception.

◆ **Secondary colors**: This is what we get when we mix primary colors. The primary red and blue colors create purple, a secondary color.

◆ **Hue**: This is a pure color, for example, red, yellow, and other such colors. Hues don't have any other color as they are a blend of the original color; they do white or black colors to lighten or darken them.

◆ **Tint**: This is what we get when we mix a bit of white or other color into a hue. We can call this lightness.

◆ **Saturation**: Think of this as how intense the color is. As a color gets less saturated, it becomes grayish. If there is no saturation, then it's a shade of gray.

◆ **Complementary color**: On a typical artist's color wheel, these are colors directly across from each other, such as, green and red, yellow and purple, or blue and orange. When complementary colors are mixed, they give us (in theory) a neutral blue. This is why, in some art, an apple will have a greenish shadowed area.

◆ **Warm/cool colors**: This depends on the visual temperature of a color. Red, yellow, and orange are warm colors. Blue, violet, and green are cool colors. Usually, if a green color has more yellow in it than blue, it may just be a warm color. If a violet (purple) color has more blue in it than red, it may be considered as a cool color. Just don't ask about the visual temperature of pink.

◆ **Core shadow**: This is an area that has the deepest shadow of an object. Depending on the kind of coloring we're doing, this shadow may be black in color or a have warm/cool tint of the complementary color of the object.

◆ **Ambient color**: While this won't put you to sleep, it is a color that permeates everything in a scene. Sunlight is just a wee bit yellow, so the ambient color outside will be a very light yellow. This also affects shadows (which, in this instance, are a complementary color, purple). Florescent indoor light is bluish, so shadows have a bit of an orange color to them.

- **Reflected light**: This is either the light from a secondary source or light that's reflected from a surface. For example, a ping-pong ball on a red table will have some red reflected light on it,

- **RGB**: This stands for **Red Green and Blue**. These are the primary colors of projected light, such as the light from our computer screens, TV monitors, and movies.

- **CYMK**: This stands for cyan, yellow, magenta, and black (the last letter of black is where the letter K comes from). These are the primary colors of print.

- **Gamut**: This is the range of colors that can be presented. RGB and CYMK can display a different range of colors. When a color can't be represented by one or the other model, it's considered to be out of gamut. Since we're creating a work using an RGB color model, some colors may appear to be muddy or slightly different when printed.

We've all seen that bit where a prism breaks white sunlight into a rainbow of colors. This is the kind of color we're using when we color using a computer and monitor. It's all light-based, and it is called emissive light. In a computer or television display, this light is broken down into three basic hues: red, green, and blue. When combined, they make white light. Manga Studio, like most other computer painting apps, perform an internal conversion from RGB to red, blue, and yellow primary painting colors so that we can mix the colors much like we can mix watercolor or acrylics.

We need to keep in mind that what we see on the computer screen (RGB of our monitors) is light-based, and what we read in books and magazines (the CYMK of print) is reflected in our eyes. Instead of muddying up our study of colors, let's just focus on RGB colors and do our research on printing on our own. In the bibliography at the end of the book are the resources that we can review to learn more about this rather intricate and involved topic.

Coloring in comics is a history

Before we start coloring our comic, we should know a little of the background of comic coloring.

In the US, comics were designed to be a cheap, throw-away method to repackage newspaper comic strips. When the demand for comics outstripped the supply of existing comic strips, publishers decided to make new ones just for these new comic books. Color was expensive (still is to this day), and publishers made do with basic four-color printing.

The process used then and until the mid-1980s had the colorist hand color the photostats of the original inked artwork with a set of dyes (usually a brand named Dr. Martin's). Then, the colorist would make notes to the engraver, the CYM (no black is used, as this is the original art) composition of the colors. These codes were percentages of the color that the colorist used. He might use 25 percent, 50 percent, 75 percent, or 100 percent (a solid color). This gave the colorist a total of 64 colors to work with. Some colors may be too dark or subtle to be printed, so the actual number of colors that could be used is close to 54.

In the 1990s, comics began to be colored using computers and the separations (which were done by hand for each of the four percentages, 25 percent, 50 percent, 75 percent, and 100 percent, and a new 70 percent for mid-tone colors) were done by the computer. This allowed a great deal of freedom for artists and allowed colorists to be truly recognized for providing a valuable artistic service. The computer programs used for coloring comics ranged from the proprietary to widely available ones.

This brings us to Manga Studio. The painting tools are quite sophisticated and will serve us well in many different styles of coloring: from the flat graphic styles of cartoons or anime to the fully rendered and modeled ones of a photo-real art.

This may get me trolled, but I've been using RGB colors when printing out my color comics for a few years now, and it's been, for the most part, all good. While there are some (albeit a very few) colors that shift when printing from RGB to CYMK, the shift hasn't been that bad and in most cases, looks just fine. This is because a number of print on demand services request RGB files, and they do the conversion themselves. It's a matter of time before the conversion will be perfected as the digital technology progresses. In short, don't sweat it; just color the artwork in RGB, and let your experience guide you. The more we stay away from fully saturated colors, the better our results.

Examining the color tools

There are two types of color tools in Manga Studio: the color choosing tools and painting tools, which are a subset of the marking tools. Although these tools are used in conjunction with one another, we'll look at them separately in order to get a better understanding of how they work.

Color choosers

Color choosers are the color wheel, color sliders, color palette, intermediate color palette, and approximate color palette. We can also use the eyedropper tool to select colors on our canvas and use the color picker on images in the subview palette.

Manga Studio's color wheel

The color wheel is the main color selection tool. Here, we can choose practically any color. The color we choose here can affect other palettes. This palette can also show us the RGB and other color mode values. Like most powerful tools, it's quite simple, so let's get to it!

Time for action – using Manga Studio's color wheel

This should be the default color picker that appears when the color wheel palette is chosen. If it's not visible, go to the **Window** menu and choose the **Color Wheel** menu item, as shown in the following figure:

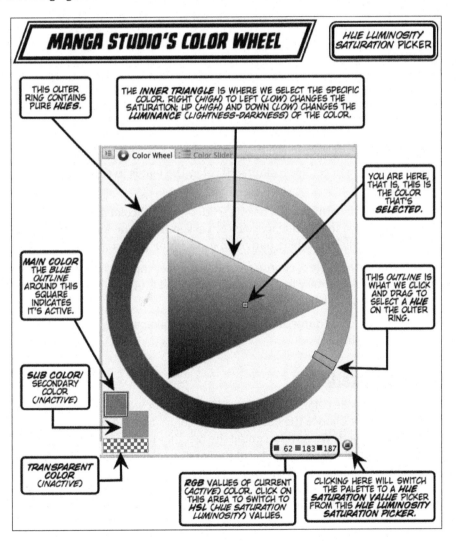

This color wheel should look familiar to those of us who have used painting apps such as Corel Painter. We can choose a color by performing the following steps:

1. Click on the outer ring to select a color; drag it to get a more precise color.

2. In the **Hue Luminosity Saturation** (**HLS**) triangle, click and drag to see what the color looks like with more saturation, less luminosity, or a combination of the two. Like the image states, the more rightward or higher you go, the lighter (higher luminosity/ brightness and less saturated) the color will get; the more leftward or lower you go, the darker (lower brightness and more saturated) the color will become.

Be sure to note the placement of the colors on the outer ring of the color wheel. Unlike the color wheels that we've seen in books and made ourselves in the color theory class, the colors of the Manga Studio color ring don't line up with complementary colors; that is, red isn't the opposite of green, for example. This is one of the aspects of digital art where it's important to have internalized the knowledge from the analog world. I've worked on acrylics and watercolor painting for so long that the color wheel and relationships between colors are automatic.

3. Choose a red color, first by going to the outer ring of the red area, and then in the HLS triangle to get a less saturated color. The hint is to click in the middle of the triangle.

4. In the lower-left corner of the palette, click on the subcolor swatch. In other apps, this is also called the secondary color or background color. Notice that the active color swatch will have a blue outline to it. This is an important visual feedback.

5. Like in the previous step, choose a color. This time, choose a dark green color. Green is complementary to red (this means that it is opposite of red on the traditional color wheel).

6. Now, we have chosen the colors to use for the main painting (main color) and shadowing (subcolor).

What just happened?

We learned how to choose colors using Manga Studio's color wheel. The outer ring of this color wheel is where we choose the basic hue (pure color), and the triangle is where we pick the specific color we want. We have accepted the fact that the outer ring, as helpful as it is, doesn't reflect the actual relationships of colors. For example, complementary colors aren't opposite each other in Manga Studio's color wheel.

Now, let's configure some shortcuts to help us switch between the main color and subcolor.

Time for action – shortcuts for switching main and subcolors

Here, we'll focus on setting a few shortcuts to switch between the main color, subcolor, and transparent color. We can set this by performing the following steps:

1. Go to the shortcut settings dialog by choosing the Manga Studio menu (Mac OS) or **File** (Windows OS) and selecting the **Shortcut settings** menu item.

2. In the **Setting Area** drop-down menu, select the **Options** menu item.

3. In the selection box, click on the disclosure triangle to draw in color.

4. Click on the **Switch Main Color and Sub Color** button.

5. On the right-hand side of the dialog box, click on the **Edit Shortcut** button.

6. Notice that a part of the **Switch Main color and Sub Color** line is now white. This means we can enter in a keyboard shortcut. Press the *X* key.

7. In the lower part of the dialog box, if the icon is a green square, the shortcut is OK. If a yellow warning triangle with **!** inside it appears, it means that the shortcut is already used. We can click on the **OK** button to change the shortcut or press the *Esc* key to try another shortcut. Let's assume that the *X* key is unused.

8. Locate the line that says **Switch between Main Color, sub color and transparent color**. Double-click on this line to begin with the editing process.

9. Press the *Z* key.

10. There shouldn't be a warning. If there is, try another key.

11. Click on the **OK** button when finished.

12. Now try out the shortcut keys.

13. Since many graphic apps use the *X* key to switch between the main and subcolors (or foreground and background colors), we used it here. The *Z* key was used because it's near the *X* key. If you're left handed (like me) and have an extended keyboard (one with a number pad), try using the *0* key for switching between main and subcolors and the dot key (decimal or period) for switching between the three colors.

What just happened?

We created shortcuts to allow us to quickly change the active color from main color to subcolor and then to transparent color. This can be very handy when we're drawing and don't want to waste the cursor movement to change the active color.

Have a go hero

Look at all the entries for color in the **Shortcut Settings** dialog. Make some of your own. Think about how you use the keyboard while drawing. Click on an item that already has a shortcut and then click on the **Edit shortcut** button. Each entry can have more than one shortcut. As our collection of shortcuts develop, it will be helpful to make a hard copy of the new shortcuts. This way we can have something we can refer to until it's firmly within our memory. These shortcut keys are part of the workspace that is currently being used. So, be sure to either save the current workspace or create a new one to ensure that these shortcuts won't be lost.

The approximate and intermediate color palettes

The approximate and intermediate color palettes are like the spreadsheets of color mixing. These palettes will take one or four colors and create a grid of various mixtures of colors. The approximate palette will take one color and create variations of it with graduated amounts of luminosity and saturation. The intermediate palette will take upto four different colors and give us a grid of various mixtures of the colors.

For example, these palettes are useful in finding different tones of colors for highlights and shadows. They are like a digital painter's palette where we can mix white, black, and other colors together to create new colors that work with established colors in our work.

We won't be delving deeply into everything that they can do; the *Chapter 12, Along for the Ride*, which is an online chapter has a complete explanation about them.

Color sets

Just like the name implies, color sets are groups of colors that we can bring up and then pick a color to color our art with. We'll go through the basic commands and options that color sets have and then our stuff's going to get real as we create a custom color set.

Locate the **Color Set** palette, either by checking the visible palettes or by going to **View** and choosing the **Color Set** menu item. Move the color set so that it shares the same space as the intermediate and approximate color palettes.

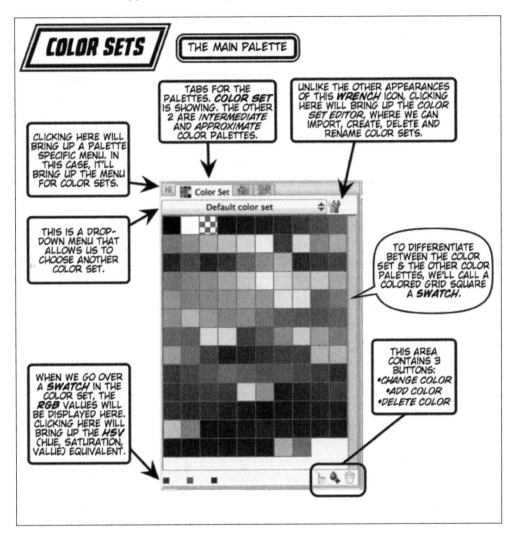

In the preceding figure, you can see the **Default color set** option. Pull down the **Color Set** drop-down menu and load the various color sets that are included in Manga Studio. This **Color Set** Palette is used just like other color palette sets in other graphic apps. Click on a color and this color becomes the selected color in the current color position (main or subcolor). Get habituated with the keyboard shortcut we made a few pages earlier.

In the bottom-right corner of this palette, there are three buttons that we can use to edit the palette. Be careful, as these are the permanent changes made to the color set. The undo option won't be able to help us if we delete a wrong color or change a swatch's color. The following are the three buttons:

- **Change Color**. This button will change the currently selected swatch (it'll have a red outline) to the current color.

- **Add Color**. This button will add a swatch of the current color to the palette.

- **Delete Color**. As if the trash can icon didn't give it away, this button will eliminate the currently selected swatch from the color set. Keep in mind that there is no undo for color sets!

The most often used dialog for color sets is **Edit color set**. We get this dialog by clicking on the wrench icon in the top-right corner of the **Color Set** palette or by selecting **Edit color set** from the palette's menu, as shown in the following figure:

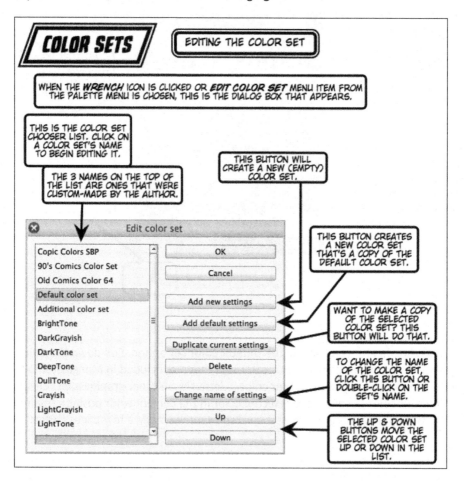

This dialog box allows us to create new color sets, delete them, and rename them. The list of color sets on the left-hand side of the dialog box includes the names of all the color sets we have currently installed. We can select one and then click on the **Up** or **Down** button to raise or lower the position of the selected color set. If we make a mistake in this dialog box, just click on the **Cancel** button and all the changes we made will be discarded. Make a note of the **Add new settings** button; we'll be using this to create a new color set in a moment.

When we click on the palette menu icon, we will get a drop-down menu with many options. Here's what it would look like:

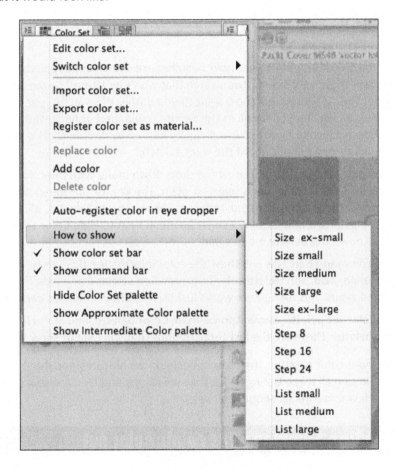

The following are the options that are shown in the preceding figure:

- **Edit color set...**: This will bring up the dialog box we just examined.
- **Switch Color Set**: This is just like choosing a set from the palette's drop-down menu.
- **Import color set...** and **Export color set...**: These will allow us to export and import both Manga Studio native color sets and Adobe .aco colors.

- ◆ **Register color set as material...:** This doesn't seem to be useful, but perhaps some of us would like to use the color pattern in a color set for a fill.

- ◆ **Replace color**, **Add color**, and **Delete color:** These do just what the buttons in the bottom-right part of the **Color Set** palette do. These are more useful in the palette, as we can easily see the selected swatch and adjust the main/sub color to our desire.

- ◆ **Auto-register color in eye dropper:** This means that if this menu item is checked (by selecting it), whenever the eye dropper tool is used, a new swatch will be created of the color the dropper is clicked on. It's best to use this option only when creating a new color set. It's a toggle item, so once it's checked, you need to be select it to uncheck it.

- ◆ **How to show:** This determines how swatches are shown in the palette. The size items will show a set size for the swatch that won't be altered by the size of the palette. The step items will show a specified number of swatches per row. The swatches will enlarge or shrink as the palette is widened or narrowed. List items will show each color in one row and can be named by double-clicking on the white space in the row to the right of the color swatch.

- ◆ **Show color set bar:** This will show the drop-down menu with the color sets when selected and hide them when selected again. The key for this menu item and the next one is that when the menu item says **Show** and you select it, it'll toggle and hide the palette it names and change the menu item to **Hide Color Set Bar** when we pull down the palette menu again.

- ◆ **Show command bar:** This will show the color information (RGB or HSV values) and the **Change**, **Add**, and **Delete** color buttons when selected and hide them when selected again. This menu item works just like the **Show color set bar** menu item.

- ◆ **Hide Color set palette**, **Show Approximate Color palette**, and **Show Intermediate Color palette:** These are the last three options that will hide or show these palettes.

Unlike the previous color palettes, the color set palette is a bit tricky and more involved, so we had to go through all these boring tasks. Now we can go and create a new custom color set and learn a few more things about color sets.

Time for action – making a 70s comic color set

Let's say we have a need to go retro and use the colors that were used in American comics during the early 70s. To do this accurately, we'll have to be able to use those colors in a color set, as mucking about in the color wheel and the intermediate and approximate color palettes won't give us the exact colors we want. Fortunately, we can search for the actual colors that are present in a graphic we can use. Then, we'll want to sample the colors from it and put those picked colors into a color set. This color set will contain around 64 colors.

We'll be using the subview palette to do our color sampling. In other graphic apps, we will have to open the file as a document and use the eyedropper tool to sample colors. With the subview palette, we can just click on the **Switch to eyedropper** button and make sure that the auto-register color in the **Eyedropper** menu item of the **Color Set** palette is chosen (we'll get the details in a moment so don't stress if this is confusing).

> There's a lot to say about the subview palette. As mentioned in *Chapter 6, Pencil Mechanics* we can use this palette to hold images for reference, but we can also use it to sample colors from. There was an image I drew that I wanted to color using shark colors. I used Google to search for images, saved them to my hard drive, and then loaded them onto the subview palette. Once loaded, I sampled the colors I needed and painted away. I also created a character sheet for a series of I'm working on that I use for both visual and color references.

1. To save us a lot of time involved in searching for the specific image, we will navigate to the **MS4B content | Ch 08 Colors | Palette_sources** folder for a file named `old-comics-64-color-guide.png` where we can use sample colors from.

2. In Manga Studio, make the **Sub View** palette visible and open. We'll need this palette to be somewhat large, so drag it on the tab to make it a floating palette. As we don't need to have a document open, we can put the subview palette where the document is present.

3. To be nice, the following figure is a recap of the subview palette, complete with callouts, so we don't have to go back and look at the preceding figure:

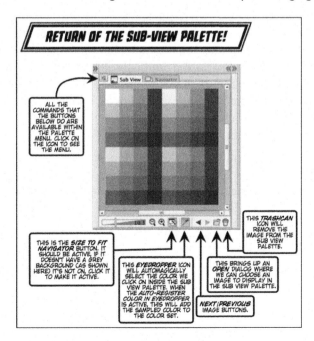

4. The preceding figure shows some of the controls of the **Sub View** palette. Click on the **Open** button. In the dialog box, navigate to where the `old-comics-64-color-guide.png` image is present. Once it is selected, click on the **OK** button.

5. Next make sure that the **Size to Fit Navigator** button is clicked. This will make sure that the image will fill up as much of the **Sub View** palette as is possible. It'll make selecting colors a lot easier.

6. Next to the **Size to Fit** button is the eyedropper button. Make sure that it's active; it'll have a gray square background when it is on. Now, when we click on the image in the **Sub View** palette, the color we clicked on will become the active color.

7. After setting up the **Sub View**, let's go over to the **Color Set** palette.

8. In the **Color Set** palette, click on the wrench icon to bring up the **Edit Color Set** dialog box.

9. In the **Edit Color Set** dialog, click on the **Add New Settings** button. You'll see a textbox in the bottom-left corner of the box; it should read something like new color set. Type in `70s Color` into the textbox. Click on the **OK** button.

10. In the **Color Set** palette, we are greeted with an empty color set.

11. Click on the palette menu icon and in the pop-up menu, choose the **Auto-register color** option in the eyedropper menu item. Don't forget to reselect this menu item to turn this option off! If we forget and use the eyedropper tool to sample colors for painting, we will add colors to the current color set. Sometimes, this is good but not so good when we're not expecting it.

12. Here's the really boring part; go to the **Sub View** palette. Starting with the colored square in the upper-left side, moving to the right, click on each of the individual colored squares, all 64 of them one by one. Thankfully, we have the one-two punch of having the **Sub View** palette and automatically sample the clicked area and the auto-register feature in the color palette to speed things up. So, one click and we move forward. There are some apps that require us to use the eyedropper tool to sample colors and then click on the color set to create new colors. Tedious is a kind description of that process.

13. When we're done with putting all the 64 colors into the color set, go to the **Color Set** palette menu and reselect the **Auto-Register** menu item, so we won't have any accidents. We can now close the **Sub View** palette if we want to keep things tidy.

What just happened?

Besides taking a chromatic trip back into the days gone by, we learned another use of the **Sub View** palette. It can be used to sample colors. Then, we created a new empty color set and filled that puppy with colors from an image in the **Sub View** palette.

Before we move on, the following are a few quick tips on color sets. They are as follows:

- Holding down the *Command* (Mac) or *Ctrl* (Windows) key and clicking and dragging a swatch will move that swatch.

- Holding down the *Option* (Mac) or *ALT* (Windows) key will fill the swatch that's clicked on with the current active color.

- Right-clicking on a color swatch will bring up a contextual menu with **Replace color**, **Add color**, or **Delete color** menu items.

- If we want to delete a contiguous range of swatches, click on the first swatch in the range. Then, in the color set palette, click on the trash icon to delete that swatch. The swatch is deleted and the next swatch in the color set is now active. Just keep clicking on the trash icon to keep deleting the swatches one at a time until the range of unwanted swatches is deleted. This is good if we still have the **Auto-register** setting in the **Color Set** palette menu and have been selecting colors with the eyedropper.

That's all for the color specific palettes. We spent a lot of efforts on this section, because color choosing and mixing are important aspects of comic coloring that really don't get much attention. The only thing that remains for us is to learn more about the color theory and apply that. Our best bet is to either take a class in color theory or research it. Color theory is a too big subject to give justice to in this book.

The eyedropper tool

The final tool we'll be looking at is the eyedropper tool. This may appear to be a simple tool (and compared to other tools, it is), but within its simplicity, it has a lot of power to easily sample colors, paint with them, and then sample other colors to keep on painting. Depending on the settings of the eyedropper tool, we can sample colors on the layer we're working on, the topmost layer, or all visible layers.

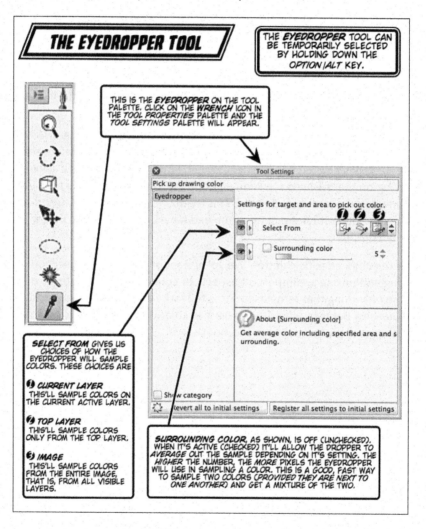

If we notice, the eye-con for the surrounding color is on (this means that we see the eye looking at us). This makes the setting visible in the **Tool Properties** palette. With the surrounding color setting visible in the **Tool Properties** palette, we won't have to go to the **Tool Settings** palette every time we want to make a change to this setting.

The **Select From** setting can be quite helpful in many situations. The three sections (numbered in the image) allow the eyedropper to sample colors from the layer we're working on, the topmost layer, and from the entire image. An interesting thing about the first two settings, **Current Layer** and **Top Layer**, is that if we sample an area that doesn't have any color in it, **Transparent Color** is made active.

The other setting, **Surrounding Color**, is good to use as either a single pixel color sampler, or when it's active (the checkbox is checked), it will sample from an area (the larger the number, the larger the sample area) and then average the colors. So, if this setting is active, set to a large amount, and we click in between the red and blue areas, the sampled color will be a purple color. This is good for the times we want to get a color that is between two colors.

As the image says, we can temporarily get the eyedropper tool by holding down the *Option/ Alt* key. It's helpful to have a button on our tablet set to the *Option/Alt* key. In this way, we can get the eyedropper faster when we're coloring.

That's it for the color mixing and selecting palettes and tools. The reason why so much emphasis was put on these parts of coloring is that color selection is one of the most important parts of coloring. Sure, anyone can select a color. However, for us, we need to select the right color to make our coloring look good.

Looking at colors IRL

Okay, this requires getting away from the computer and entering the analog world. Don't worry; our computer will still be there when we're finished. This won't be that scary.

We'll need to get about six or more blank index cards (three by five inches) or large sheets of paper. The paper should be somewhat thick (like a cover stock or bristol board). We want to color the entire card (using watercolor paint, guache, or marker) with as close to a solid color as we can get. Pick blue, red, and yellow colors. Go around to different rooms in our home and place the pairs so that one is in a lit area and the matching one is in shadow. We should have a blue, red, and yellow set of colors in the shadows and in a lit area. Look at the sheets. Even though we know that the colors are the same for the shadow and lit sheets, don't they look different?

Now, repeat this with incandescent and florescent lights. Use candles also (if you can use them safely) as a light source. Go outside and see what the sheets look like in a sunlit area and in tree shadows.

This is pure observation, so there's no right or wrong way to do this. The major thing to observe is how the colors appear to be different in different lights. As a general guide, the warmer the light, the colder the color appears in the shadow. So, a candle or incandescent light will give cold colors in its shadow, while cold light from a florescent light will yield warm shadow colors.

Basically, things have pure color, hue, and this hue can be muted or darkened depending on the surroundings. Make the colors fit the scene we're coloring. We don't need to use the exact same color in every panel. It's better that things look right than to be chained to a specific RGB value.

Now, when we color our comics, we can recall this exercise to add a bit of realism to our coloring.

Using the color marking tools

While the title of this section sounds odd, it's perfectly logical as any marking tool in Manga Studio can be used to color with. There are some tools that are specifically meant for working with colors (and they will work with just black, white, and gray if we're so disposed). The following are these tools:

- **Pastels**: These are located on the Pencil subtool palette, and they work much like their analog counterparts. They blend together, but in a rough manner, as the tooth (texture) of the paper will give them an irregular pattern.

- **Watercolor**: This is present on the Brush subtool palette, and it works just like analog water colors. Colors bleed and blend together easily. We can even set the watercolor border value to give a light outline to our stroke for an even better watercolor impression.

- **Oil Paint**: These are brushes that lay down thick, gray color and blends with subtlety or contrast, just like real oil paint. The best thing about it is that it doesn't have any oil paint smell.

Keep in mind that although we can drag a tool from the **Sub tool** palette into the **Tool** palette, this can cause the **Tool** palette to get filled up rather quickly. When we have used Manga Studio for some time, we can get a good idea of what tools we want in the **Tool** palette and which tools should remain as a subtool set. Adjust Manga Studio to the way you find yourself working, and things will be much more streamlined.

All other marking tools can be used to color. In the Pencils subtool group, there's a colored pencil tool. The **India Ink** group in the Brush subtool palette has a number of good brushes that can be used to color and give excellent results. Don't be afraid to experiment.

Don't forget that we have the bucket fill tool and the gradient fill tool to use.

But wait! There's more! We have blending modes for individual layers and a plethora of tonal controls that can finely tune colors to refine what we've done.

Combine these tools, selections, and masks; we have all the tools we'll ever need to do good quality coloring within Manga Studio.

A process for coloring comics

Like with most new ways of doing things, they become codified with time and an efficient way of doing it comes forward. This has happened with comic coloring. When a colorist gets the digital inks, the work begins as follows:

◆ Each object and part of an object gets a flat color added to it. So, a character will be painted with a flat color for the skin, clothing, and other accessories that it has. Think of a colored page in a coloring book.

◆ The colored areas are not anti-aliased and are usually below the layer that contains the inks.

◆ Background and props are colored in the same way, sometimes on the same layer as the figures/foreground and sometimes on a layer below it.

◆ These solid areas of color are needed so that the magic wand selection tool can select all the areas of that specific color. At that point, the selected color is shaded and rendered in color on the original layer or on a new layer above the flat color layer.

This process is called flatting, and we can think of it as our color rough draft. It's a good way to get a feel of the overall balance of color on a panel and page. As the colors are flat (not shaded), they are very easily selected to change their color. It's quite common for some mainstream colorists to hire people who just to do the flatting work.

Once the flatting is done, as stated in the last bullet item earlier, we can begin the actual shading process and add textures to our art.

So, what we're going to do is have some *Time for action* sections that mirror this process. Before we do that, there is one last thing that we need to cover.

The name of this section is *A process for coloring comics*, and not *The process*. There is no reason for an independent artist to color his/her comics as one would paint a picture. However, by performing the following steps, we can really get a good grasp of what we can do with colors and digital painting with Manga Studio. Like the old saying goes, "You have to learn the rules before you break them."

By this time, we should have some fully inked-in artwork. If the earlier *Time for action* sections for inking (*Chapter 7, Ink Slingers*) were followed, the inks are on one layer. For those of us who are adventurous, these inks are on a vector layer. This will be somewhat important when we learn about Manga Studio's anti-overflow settings for all marking tools. If you don't have a Manga Studio file with vector inks, there's a Manga Studio file in the `Downloads` folder. It's titled `MS4B_ColoringExercise.lip` and is inside the `Chapter 8 resource` folder. Alternatively, you can ink a penciled drawing on a vector layer; remember that all the tools can work on a vector layer. Just don't forget to make a black fill layer as outlined in *Chapter 7, Ink Slingers*.

It wouldn't be a bad idea for all of us to check out the coloring exercise Manga Studio file. Open it up in Manga Studio and click on the **Layer** option. Make sure that the **Enable Mask and Show Mask Area** settings are on (it's present right next to the Lock Transparency icon). Notice how there's a blue area that goes around the enclosing box but doesn't extend into the Pencil and the guy's nose and fingers. This was done by working in the Mask sublayer. Go back to *Chapter 6, Pencil Mechanics,* for details on how to use masks.

We'll be creating some new brushes just for use to make our flats, so (*ahem*) brush up on the **Tool Settings** palette, because only the recipe for brushes will be included; no images, except for the **anti-overflow option,** will be shown. The process of creating new layers and adjusting their settings will be equally brief, as we should be old hands at it by now. Let's go to the **flat** cave!

Time for action – setting up our file for flats

To make our lives easier and less frustrating, let's make sure our layers are named so that we won't get confused. The layer containing the inks should be named `Inks`; if there's a background inks layer, it could be named `Inks BG`. Any pencil layers (if they're not required) should be hidden. We could save the Manga Studio file with the suffix `Color`, and then delete the pencil layers in this copy. This can enhance our computer speed, as color layers can weigh down Manga Studio, and on some less speedy computers, it can take a while to save files and even cause a lag when we make a pen stroke.

This is an important point: if we find that our computer is lagging when using Manga Studio, we can do a few things to speed things up. The first is to reduce the number of layers. Make a copy and delete any unnecessary layers in that copy. If things are still slow, we can try to combine as many layers as we comfortably can. If things are still sticking in the mud, we can reduce the DPI of our file. Remember that we don't need to have files that are larger than the printed size. We only used 600 dpi to get the details that will get smoothed out and will reduce down to 300 dpi. So, just making a 300 dpi file won't adversely affect our final work. However, we'll lose the smoothness that reducing down will provide. Unfortunately, Manga Studio won't retain any cropping or margin information when changing a canvas' resolution. This is a subject we'll cover in *Chapter 11, One More Thing*.

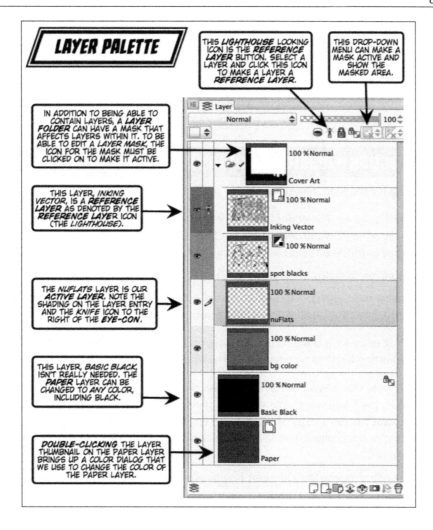

In the preceding figure, the layer thumbnails have been set to large so that we can get an idea of what the canvas area looks like.

1. Open the file that is to be colored.

2. Locate the layer with the inks.

3. Select that layer.

4. Click on the Reference Layer icon in the **Layer** palette.

5. Select the layer below the ink layer.

6. Create a new raster layer; make sure it's a color layer.

7. Give the new layer a meaningful name, for example, color flats.

What just happened?

We will not do much on the surface. However, what we did is prepare for the coloring. Like a painter who coats his/her canvas with gesso, our file is now primed and ready for colors. Setting the ink layer as a reference layer is crucial for us so that we can take advantage of the anti-overflow feature. Now that we have our document all set up to begin coloring, let's create a new brush that we can use to make our color flats.

Time for action – making a flatting brush

We are looking for the following three things in a flatting brush:

- **No anti-aliasing**: The edges it produces must be distinct. This will help us if we need to make a magic wand selection based on color; we'll get a good smooth selection without any little bits that won't be selected.

- **Responsive to stylus pressure**. We'll need to color small and large areas.

- It must produce solid, flat, unblended colors, for example, the gauche paint. The brush cannot blend colors while coloring over another color.

We'll be starting out with a basic oil paint brush, make a copy, and then create a new tab group for our flatting brushes by performing the following steps:

1. Open a file that has an ink layer (or open the `Packt Cover MS4B Vector Inks 02.lip` file if you want). We won't be saving any of our changes, but to be sure, you may want to save a copy of the file and work on that copy just to be safe. Make sure that we're on a color raster layer. If we're on any other kind of layer, options may be grayed out.

2. We need to choose the **Oil paint** brush, as shown in the following figure:

3. Make a copy of the **Oil paint** brush subtool as we've done many times so far. Name the copy `Flats brush`.

4. Let's make some modifications to this brush to make it the ideal flatting brush. Open up the **Tool Settings** palette by clicking on the wrench icon at the bottom of the **Tool Properties** palette.

5. Now, we're going to go from category to category and list the following settings we want this new brush to have. If a setting isn't mentioned, it's a safe bet as it's either set to zero or not turned on.

❑ **Brush Size:** We want to color with nice thin-to-thick strokes. Set the **Brush Size** between 20 and 30 and the pressure settings (on the far right of the brush size number setting) is set differently than previous pressure curves, as shown in the following screenshot:

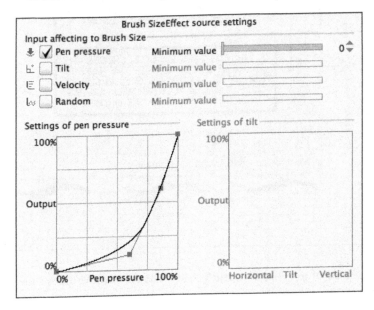

This is done so that we can get a finer line when using light to medium pressure and get really a thick line when we press harder on our stylus. We can always go back and readjust the pressure settings to fit our individual work process better.

❑ **Ink: Opacity** needs to be set at 100, **Mix Ground Color** should be unchecked; we don't want any colors to be mixed with this brush. **Mixing Rate of Sub Drawing Color** (the very last setting) is set to zero. Again, no mixing!

❑ **Anti-Aliasing:** Choose **None**. It's the first choice in the drop-down selection menu.

❑ **Brush Shape:** There is nothing that we need to change here; move along now.

❑ **Brush Tip:** The **Tip Shape** is set to **Circle**, **Hardness** and **Thickness** to **100**, and **Direction of Applying** to **Horizontal**. **Direction** is set to zero, **Brush Density** is set to **100**, and **Adjust Brush Density** is unchecked.

- ❑ **Spraying Effect**: This isn't used, so it's unchecked.

- ❑ Stroke: **Space** is set to **Narrow** and all other settings are unchecked.

- ❑ **Texture**: This isn't needed for this brush. Make sure that the **Texture** option is set to **None**. If there is a texture, click on the Trash icon to the right of the **Texture** option to delete the texture, and the button will read **None**.

- ❑ **Correction: Stabilization** is set to **2. Correct by Speed** is unchecked. Everything else is unchecked except for **Possible to Snap**. It's good to have our flatting brush snap to rulers and such options. If there are no rulers, having this setting on won't matter.

- ❑ **Starting and Ending**: This is set to **None, Method** is set to **By Length, Starting and Ending** are checked and both are set to **20**, and **Starting and Ending by Speed** is checked.

- ❑ **Anti-Overflow: Do Not Exceed Line of Reference Layer** and **Stop Filling at Center Line of Vector** are checked, **Color Margin** is set to **10**, and **Area Scaling** is unchecked.

6. Whew! Now all we need to do is click on the **Register All Settings to Initial Settings** button so that our new flatting brush will be saved with the settings that we spent so much effort on.

7. Since this flatting brush colors and behaves very different from its oil brush cousin, let's create a new tool group for it to live in.

8. Click on the brush subtool entry in the **Sub Tool** palette and drag it up to the tabs. A vertical red line will appear where the new sub tool group will be. If there's a red outlined box, this means we're dropping the brush into another group; move the cursor a bit until there's a red vertical line. Let's have it on the left-hand side of the rest of the tabs. When it's were we want it to be, release the stylus or mouse.

9. A new tabbed group appears. Right-click on the new tab and choose the **Settings** menu item from the **Sub Tool** Group. Name the group `Comic Flatting`.

What just happened?

We modified an oil brush to serve as our flatting brush. We then made a new sub tool group with this brush. We made sure that anti-overflow is active on this brush. Now we can begin coloring. Finally!

Coloring our flats

The main concept of flats is that there are solid areas of color that we can select and render in highlights, shadows, and textures. This rendering can be on the flats layer or, more preferably, on a new layer.

This is when we begin to color our work. Usually, the creation of flats takes very little time and can save a lot of work, as changing colors can be easy with some adjustments on the Fill (Bucket) tool. If this was a digital painting, we could call this activity *color blocking*.

In this section, we'll start out by using the Fill (Bucket) tool with a few adjustments. Then, for details, we'll use our new flatting brush and see just how overflow protection/anti-overflow works on flatting an inked drawing. Then, we'll move on to finishing our flats. This section will wrap up with an overview of selections and adjusting the Magic Wand and Bucket tools to use them where flat colors are required.

Making use of overflow protection

Overflow protection is a great feature of Manga Studio. We'll call this feature either overflow protection or anti-overflow. Both terms mean the same, however, overflow protection sounds better. In any case, this feature was introduced in Version 5.0.2, and it has drastically changed how flats and other coloring techniques are implemented. The following is an example of **ANTI-OVERFLOW** in action:

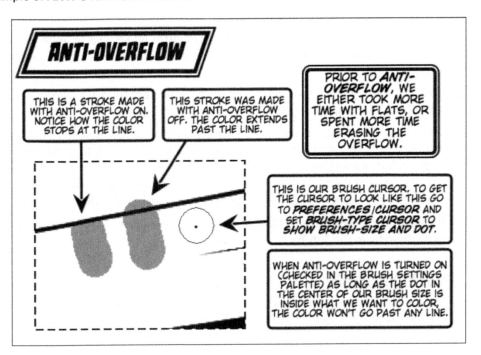

Both strokes were made to look as alike as possible. Both strokes in the image ended at the same (relative) place. The most important aspect of **ANTI-OVERFLOW** is the *center* of the brush. In the figure, this center dot is exaggerated a bit to be more visible; on our monitors, the dot may be a bit smaller.

Be sure to go to **Preferences** and change the setting, as indicated in the image's text. The brush tool and the center dot make it quick for us to see that this is a coloring brush.

In the **Tool Settings** palette for our flatting brush, it may be a good idea to make the **Anti-Overflow** setting visible in the **Tool Properties** palette. This can be done by clicking on the eye-con button on the left-hand side of the **Anti-Overflow** setting in the **Tool Properties** palette.

Our process of coloring the flats can be completed by performing the following steps:

1. Use the paint Bucket tool to fill in large areas with color.

2. Switch to the flats brush to add in details.

3. Change the colors of areas so that they are more harmonious with the color scheme we're using.

4. Make sure that the colored areas are within the inked lines, only if we want them to be.

In the following exercises, we'll see examples using the `Packt Cover MS4B Vector Inks 02.lip` file. Feel free to use the copy of this file in the MS4B download package or your own artwork. Just make sure that it has a layer of inked art and a layer for flats. Now, let's make like a prism and spread some colors!

Time for action – coloring the flat color layer

The Manga Studio file that we want to color should be open. Select the flats layer. Let's double check that the inks layer is set as the reference layer. Keep in mind that only one layer at a time can be the reference layer. We can, however, color in any layer and still use the same reference layer. The settings for using a reference layer (sometimes, it's called the referring layer in the Manga Studio interface) reside in the **Tool Properties** and the **Tool Settings** palettes. We set up the inks layer to be a reference layer in an earlier *Time for action* section; here is where it really comes into play. We can color the flat color layer by performing the following steps:

1. Create a custom fill tool.

2. Select the Fill (Paint Bucket) tool. We'll need to make a custom Fill tool, so let's do the usual process:

    1. Duplicate the tool.

    2. Name the duplicate tool `Fill Flats` and give the icon background a color that is different from the default. This is to make sure that we can identify which tools we create and which tools are the defaults.

3. Open up the **Tool Settings** palette for our new Fill Flats tool. Make the following changes to the Categories:

    ❏ **Fill: Follow Adjacent Pixel** is checked. This makes the fill occur in areas that are enclosed, that is, connected.

    ❏ **Close Gap**: This is set to **5**. This will automatically treat a gap (in this case, a medium-sized one) as being closed. This avoids a flood fill when some lines are not closed.

    ❏ **Soak into narrow area**: This should be checked. This will fill in areas that are close together, such as parallel lines that are really close to one another.

    ❏ **Color Margin**: This is set to **10**. If we're working with more than one color in the reference layer, the larger this number is, the more colors it'll include when considering lines as borders.

    ❏ **Area Scaling**: This is checked. This scales the filled area outwards with the amount entered. To use offset printing terms, this is an adjustable overprint for our filled color. It works best when set between **2** and **5**. Here, it's set to **2**.

    ❏ **Zoom Method**: This has **Rounded** selected. This is the middle option in the set of three options.

    ❏ **Select From**: This is where we tell the Bucket tool to get the outlines we're filling.

    ❏ **Multiple Referring**: This is checked. It has **Referring Layer** (what is called the reference layer in the **Layer** palette) selected. Non-reference layer is where we refine additional sources of where the Bucket tool gets its information from. A button is on when its background color is darker. It's off when it's lighter. All of these should be on except for the editing layer and locked layer. This way we can use the layer we're coloring on as a referring layer and manually close gaps with a painted stroke. The Bucket tool will respect this line and not go past it when filling an area.

    ❏ **Stop filling at center line of Vector**: This is checked.

    ❏ **Ink**: This has **Opacity** is set to **100** and **Combine** mode is set to **Normal**.

    ❏ **Anti-aliasing**: This is unchecked. For flat fills, we need hard-edged lines. Anti-aliased edges can cause some issues while filling in an area drawn by a flats brush. One notable issue is that a fringe of lighter color may be selected. This can be the exact opposite of what we want.

4. Click on the **Register all settings to initial settings** button to save our changes to this tool.

What just happened?

By going through all the appropriate categories and adjusting the settings, we changed an oil brush into an ideal flatting brush. There's no aliasing or blending in this brush. It'll lay down a solid color and be responsive to the pressure we apply on our stylus. Now we can go on and make our flat color layer!

Laying down the flat colors

A guided example for filling in flats would tend to encourage a fill-in-by-number mindset. We know all we need to do this. Be adventurous, fill in areas, and strive to have something that looks harmonious and dynamic or noir or moody, whatever is the best for what we're working on. The following are some general guides and tips:

- Now, we have to specifically set up two tools that we can use for coloring in flats: the Flatting Brush and the Flat Fill Bucket.

- Open up the **Color Set** palette. We can choose initial colors from this palette or make custom colors using the color wheel.

- Use the intermediate or approximate color palettes to choose lighter or darker tints of the chosen color.

- We can use the *Option/Alt* key to sample colors from our canvas.

- The Bucket tool can be used to refill an area. We will have to do this sometimes if some color spills out from a smaller area. If this happens all the time, reduce the value of **Area Scaling** in the tool properties **Fill** category.

- Undo is our friend.

- If an area we're trying to fill ends up flood filling (filling in the entire layer), check to see if there are any gaps—areas where the ink lines aren't connecting with one another. This is solved using the flatting brush, with the color we want to fill the active area, and outline the inside of the area we want to fill. Once this is done, use the bucket to fill in the area. This is why the bucket and the Flatting brush have anti-aliasing off. Now, when we fill in an area drawn by the flatting brush, we won't get a fringe where the fill ends.

Time for action – using the auto select (magic wand) tool

In our early stages of coloring, this is our third most used tool. It automatically selects the color that it's clicked on. Let's look at the Magic Wand tool settings:

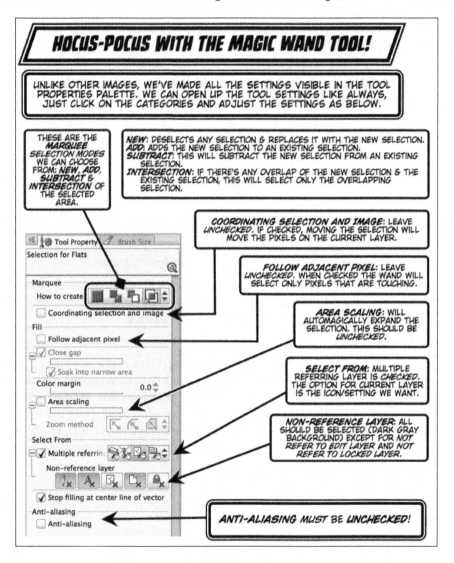

We can do this by performing the following steps:

1. To get what we'll end up with in the preceding figure, we'll need to select the Magic Wand tool (called the Auto Select tool).

2. As we did earlier, make a copy of this tool.

3. Name the copy `Flat Selection`.

4. In the **Marquee** category, in the **How to create** section, select the **New** option. We can change this setting when we need to in the **Tool Settings** palette (and the eye-con can be checked, so it'll appear in our tool properties palette as will the other settings listed here).

5. In the **Fill** category, make sure that **Follow adjacent pixel** is unchecked. When we're creating flats, we should be able to select everything with the same color.

6. **Color margin** should be set to zero. Flat colors are single colors. They do not include any blending or aliasing, provided we used the flatting brush we made a while back.

7. **Area Scaling** is unchecked. Unless we want to add a glow or some other effect, we will select just the color, nothing more or less.

8. Under **Select From**, **Multiple referring layers** should be checked. The Fill current layer should be the only option selected. In this context, Fill refers to selecting pixels and not filling pixels with color.

9. All the options in the **Non-reference layer** setting should be on, except for Not Refer to Edit layer and Not Refer to Locked layer.

10. **Stop filling at center line of vector** should be checked. This works in conjunction with overflow protection.

11. **Anti-aliasing** must be unchecked. If this were to be checked, our selections would have fringes of intermediate color that would look bad and be very time-consuming to correct.

What just happened?

Earlier, we created a custom paint bucket (Fill), and now, we created a custom Magic Wand (Auto Select) tool that we can use for coloring in our flat color. This is an important part of our colored comic. Here, with just flat colors, we can evaluate whether our color scheme is working or not. At this stage, it's very easy and quick to make changes just using the new Selection for Flats Magic Wand subtool to select the color we want to change. Then, all we have to do is choose the replacement color and click on the bucket icon in the selection bar. The selection will be changed to the new color.

We do not have a *Time for action* section for the actual creation of flats, as there are so many variables, and as with the rest of the exercises in this section, it is recommended that you just do it. Think of flatting as filling in a coloring book. Experiment with the tools. You'll find your own way in no time.

Have a go hero

If there are areas that just won't fill in properly, check the anti-overflow settings and look at the reference layer for lines that don't meet up. What if we took a marker tool (with anti-aliasing set to none) and used that tool to close up the gaps with the color we want to fill in the area? Of course, the marker would have to be made smaller. Any problem can be solved if we have both sides of the equation: problem + workaround = solution. We just need to figure out what the workaround is. At this point, we should be comfortable enough with Manga Studio to figure it out.

Painting our comic

The final piece of coloring is here. When painting over our flats (either in the same layer or in a new layer), the most important thing that we can do is keep the importance of contrast in mind. In addition to different colors contrasting with each other, the one factor that will either bring out the best in those colors or muddy them is how the colors blend. Is the blending a gradation or an edge? Is the gradation long and gradual or short and sweet? Are the edges between the colors a smooth line or is the edge rough and distinct? In this section, we'll look at different ways of putting two colors together and the visual effects the different ways can provide us.

As artists, we have an interesting dilemma: we need to engage our viewers by providing a consistent visual appearance. Still, we don't want to bore them, so we try out different ways of doing things. It's a tightrope to be sure. On one hand, we're providing our style. On the other, we need to occasionally change things so that our work won't look stale and repetitive.

The techniques presented here are just starting places. It's up to each of us to find what works best, not only for the way we individually do things but for the work itself. Paradoxically, this is not only the most important section, it's also one of the briefest, because it requires work on our part that none of the canned tutorials can give us. One of the best teachers for this is not the photorealistic artists but the impressionists. It's more important to capture a mood, a feeling in our coloring than to be totally slavish to reality, which is subjective when we really think about it. Enough of this navel-gazing, let's paint!

Time for action – tool settings for painting

Here, we'll look at some of the tool settings that make a marking tool a painting tool. We passed them by when setting up our flatting brush; now, let's look at some settings and see just how they can help us paint our comics by performing the following steps:

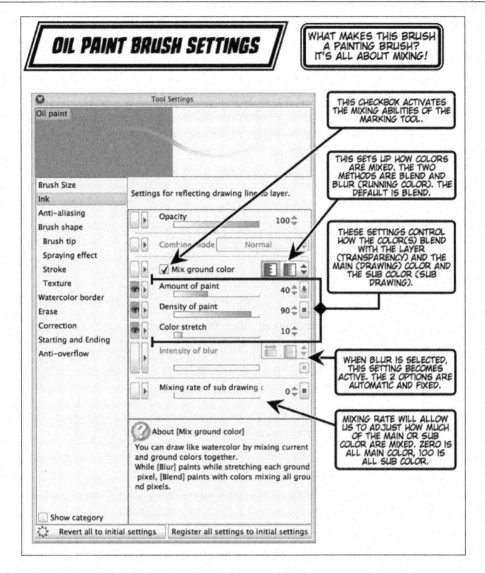

1. Open a file that has an inked drawing. We may want to save it under a different name, as we'll be just experimenting with coloring and don't want to mess up our original. We can always delete this file later. Overflow protection works best with vector lines, but raster lines are still okay to use.

2. In the Tool palette, choose the **Oil Brush** tool.

3. Make a copy of the tool and name it `Comic Painting`.

4. Click on the wrench icon to bring up the **Tool Settings** palette.

5. In the **Tool Settings** palette, click on the **Ink** category. This is the category that chooses the major settings for making this brush a painting brush.

6. The section that begins with a checkbox marked **Mix ground color** is the beginning of the painting settings. This is also where the current version of Manga Studio (Version 5.0.3) has some oddness with the interactive help, for example, Blur is sometimes called Blue or Running Color (which could be a neat name for a character from a Western movie) among others.

7. Once **Mix ground color** is checked, there are two options from which we can choose one.

8. Blend does pretty much what it says. As the stroke progresses, it blends the main color into the stroke from the subcolor. This gives really nice results that look remarkably like paint strokes.

9. Blur or Blue running color will blur the colors as they mix. This basically gives a solid stroke with just a bit of blur on the edges of the stroke. If we want smooth blending, we'd have to supplement this tool with a blur tool to blend the colors smoothly.

10. The next three settings, **Amount of paint**, **Density of paint**, and **Color stretch**, all work in relationship with one another. To get a feel of what they do, move one to an extreme and paint a few strokes. Set it back to what it was and do the same for the next setting. Make a note of the results that you find interesting. We can go back and make a new custom oil brush tool with these settings.

11. If Blur is selected in the mixing section, the intensity of Blur is where we adjust how blur works. Like with the previous step, experiment with the settings.

12. Now, create a new color document; the resolution can be anywhere between 150 to 300 dpi.

13. In *Art School Instructor* terms, go crazy. Choose a color, paint a few strokes, make a large area of one color, and then pick a complementary color.

14. Using this color, blend it into the earlier color.

15. There is no right or wrong way here. Do what looks good to you.

Time for action – basic painting techniques for comics

In this section, we'll be taking a different approach compared to other exercises. Here, we'll search out paintings and other examples of colored comic art to serve as both inspiration and learning exercises. By looking at these examples, we can then try to emulate them in our own coloring. There is no right or wrong way in this. We are expanding our artistic horizons and challenging ourselves to go outside our comfort zone. The more we put into this exercise, the more we'll get out of it. We can do this by performing the following steps:

1. Find some examples of different kinds of artwork for examples of coloring and for inspiration for experiments:

   ❏ Search the Internet for impressionist and abstract paintings.

   ❏ Also, search for colored comic pages from the 60s, 70s, 90s, and the current day.

   ❏ As we search, keep the links to the images that we like best and least.

   ❏ Now try to identify what we like best. Be specific. This is to help us see what is good and not so good. Is this the color that makes an image look good? Is it how the colors are blended? Is it just the subject matter?

   ❏ Look at how the colors are blended to the colored comic pages. Is there no blending, just one color up against another? Is the blending an airbrushed-like gradient? Is the blending going with the shape or does it look mechanical?

2. Working with edges can add some different looks to how artwork is colored. It doesn't have to be smooth blending from one color to the next. Sometimes a rough edge between one color and the other can be much more visually interesting than a bland smooth blending:

   ❏ Edges are where painting occurs. Using edges, the blending is done, and they allow a colored comic page to achieve its look and feel. Is the edge smooth, like in anime and other cartoons? Is the edge distinct but rough like a brush that was just flicked across the area?

   ❏ To experiment with edges, go to our custom **Flatting** subtool brush we made earlier and bring up the **Tool Settings** palette.

   ❏ In the **Brush tip** category, choose **Material** and click on the area that asks to be clicked within.

   ❏ In the dialog box, click on the right-hand side tag that says **Painting_Material**.

   ❏ On the left-hand side scroll to find a material named **Fabric C**.

   ❏ Select **Fabric C** and click on the **OK** button.

   ❏ Now, in a test document, paint a few strokes of different colors with the brush. Notice how the edges are irregular.

   ❏ If you can't see any effect, check the texture density and size ratio. Make them higher and larger, respectively.

3. Sometimes a smooth graduation between colors are needed. For that we can use Manga Studio's gradient tool:

- Gradients are good to use for inanimate objects. They tend to make organic objects look artificial. We can only have gradient blends that are straight or circular. There are no ovals or curved gradients unless we do them by hand.

- Gradients are excellent for laying down a background color blend of two colors

- The **Gradient** tool has a number of presets; experiment with them, we'll have more on how to use this tool.

What just happened?

We made our first foray into learning about coloring and painting. The exercises in this chapter focused on just the tools we can use. How to use them is up to us and our experimenting with them. There are many resources better suited to learning painting and coloring than this one. As artists, we must always be learning from as many different sources as possible. Don't just stay in one genre or type of art. There's much we can learn from museums and art books from libraries.

We can just incorporate these learnings into our work in Manga Studio. Try to emulate coloring/painting styles from all periods of time, from Renoir to van Gough to Robert Williams. It's all out there to see, but we must learn to look.

Have a go hero

With the new texture (**Fabric C**) on our brush, how would making the **Scatter** category (in the **brush settings**) active change the brush's look? If we have analog art tools, what if we made some splatters and smears with ink, and then took digital photos of them or scanned them into our computer? We could edit them to just include the splatter or smear and then save them as materials in Manga Studio like how we did for the Kirby dots in the previous chapter. What kind of brush effects would they give us?

Go through all the different brushes, see what they do out of the box, and then make a duplicate of them and look at their settings. Make changes to the settings and see what these changes do. It's best to change one setting or category at a time and then see the results, reset it back to the original state, and then change a different category. This way we can see what each category does in an isolated way instead of a chaotic display.

Pop quiz

Q1. Anti-Overflow prevents color from which of the following?

1. Coloring the inked lines of a reference layer

2. Coloring outside the inked lines of a reference layer

3. Coloring within the inked lines of a reference layer

Q2. Hue is another word for color.

1. True

2. False

Q3. Early comics were limited to 64 colors because of cost.

1. True

2. False

Q4. Which quality isn't good for a Flatting Brush?

1. Anti-aliased edges to allow blending

2. Solid color strokes

3. Brush size that's responsive to stylus pressure, so we can vary our brush size

Q5. A warm light gives us warm shadows.

1. True

2. False

Summary

What a long journey this has been, from color theory to different kinds of color palettes to creating color flats and using them to create our final colored comic page. Now we have all the tools we need to create colored pages in Manga Studio. All we need now is practice.

So, have fun with making brushes and coloring comic art. Next, we go from the world of up and down to adding depth. Yes, welcome to the 3D zone as brought to us by Manga Studio. We'll explore this zone using some of the 3D content that is included and learn how to pose a 3D figure, all within Manga Studio.

9
Adding a Third "D"

Manga Studio can use 3D objects. There are a few 3D objects that come with the program itself, in the materials palette. We'll cover some of their uses. While we won't cover how to create 3D objects, we'll investigate how to import 3D objects into Manga Studio. The topic of 3D is complex; we'll just cover the basics on using the 3D abilities of Manga Studio in this chapter.

In this chapter, we'll cover the following topics:

- ◆ The basics of 3D objects in Manga Studio
- ◆ How to place and manipulate a 3D object in Manga Studio
- ◆ Placing and posing a 3D mannequin in Manga Studio
- ◆ Creating a color-still life of 3D objects in Manga Studio

3D objects in Manga Studio

If you don't have any interest in using 3D within Manga Studio, feel free to skip this chapter. With that being said, there are uses of 3D in Manga Studio that can help us in our comic creation.

A basic primer in 3D

What we've been dealing with in Manga Studio thus far has been working in just two directions; up/down and left/right. In other words, just flat drawings. We've had encounters with x and y positioning (when importing graphics, aligning objects, and so on). We can say that we've been dealing with things on x and y axes. That's 2D. When we add depth (or the illusion of it), there's an added dimension to our work, it exists in what's called the z-axis.

We've been using coordinates all along. When we create a page that's 10 and a half inches tall, that's setting our y-axis to that height. Other raster and vector drawing apps use *x* and *y* coordinates. Manga Studio doesn't display *x* or *y* coordinates in most instances. Here's an illustration to help you understand all these Ds:

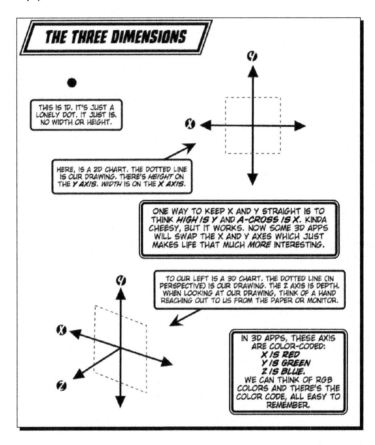

Remember Algebra? All that stuff about *x*, *y*, and *n*? This is where part of that gets applied. Drawing software such as Manga Studio may hide it, but all drawings are nothing more than huge datafiles that keep track of whether pixels are filled or not, what color the pixels are, and if the colors are RGB or CYMK. Pixel locations come in pairs, one number is located on the x-axis, and the other is located on the y-axis. A line could be described by a set of *x* and *y* coordinates to start and another pair of *x* and *y* coordinates where it ends. 3D adds the z-axis to the mix. This new axis adds depth to the data.

If that's not confusing enough, hold on. Each object in the 3D world has its own set of coordinates, their local set, if you would. And we see the image through the lens of a camera that has, you got it, its own set of coordinates.

Thankfully, Manga Studio hides a lot of this from us. It saves us time and sanity.

3D in Manga Studio 5

Beyond what we can create with the drawing tools, we cannot create 3D objects in Manga Studio. We can use objects in the **Material** palette under the **3D** tab. If we want to use custom-made 3D objects, we need to use another program. 3D programs can be somewhat pricey and always hard and involved to learn. Blender is a good solid 3D app. It's open source and is free to use. Go to `www.blender.org` to get started. Packt has an excellent book on *Blender 3D Basics for Beginners* by *Gordon Fisher*, in case you're interested. Google SketchUp is another alternative for 3D that's been used quite a bit.

In the rest of this chapter, it's best for us to be patient. The 3D objects we'll be using will slow down Manga Studio, depending on your computer system.

Dealing with 3D objects

Let's get acquainted with the options in the **Material** palette for 3D, and then we'll learn how to use the 3D stuff in *Time for action – placing and manipulating a 3D material*.

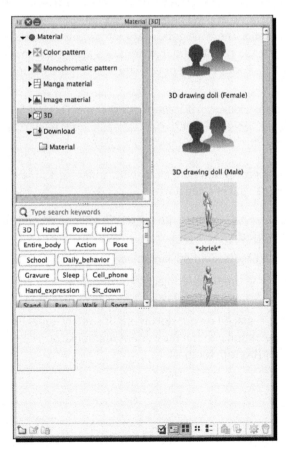

Open Manga Studio and create a new document. Open up the **Material** palette. As shown in the previous screenshot, click on the **3D** entry. Take a few moments to scan what is there under the **3D** folder. There's:

- ◆ **Body type**: Here, there's a 3D drawing doll for males and females
- ◆ **Pose**: Click on the disclosure triangle and be treated to dozens of different poses for the body and hands
- ◆ **Characters**: There's just one guy and two gals here, in the typical school-kid garb
- ◆ **Small object**: An assortment of various props
- ◆ **Backgrounds**: A limited selection of miscellaneous locations
- ◆ **Motion**: An empty folder

Locate a small object named **Mug A**. We'll be using this in the next section.

Time for action – placing and manipulating a 3D material

We'll be taking an ordinary object and getting a good idea of how to perform basic 3D operations in Manga Studio. There's a good lot of info in this exercise. A simple mug was chosen as it's easy to see the results of our actions; it's also small enough for us to get a good feel of the actions without the lag time a larger and more complex object will have.

> When working with 3D objects, moving an object is called translating or translation. Rotating used in 2D is still called rotating in 3D, but the direction and axis are usually mentioned.

We should still have Manga Studio open, along with a blank document. Save that document with the name 3dtest.lip. Let's get started.

1. With the **Material** palette open, go to the **3D** folder. Within that folder is another marked **Small objects**.

2. Inside the **Small objects** folder is an object named **Mug A**. Click on that to select it.

3. We can either drag the **Mug A** object to our document or click on the paste button on the bottom of the **Material** palette.

4. When the mug is placed on our document, it's really huge. Before we scale it down, let's look at the options on the movement manipulator (the top toolbar) and the object launcher (bottom toolbar).

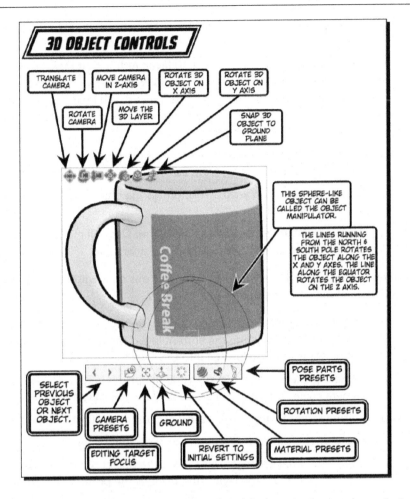

There are a lot of buttons here; let's go through them and get to know just what each one does. There are two bars on the object. The top one is called the movement manipulator; its buttons are:

- **Translate camera**: This moves the camera that we're viewing the 3D object through, up, down, left, or right. The movement doesn't change the perspective of the object.

- **Rotate camera**: This will rotate the camera on the *x* and *y* axes. The perspective of the object changes with the movement of the camera.

- **Move camera on z-axis**: This moves the camera closer to the object or further away from it.

- **Move 3D layer**: This moves the 3D layer. Although it looks like it does the same thing as the translate camera, look at the 3D grid that appears when the object is moved. The grid doesn't move. While using the translate camera, the grid moves. This will become an important distinction when we add objects to this layer.

- **Rotate 3D object on x-axis**: This rotates the object on the x-axis, like it's tipping toward us or away from us.

- **Rotate 3D object on y-axis**: This rotates the object around its center, like a spinning top.

- **Translate 3D object on the ground plane**: This will move the object on the 3D ground plane, like sliding a mug on a table.

The bottom bar is the **Object** launcher. The buttons on it will change according to the type of object that's selected.

- **Select previous or next object**: Clicking on the brackets will select the next or previous 3D object on the current layer. The order is determined by when the object is inserted/pasted into the layer.

- **Camera presets**: This brings up a grid of buttons with a visual indication of the camera angles available. Once selected, the object will change accordingly.

- **Editing target focus**: This button will center the 3D object on the canvas.

- **Ground**: This puts the object on the 3D ground plane.

- **Revert to initial settings**: This reverts the object to how it looked when it was first placed on the layer. This includes the position and rotation.

- **Material presets**: All 3D objects have what's called a material that's applied to it. This button will display other materials that the current object can have.

- **Rotation presets**: This will display buttons with icons that show various rotations, usually front, left, right, and back.

- **Pose parts presets**: If the object has moving parts, those parts have presets that this button will display. For example, a book that's open or closed, or a room with a door that can be open or shut.

The buttons that are shown depending on the kind of object selected are:

- ❏ **Register pose/Body shape**: This is used usually for the posing doll or characters. If we've come up with a pose or body shape we like, this button will save it.

- ❏ **Flip horizontal**: This is pretty much what it says.

- ❏ **Initial pose**: This will discard any changes to the pose and return to a natural pose from the first time we placed the figure on our canvas.

- ❏ **Face options**: This shows us options for the face. There may be a button for selecting the specific face and another for selecting expressions for the face.

- ❏ **Hair options**: This is used to choose different hairstyles.

- ❏ **Clothes options**: This is where different costumes are selected.

- ❏ **Accessories**: What good is fashion if we can't accessorize? Hats, cat ears, and so on are here.

- ❏ **Drawing doll options**: There are a few buttons that allow us to fine-tune the drawing doll from heroic proportions to chibi ones.

There are more options, but we have a good base of them from this list. For the rest of this exercise, do the following:

5. The top control buttons position the camera and the object itself. Now rotate the mug so the handle is on the left side.

6. Rotate the mug so that it appears to be on its side, as if it's tipped over.

7. Change the color of the mug to red (or any other color that's available) by using the material presets.

8. Click on mug and see the object manipulator appear. This is a virtual sphere that shares its center with what's been chosen as the center of the object. The arcs on this sphere are red, green, and blue. When we click and hold on one of these arcs, it turns yellow (which is hard to see on a white background), and when we move the cursor, the object rotates on that axis. Use this manipulator to place the mug back on its base.

What just happened?

We went to the **Materials** palette and placed a 3D object on our canvas. We then examined the various ways the interface allows us to manipulate the object. With this knowledge, we moved the mug to a custom position and changed its color.

Have a go hero

With a 3D object inside a layer, click on the **Tool navigation** button in the **Layer properties** palette. Look in the **Tool properties** palette settings for the 3D object. Experiment with the settings. Go to the **Tool settings** palette and see more settings and options for the object. Make the outline of the object thicker. Turn on the light source settings and make the light come from the bottom. Notice how the object is shaded. Try all of the settings to see just what they do. Hint: adjust one at a time, restore it back to what it was and move on to the next settings. When we're sure we know what each one can do by itself, adjust more than one.

Using a 3D mannequin

If we've used Poser or DAZ Studio, we know the basics on how a 3D mannequin moves and its limitations. When drawing a figure, we can exaggerate and distort our figures to fit an emotion or action. When using 3D, we're limited to the range of motion that the 3D model allows us. This can result in stiff, wooden figures. If we're using 3D figures as a way to trace over to get our proportions correct, we would be better off if we just purchased a wooden mannequin from an art store and draw from that. The advantage is that drawing from life, even from a mannequin, improves our eye. Tracing over figures gives us false confidence and awkward drawings.

 It's time to mention the mannequin in the room: QUMARION. We've seen it on the Manga Studio application menu. It's a doll that connects via a USB connection to the computer. It can be posed, and in Manga Studio, the drawing doll within the document will reflect that pose. It sounds neat and cool. But the setup costs several hundred dollars and is sold (at the time this book is being written) only in Japan. A better use for that money would be a larger graphic tablet and/or life drawing lessons. But that's just my opinion.

Time for action – posing the 3D mannequin

Although we'll be using the drawing doll, the same principles apply to the 3D characters. We'll be posing the doll as if it's waving to us or warning us of an upcoming apocalypse.

Save the document we worked on in the previous exercise. Name it MS_objects.lip. Close that document and create a new one. We're doing this because 3D is very processor-intensive, and if we pile on lots of 3D objects without saving, we run the risk of our computer getting bogged down or Manga Studio crashing and us losing work. Sometimes, Manga Studio can begin to act a bit odd when too much 3D is being done. When this happens, save your work and quit Manga Studio. Restart Manga Studio and reopen the file we were just working on.

With a shiny new document created, go to the **Materials** palette and find the drawing doll 3D object. It's inside the `Body type` folder. We'll be using the female drawing doll in this exercise, but choose whichever one you'd like.

1. Drag the drawing doll from the **Material** palette and drop it onto our document. Although we could use the **Paste** button, dragging-and-dropping works a bit better as we don't have to find a button.

2. The drawing doll fills up our canvas. That's fine, as we can easily resize it later by moving the camera in the z-axis button.

3. We want to click on the shoulder area and rotate the arm down to the doll's side, as shown in the following screenshot:

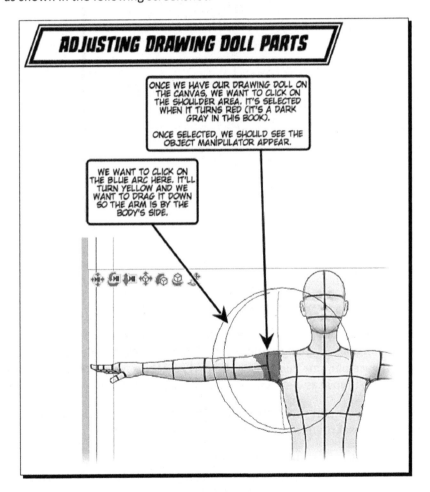

4. Now, we want to do something similar to the other arm, only this time raise it up. We're going for a waving-hello pose, remember?

5. We should end up with something my opinion shown in the following screenshot:

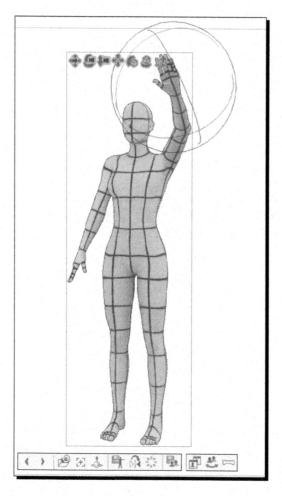

For the waving arm, we had to adjust the shoulder, forearm, hand, and back to the clavicle on the doll. Manga Studio doesn't indicate what's selected by name, so we need to take our time and choose the parts we think will work and move them. If they don't move as we want them to, we can undo it and select another part.

6. Posing hands can be time-consuming. We can avoid that hassle and frustration by using preset poses for the hands in the **Material** palette.

7. First, we click on the palm of the raised hand. The part will turn red and we'll get the object manipulator. When we move our cursor away from the hand, the red highlight will vanish. That's okay, as long as we still have the object manipulator, as that shows us something that's selected.

8. In the **Material** palette, open up the `Poses` folder in the 3D section. Go to the `Hand` folder. Within the `Hand` folder are many poses for hands. Let's say we want her to be greeting fellow metal heads, so look for a hand pose named finger sign.

9. Click on the finger sign and drag it over the hand of the doll on our canvas. Although it's not necessary to drop it over the hand, it's good for us to do so as it keeps what we're doing foremost on our minds.

10. After a moment, our doll has the hand sign we want her to have.

11. Now select the palm of the other hand and choose a relaxed pose from the **Material** palette.

12. Wave back to our canvas. We just posed a figure.

13. We can use the camera controls to make the figure smaller and dolly (move side-to-side or around) the camera so that our model doll is positioned where we want. Now if we want, we can create a new layer above it and use a pencil to draw over the model, so we can have a correctly-proportioned figure for our comics.

14. Save the document. It's an excellent idea to save after inserting a new 3D object and after inserting a pose into a 3D object. You can never, never save too many times! It's better to save a dozen times than to crash once.

What just happened?

This time, we imported a 3D mannequin and learned how to pose its body parts. We found out that each part of the body can be moved, and with some forethought and planning, we can make pretty convincing poses.

Have a go hero – posing the 3D mannequin

Now insert a character (from the **Character** folder of the **3D** folder in the **Material** palette) into a new document. Using what we just did with the drawing doll, make this character wave to us. Experiment with hairstyles and facial expressions, and don't forget accessories!

Time for action – making a scene

We've covered using a single object earlier. Now, let's add a few more objects and make it look as if they all belong together.

1. Open the scene with the mug we created earlier.

2. From the small object folder in the **3D** section of the **Material** palette, locate a pair of props that would go with the mug. In the upcoming screenshot, text, note book, and pile of books were chosen.

3. Make sure that the layer that has the mug is the current active layer. If we have any other layer active, a new 3D layer will be created. We want all three items to be on the same layer.

4. Drag the first object onto the mug layer. Don't worry about its position, we'll adjust it in a moment.

5. In the movement manipulator toolbar, click on the translate camera button and drag the cursor around. Notice how both the mug and the new object moves around? Cool, isn't it? It's a big time saver, as we only need to worry about the actual position of the second object.

6. Click on the second object so that we see the object manipulator sphere.

7. In the object launcher toolbar on the bottom of the objects, click on the **Focus on editing object** button. This ensures that we're just going to be moving around the object we just clicked on.

8. Using the object manipulator arcs, rotate the object so it looks good next to the mug. We want to just move the blue arc that rotates the object on the z-axis (remember the spinning top). We can click within the object manipulator sphere to move the object around. This may raise or lower the object, so we want to click on the **Ground** button to put the object back on the same ground plane as the mug.

9. Repeat the same procedures with the next object. We now have a nice little still life scene.

What just happened?

We used multiple objects to create a single scene. We also learned how to use the camera controls to affect all objects. By using the **Focus on editing** button, we can rotate and move individual objects without changing other objects that we want to be left alone.

Have a go hero – making a scene

Now, try to place an interior background into the canvas. Try putting it on the same layer or a new one. If the canvas turns all black, it means that the camera is inside something, so the background needs to be moved or the camera adjusted.

Manga Studio's 3D features and the future

At the time of writing this (November 2013), there's some speculation around the Manga Studio orientated 3D modeler. Details of this software will be mentioned on Smith Micro's newsletter and in the Manga Studio forum at `http://forum.runtimedna.com/forum.php`.

A search on this forum will give us a number of good posts on crafting our own 3D objects for use in Manga Studio.

As mentioned earlier, the Blender app is a good option to use to create 3D objects. Its interface is a bit confusing to the novice, but there are many tutorials that can help novices with this. The Google SketchUp is another option that's well-used by some.

For Macintosh users, there's Cheetah3D (`http://www.cheetah3d.com`), a low-cost 3D app that can be used to create 3D objects. The interface is very Mac-like and quite easy to use.

While the 3D features of Manga Studio 5 may seem to be cool, in my opinion, the 3D features are added to inflate a bullet-point list of features that leave much in the way of usability and ease-of-use, which become the talking points instead of functions used daily.

Pop quiz

Q1. The colors for the *x*, *y*, and *z* axes are like the colors for...

1. CYMK
2. RGB
3. Rulers

Q2. The *x* in *x, y, z* 3D coordinates is for depth.

1. True
2. False

Q3. In 3D, to move an object is to...

1. Rotate an object across a plane
2. Translate an object
3. Dolly an object

Q4. To use more than a single 3D object in Manga Studio, we need to...

1. Create a new document for each object
2. Create a new layer for each object
3. Insert the object in the same layer with the existing 3D object

Summary

Although Manga Studio does come with a good selection of 3D objects, using them requires a bit of planning and knowledge of how 3D works in Manga Studio. We can use the 3D out of the box, if we need to. Most times, we may find it quicker to just draw the object ourselves, as it will look like it belongs in our art.

Now, we'll leave the 3D realm, venture forward into getting our comic story out, and share it with other apps and people. We'll explore the ways we have to export our story and the many ways available to us to share it with the world.

10
Caring about Sharing

We have our page all done. Now what? Well, there's this thing called exporting that we can learn about. We can even print out our comic if we want. This chapter covers it all, from pixel size to what the heck does CYMK mean and why we should care about it. We'll look at the various ways in which we can digitally export our comic story and learn about CBZ, CBR, PDF, and ePub formats. We will use not only Manga Studio but also add Comic Life 3 and other apps into our toolbox for this penultimate chapter.

In this chapter, we will cover the following topics:

- Ways to export our art
- Formats for exporting our art
- Considerations about the destination of our art (print or pixel)
- Other programs that can help us in these endeavors

Art is just part of the process

Unless we're going to have our comic published by a publisher, it's time for us to get into some technical aspects of our job. This chapter is where our work on the comic comes together to get out into the world.

Throughout this book, we've been so caught up in making art that some finer points of what we're doing may have been understated. Let's sit back and understand what we're doing here.

Manga Studio is a means to an end, and the end of the game is to tell stories, whether it's a series of pin-ups featuring our favorite characters or our own creations, illustrations of far-off fantasy or science-fictional worlds, a comic strip, or a comic book. It's all about the story: the drama of the setting and the conflicts that the characters find themselves in. Each of the earlier examples will have different requirements at the beginning, and now, at the end, these requirements may converge, albeit for a short time, but they will all go in different directions.

In this chapter, we'll anticipate the possible needs that all these kinds of stories may require. There may be times when a second application may be needed. I am Mac-based, so apps for this operating system will be examined. Whenever possible, a Windows OS analog will be mentioned. We will have to learn the actual use of these apps, as this book cannot devote much more than a mention to apps outside of Manga Studio.

Whenever possible, do stray from the instructions. As long as we're working on a copy, the worst that can happen is that Manga Studio may not give us the results we want.

After exporting the art, we'll look at the many different ways in which we can get our work done. Some of the ways are as follows:

- Print on demand services
- The local copy store
- Web-based communities devoted to comic art and comics
- Our own web comic
- Digital versions of our work to view on computers or tablets

The real key here is to know a bit about all of the ways just mentioned. We may have our favorites, but we all need to be flexible. Now, let's get going to get our work out of our computer and into the world outside!

Exporting from Manga Studio

Like with most things that relate to computers and are digital, if we have a solid foundation to work with, our work will be easier and much less frustrating. Throughout this book, we've mentioned the need to name things, whether they're layers, documents, or folders with meaningful names, names that will describe what they are better than `Folder 1`, `Layer 1`, or `untitled.lip`. This is where all the work in naming files and folders really shows how important this concept is. The following image shows an illustration of a folder structure used for my comic story called "The Quantumneers":

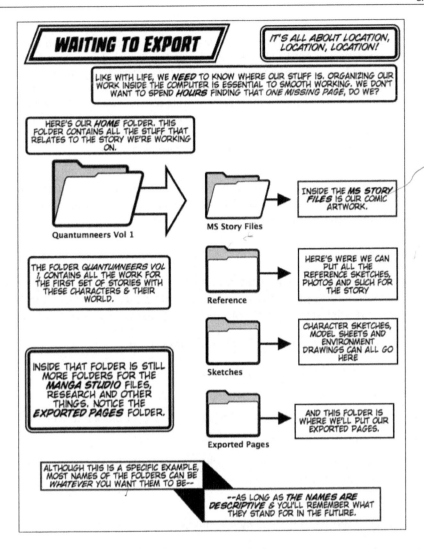

A method when organizing our work isn't just a theory or some kind of OCD thing; it's a good work habit to get into. It will save us a lot of trouble as we create more stories and artwork.

In one of my hard drives, there's a folder named `Comic stories`. Within this folder are many different folders that mirror the setup in the previous screenshot. The advantage of subfolders is that the stories (or series) are laid out in a way that makes it quick and easy to find the one story that we want to work on.

As an artist, I attend a lot of local Northern California comic and Manga conventions in Artist's Alley. The pre-con preparation is always at the last moment, and after a few times of staying up way too late printing out art to sell, I spent some time organizing my work and planning out what to sell. It became really easy to see the art that I want to bring with me, without the hassle of figuring out where I put that one file (which is always not where I thought it was). So, I was able to cut down on the time wasted in searching and put that time towards actual preparation for the convention.

As usual, with anything digital, make backups regularly. Don't just rely on the cloud to store backups. The Internet will go down just when we need it most. Invest in a few 4 GB (or larger) flash drives to use as backups.

Paper or pixels

Part of getting our art out of Manga Studio is deciding which media we want. If it's for a web comic or a digital comic, it's pixels all the way. If we want a tangible object, whether it's a printed comic or art print, it still begins with pixels regardless of the final form of the work.

We should review the entire process of our comic work so far:

- Idea of the work, story, plotting, and character work.
- Scripting and page layouts.
- Penciling, lettering, inking, and coloring (or toning for black and white comics).
- Review and proofreading (this is where we're now).
- Artwork pre-press: getting the artwork/story ready to be printed or distributed via the Web or online stores.
- Promotion of our work.
- Go back to step 1 and start all over again for the next issue or graphic novel.

Let's examine what's involved in review and proofreading.

Proofing and reviewing the work

In a prose novel, this stage would be where the novel is read by a proofreader, and errors in spelling, punctuation, and grammar are noted. However, this is a comic, and there's an additional level of proofing to do, that is, reviewing the work. Ideally, we should have our comic read by somebody else to catch as many errors as possible, to point out whether our storytelling (panel-to-panel continuity, how the story is understood by the reader) is working or not, and to catch things such as thumbs being on the wrong side of a hand, and unexpected costume changes. Ideally, this kind of review should be done at various stages of the comic's completion, such as when it's penciled and lettered, before it gets inked. It's easier to correct our pencils than to have to redo pencils and then re-ink. As far as the lettering goes, often when the text is corrected, our balloons or caption boxes may need to be resized. This is best done before we ink our work.

Tips and hints about spelling and grammar

If we're using Manga Studio to letter our comic, keep in mind that Manga Studio doesn't have spell check. If we've written our script on a modern word processor, spell check it in that app and then copy and paste it into the text block in Manga Studio.

Here's a tip to avoid incurring the wrath of the grammar police (oh, they are out there, trust me). Use contractions properly! This means using "you're" instead of "your" when you mean "you are." You're and "your" may sound the same, but they are two different words.

"You're" is a contraction of "you are". For example, "you are serious" becomes "you're serious" and not "your serious." If we're not batman, we cannot possess seriousness.

"Your" is a possessive pronoun. An apple that belongs to you is "your apple" and not "you're apple." If we expand this contraction, it reads as "you are apple", which makes little sense if we're talking about the fruit.

The same applies for "it's" and "its".

"It's" is a contraction of "it is", so "it is time" becomes "it's time".

"Its" is a possessive, nongender specific pronoun. An object that has lost the marbles that it contains can be said to "have lost its marbles."

An excellent way to avoid these mistakes is to read the sentence out loud and substitute the word (you're, your, it's and it is) with the two words. If it sounds wrong, chances are you're using the incorrect version. Both these words sound the same, but when reading the word as an expanded contraction, we can get a better feel of the correct way.

Do check out the book, *Elements of Style*, by *Strunk and White, published by Dover Publications Inc.*, for a great concise primer on grammar. Our readers will thank us for it. This is because in the end, we are responsible for what's written.

Sometimes, we won't be able to have a reader review our work. This is not optimal, as authors make the worst proofreaders. We get used to mistakes that we make often. In these cases, let the comic cool off by leaving it alone for a few days (or a week, if we have the time). Then, when we get back to it, it'll be new to our eyes and mistakes will just pop up at us.

Flip the artwork horizontally using the button in the command bar. Often, mistakes will become a lot clearer when reversed.

One thing to always keep in mind is that no matter how much we try, mistakes will always avoid detection until we have them printed out. Then, we can correct them, so the second printing will not have them.

Now that we have our work reviewed and proofread, we're ready to prepare the work, so it can be printed. If we want to get all fancy like a graphic designer, we can call this "pre-press."

Printing our comic

There are three ways we could do this. They are as follows:

- Print the comic on our own printer
- Using a local copy store to print out the comic
- Go online and use a print on demand (POD) print service

Each one of these methods has advantages and problems. We'll examine them as we go.

Using our home printer

Think of a DVD player. It's a digital medium, and the picture is perfect. Now, imagine watching "The Incredibles" on a small-screen, black and white, 70s television. It's not very pretty.

The same thing goes, not as far though, for printers. As a general rule, if the printer can output decent photographs, then it should do well printing out our work, especially if it's color. The second most important thing, apart from printers, is paper. While copy paper is fine for e-mails and text, we need something a bit more sturdier for artwork. Since we'll be printing out artwork, it will saturate the page with ink (or toner if you're using a laser printer), and if we use inexpensive paper, it will buckle and get more wrinkly than our great-aunt Agnes.

If you're serious about printing out your work, for sale or just to show around, always have a spare set of ink cartridges with you. We will always run out of ink at 2 p.m. in the morning, and the only place we can get ink is from a 24-hour store and the price is probably much higher than where we usually get the ink from. Be on the lookout for sales and specials for ink cartridges and stock up if we can. Don't go too crazy though; inkjet printer ink does have a shelf life. It may be better to buy just what we need and not have to throw out unused cartridges because they aren't good. Keep all receipts and maybe we can get a replacement. Some office supply stores will give in-store credit for recycling used cartridges, so keep the empties. One last tidbit: depending on how we use color, there will be a specific color we will use less than the others. In my case, it is yellow. This is where using the recycling program makes the pain of getting rid of an old but unused cartridge a bit less.

Since there are many different printers out there, it'll be insane to cover them all, so let's just look at the basic Manga Studio page.

Time for action – setting up printing at home

Right off, most inkjet printers will print just fine from an RGB file, so there's no need to convert to CYMK, as the printer driver will just convert the CYMK back to RGB and then to it's own interpretation of CYMK. So, instead of muddying up the colors with unnecessary conversions, just use the RGB from Manga Studio to print from.

We need to start with a colored Manga Studio file. If we're just printing out a black and white copy (with tones or gray-scale fills), we don't need to worry about color, of course. In this case, we just need to set our printer dialog to print black and white documents. Otherwise, we could get printouts that have a bluish tint.

1. With our document open, navigate to **File | Print settings**. We'll see a dialog box with many options.

2. Next, we'll hit the highlights of this dialog box.

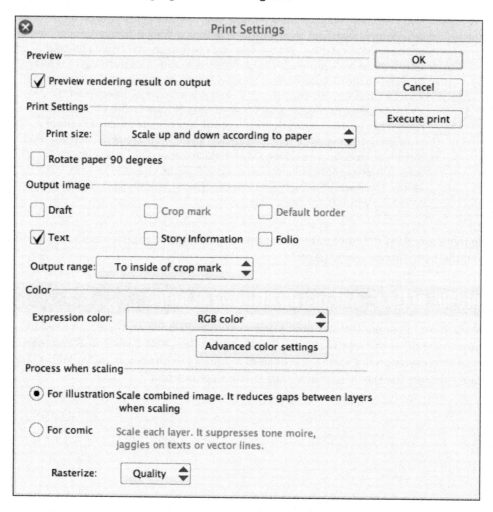

3. Under **Preview**, check **Preview rendering result on output**, as it'll give us a representation of what our page will look like before it gets printed. This way, we can stop the printing if something is wrong and correct it.

4. The **Print size** settings comprise the following options:

- **Same as detail**
- **Scale up and down according to paper**
- **Pixel size**
- **Dual page**
- **Spread**

5. For most printing, we can use **Scale up and down according to paper**. This will allow us to print on large and small sizes of paper by letting Manga Studio and the printer driver do the scaling.

6. Under **Output image**, if we have layers that are set as a draft layer and we want that layer to print out, the **Draft** checkbox should be checked. Except for **Folio**, the other options are self explanatory. That seems to do very little, or whatever it does is pretty hidden.

7. The **Output Range** comprises the following options:

- **Full page**
- **To offset of crop mark**
- **To inside of crop mark**

8. If our art extends to the very edges of the document and we want to print all of it, then we'll choose **Full page**. If we want to crop to the active area or what's called the Manga draft area, we'll want to choose either **To inside of crop mark** or **To offset of crop mark**. Although the terminology is different (and it would be of great help if Celsys would standardize on it), we can just think about what the terms used mean and what we want to do in order to select the right one.

 A quick and easy way to avoid all this confusing terminology is to create a layer above all others in the document. In this new layer, select the area that we want to print, invert it, and fill the new selection with white (make sure its pure white; any tints will get printed). Then, in this **Print setup**, choose full page, and things should get printed without any issues. This could be set up as an auto-action.

9. The options in **Expression color** are as follows:

- **Auto detect appropriate color depth**: Manga Studio will decide the best method to print out the work.
- **Duo tone**: This isn't like other implementations of **Duo tone**, where there's one (or two) color/s and tints of that color. In the world of Manga Studio, **Duo tone** means black and white, not grays.

- ❑ **Gray**: Prints a gray scale version of the illustration.

- ❑ **RGB color**: Prints the image with the RGB values that the printer translates into its own printing colors. This gives the best results for printing out color illustrations in Manga Studio.

10. For **Expression color**, choose the selection that best matches our piece. If we're not sure, choose **Auto detect** and let Manga Studio decide. Choose **RGB color** if our work is in color and **Gray** if it's in gray scale or uses tones with no colors.

11. Let's click on **Advanced color settings** and see whether there's anything we can use.

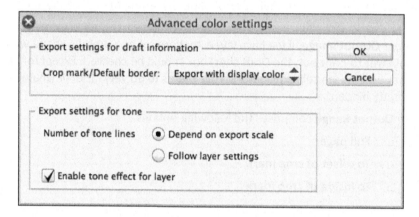

12. Strangely enough, the most important settings here have very little to do with actual color.

13. The first area, **Export settings for draft information**, refers to the active area and trim borders on the page. If we have the checkbox in the main **Print settings** dialog checked, we can change how these lines are printed. The **Crop mark/Default border** drop-down menu determines how these lines are printed. The **Crop mark/Default border** drop-down menu has following options:

- ❑ **Export with display color**: This will print out the page border/active area borders in the color that we have set it to in **Preferences**.

- ❑ **Export with black**: This prints out the borders in black.

- ❑ **Export with cyan**: This exports the borders as cyan (actually close to non-photo blue). It is a good setting if we're printing out penciled pages for analog inking (in which case, the penciled pages also need to be printed out in non-photo blue).

14. The next section, **Export settings for tone**, will affect how tones are printed out. The wrong choice here may result in poor tone printing. Of the two choices, **Depend on export scale**, may be the best for our needs. However, **Follow layer settings** may work best for settings that have been tweaked by us. Make sure that **Enable tone effects for layer** is checked, so any layer tone effects will get printed.

15. The final area of **Print settings** is a choice between two ways of processing the work:

- ❑ **For illustration**
- ❑ **For comic**

16. The main difference between these is how things get scaled for printing. **For illustration** combines the images (all layers merged) and then scaled down. **For comic** will do each layer separately and then combine them. If we don't use many tones, then the **For illustration** setting is good to choose. If we use a lot of tones, then the **For comic** setting could help us if we're experiencing a lot of jaggies and moire patterns.

 If we want to get clever, we can just rasterize all tone layers in our work. This will make tones a bit better for printing; in some cases, it may make the tones slightly fuzzy, which may be a good effect.

17. The final setting is a drop-down menu choice among **Rasterize**, **Fast**, and **Quality**. If we are just printing out a copy for proofing, **Fast** is good to use. Otherwise, opt for **Quality**.

What just happened?

Even without using features that are unique to our specific printer, there's a lot to keep track of when printing out from Manga Studio. Keep in mind that each printer is different, and we may have to adjust the steps to give us the best printout that our printer can. Be sure to check out any area in the dialog boxes that may contain printer-specific options that may make the difference between a bad printout and an excellent one.

Using our home printer to produce multiple copies of a comic may not be the best option, as we can burn through ink cartridges quite quickly. For color prints, our printer may work just fine for a small number of copies (five to ten copies of a print). However, what do we do when we want to print out more than one copy of our comic? We'll have to leave our studio, venture out into the world, and go to a copy store.

Using a copy store

We would go to a copy store, such as FedEx Office (formerly Kinko's), giving the clerk a file (on CD-ROM or flash drive) and having them print it out. Here, the main thing to keep in mind is that we have to make our work as simple as possible so that very little is left to chance.

We're just exploring a copy store, not going to an offset printer. While the principles are pretty much the same, if we are going to use an offset printer, it's best to contact them directly and see what their requirements are. Some will accept digital files, while others do best with a print out that they will take a special photo of (called a Photostat) and then use it to make a printing plate to print with. Offset printing is costly, and the results can be stunning. However, copy stores and print on demand services are rapidly overtaking offset printing for most (if not all) Indy creators, because the quality of these services are approaching those of offset printing.

If we're going to a copy store, then we should be printing multiple copies (more than two comic books worth) that would be way too expensive to print out on our home printer. The main advantage of going to a local copy store is that we can get our copies within a few hours or a day or so.

When we're printing out black-and-white copies, there's little to go wrong. If it's color, insist on looking at a sample printout before the actual print run begins. Most copy stores will do this without any hassle. If they resist, go someplace else.

If we live near a college or business park, go to a copy store that's far from these places. The reason is because those printers are used more often and may not give good (to us) results. We want our copies to look as good as possible, and this is a challenge if the copiers we're using have already been heavily used. See, the more use a copier gets, the more likely it may do, what's called, solarization. That's when a large solid black area goes all white and spotty in the center. This is not good for us, not at all.

If there's no other choice, then use the machines well before mid-terms (when papers would be due) or prior to the fiscal quarters (when the suits would need to print out reports for investors). The beginning of the week is best, as realtors would be doing their print jobs near the end of the week, prior to the weekend when they would be showcasing houses. Just like good comedy, it's all in the timing.

When in doubt, ask the clerk which machine would give the best results for our art. You'd be surprised how helpful they can be (mostly because they themselves could be struggling artists like us).

So, how do we make sure what we give to the copy store is as foolproof as possible? This is the focus of the following *Time for action – exporting for copy stores* section.

Time for action – exporting for copy stores

Our art for this section is black and white, using a page of 10.5 x 7 inch that we created way back in *Chapter 2*, *Messsing Around with Manga Studio 5* (ah, those were simpler times). We may have used some tones and/or gray scale shading for this.

1. Our document(s) should be opened. Each page will save its own print settings, so double-check that the settings are either the same or exactly what you want.

2. Usually we can export TIFF files, and most copy stores will accept them. We should either have a flash drive or a DVD/CD-ROM burner, so we can copy the files to either one of those types of media.

3. On the hard drive where we have our comic, we should make sure there's a folder that is dedicated to use just for the exported images, like in the first image in this section. Having a folder with just the exported images is good, as we can just drag-and-drop the entire folder onto the flash drive or disc burner software. The better organized our work is, the less likely we are to forget something.

4. With all of this done and checked, we navigate to the **File menu** | **Export (Single layer)** and select the **tiff (.TIFF)** menu item. Make a note of the other kinds of formats that are available, especially the PNG format that we'll be using later in this chapter.

5. Manga Studio will then ask us where we want to save the file. Navigate to where the export folder for the story is, select that folder, and click on the **OK** button.

6. Now we're presented with a dialog box with oodles of options, as shown in the following screenshot:

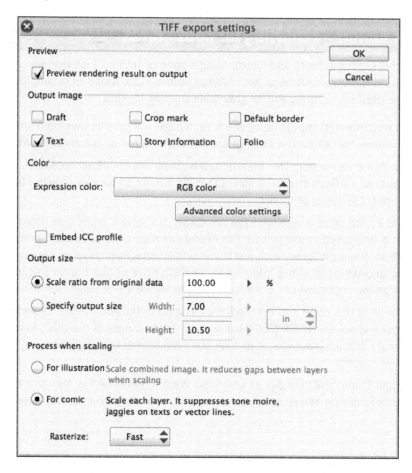

7. This dialog looks a lot like the **Print settings** dialog box. It shares a lot of options with that settings dialog, except for the output size.

8. Check the **Preview** checkbox. This will open up a large dialog box that will have an approximation of what the file will look like when exported.

9. In the **Output image** option, check the options that we want, to print. In this example, **Text** is the only option that we want to export.

10. In the **Color** section, for **Expression color**, we'll choose **Gray** from the drop-down menu. If we were working on color, then we'll use **RGB color**.

11. Select the **Embed ICC profile** checkbox by navigating to **Preferences | Color conversion**. Here, we can choose a profile for the colors. Adobe 1998 is a good selection. The RGB is a good setting, but it tends to be geared more towards a one-size-colors-all setup and may not be good for intensive color work.

12. For **Output size**, we can either set a percentage or specify an output size. If we did our homework correctly, the work is already of the correct size. Usually, the copiers used by copy stores can deal with any dpi and reduce it automatically to the best resolution for the copiers.

13. Under **Process when scaling**, **For Comic** should work well for black and white printing.

14. The **Rasterize** option should be on **Quality** for the best results.

15. Click on the **OK** button.

16. The **Preview** window dialog will appear. It's okay if it looks a bit grainy or aliased. Zoom in to 100 and it will look a bit aliased with stair steps. This is okay for printing to a digital copier. It can't print grays; it will automatically produce its own halftones for visually simulating grays. This will give us nice crisp lines when printed.

17. Click on the **OK** button on the preview. The file is saved in the location we specified.

18. Repeat the preceding steps for every page.

What just happened?

Although we went through many steps, each is needed to give us the proper files that we need so that a copy store can print them out correctly. As we do this more often, these steps will become our second nature. We may find that some steps can be avoided (such as preview image) and some can be changed (such as the ICC profile). Only with regular use and experimentation can we streamline our workflow, so it'll work with the store we're using.

Now, all that remains is to copy the files to a flash drive or burn them to a CD-ROM/DVD and take it to the copy store.

Going for print on demand

When using a POD service, the best thing to do is to read and follow the instructions and requirements that the specific service requires. Some will only take PDFs, others will accept TIFF files. When dealing with color files, most will accept RGB files and the odd few will take CYMK only.

The next best thing for us to do when using a POD service is to have patience. If we're making comics for a convention or other event, we should send out our POD order at least a month (or two) in advance, especially if we're ordering close to a major comic con, such as the San Diego or New York comic con. When we plan these things out, we don't need to pay to expedite the order, which is very costly and ensures that we'll lose more money than we need to.

Now, the insistence on following a template (way, way back in *Chapter 1, Installing and Setting Up Manga Studio 5*, and *Chapter 2, Messing Around with Manga Studio 5*) pays off big time. Since we followed a specified template, all we need to do is just hit the export menu command, export our files as TIFF, and we're done! If we did our work at 600 dpi, we'll need to reduce it down to 300 dpi (mostly to keep the file size down, as we'll be sending the files to a remote server). As good as Manga Studio is for laying out, drawing, inking, and coloring our comics, it's not really an image editor in the sense of changing the dots/pixels per inch for a document. Manga Studio will get rid of all the active area and crop area guides when the resolution is changed.

When we export our image, we need to reduce it by 50 percent. We'll also need to open the exported file in an image editor (such as GIMP and Photoshop) and change the image size to the size we want at 300 dpi. This is basically changing the way the data of the image is displayed and isn't changing anything with respect to the actual pixels.

- Keep in mind when exporting pages that have text or lettering, you should rasterize the text before exporting it:
    - In the **Layers** palette, make a copy of the text layer
    - Then, right-click on **New layer** and choose **Rasterize** from the contextual menu
    - Now, just hide the original text layer

This way, we can be sure that the text will export the way we want it to. Manga Studio has a habit of doing wacky things to the text when exporting, and by rasterizing a copy of the text, we make sure it won't happen. Hidden layers won't export, so we can always change the original text if there's a typo and make a copy of the changed text and rasterize it.

The process of exporting for a POD is exactly like the one for a copy store.

As we see, all the planning that we did prior to our actual drawing saves us a lot of time when printing out our comic. Now, what about putting our work on the Internet?

Web comics and other Internet graphics

While Manga Studio doesn't allow us to create slices (like Photoshop and other image editing apps allows us to), we can export specific pixel dimensions. So, open up a Manga Studio file and let's export it out.

Time for action – exporting for the Web

Before we begin, let's set some guidelines:

- The resolution is 72 pixels per inch. While some monitors may be 96 PPI or in the case of retina displays, they can range from 220 PPI to 326 PPI for desktop and tablets, we can use 72 PPI as our base to figure out how large we want our image to be.

One thing about the new high-definition computer and retina displays of tablets is that the resolution of the displays matches the print quality (more than 200 pixels per inch). We are given more freedom to create high-definition artwork that isn't as tied to the 72 or 92 pixels per inch of monitors of yesterday. We can be secure by the fact that our art will be scaled to the right size by the browser or operating system that the reader is using. Of course, there may be a few who are still using older systems, but sometimes, we have to sacrifice a few readers in order to make things nicer for the rest of us.

- Some image-sharing site may have restrictions on the size for both the dimensions and the file size of the image. Get the maximum dimensions and see how our art can fit into it. It may require some cropping, which may be best done in another app. Some WordPress blog plugins (like ComicPress and ComicEasel) allow flexibility in the size of the uploaded image.

- We need to balance the way the image will look on the Web versus the file size. If the file size is too large, it'll take forever (which takes about 4-5 seconds on the Web) to load up on the browser. If we're using our own hosted website, this can significantly increase our bandwidth and could incur additional costs from our web-hosting provider.

- If the preceding points make no sense to you, it will become understandable in time. The Web, as usual, is in a state of flux, and it's up to us as content creators to keep up with the current state of things on the Internet.

It may be our second nature to use JPG format as the export format for our Manga Studio files. The file size may be smaller, but if we need to edit files, the JPG format will make the revised files look inferior, because JPG is a Lossy format. Information is being dumped to save file size. If you export your work in the PNG or TIFF format, they don't dispose of data and will look crisp and sharp, no matter how many times you resave the files.

1. Navigate to **File | Export (Single Layer)** and choose **png (.PNG)**.

2. Choose the folder where we want to save our web-exported images.

3. In the **Export settings**, use the same settings we used earlier.

4. Under **Output size**, click on the **Specify output size** radio button.

5. In the drop-down menu to the right, choose **PX** from the options. PX stands for pixels, and that's what we're concerned with here.

6. The numbers we enter in the **Width** and **Height** are linked. This means that when we enter in a number in either one, the other will change to keep our exported image proportional. Depending on what kind of comic we're exporting (comic strip or comic page), the width can be anywhere between 700 to 1025 or more pixels wide.

However, what about retina displays? In this case, we can double the width of the site we're posting the work on. If the limit is 800 pixels wide, then just double it to 1600 pixels. In the web page code, just make sure that the image width is set to 800 pixels wide. The browser will resize the image to fit the display. If people zoom in on the image, they will see more detail, and our art will still look great. A number of web comics are beginning to do this and it can work well.

7. Next, in **Process when scaling**, choose **For illustration**, as this will alias the lines and give some smoothness to the exported image. Since all displays can show grays and colors, having aliased edges here will look bad.

8. **Rasterize** is set to **Quality**.

9. Click on **OK**.

10. In the preview, look at the image at 100 percent to see if it'll work. If it doesn't, click on **Cancel**, go back through this section, and change the settings so that you get a better image. (The **Output size** can be changed; sometimes a difference of 10 pixels or so can make a difference or switch the **Process** for scaling.) If it looks fine, click on **OK** and we're done.

11. Rinse, lather, and repeat the preceding steps for all pages of the story.

What just happened?

We learned that printing out to pixels is much like printing out to paper. Except that in this case, we're controlling most of the printing. We have a set of nice PNG files that we can now put on the Web or put into other files for reading.

Other ways to display

In the introduction to this chapter, files such as CBZ, CBR, PDF, and ePub were mentioned. Here's a brief rundown.

CBZ and CBR

The CBZ and CBR formats are nothing more than a group of image files inside a folder that's been compressed with a ZIP or RAR compression. Yes, they are either a ZIP or RAR compressed file. The name of each file needs to end with a number and then the extension. So, the first page of a story that's been exported as a PNG file would be `Page_001.png`. The next page would be `Page_002.png` and so on. The name of the original folder would be the name of the comic story or comic book issue. The folder is compressed (usually, it's zipped, as this is more common) and the extension is changed from ZIP to CBZ or RAR to CBR (if we're using the RAR compression). These files can be read by a comic viewer. A search for comic viewers should bring up a number of good apps (most are free or low cost) to view CBR/CBZ files.

PDF

To create a PDF, we'll need the TIFF files (like what we created in the copy store section) and an application that can create PDF files.

ePub

These are files that are created either by hand or by a program (such as comic life, which can also export CBZ and PDF files), and the `.epub` files can be read by iBook on iOS and Android devices. If we want, we can learn more about ePubs through a good search. ePubs are zipped folders that contain XML/HTML files and images. ePubs can not only contain static images and text, but they can also contain videos on iPads and iPhones. This is awesome but something we'll experiment with outside this book. If we use comic life, we can export our comics in the ePub format.

Applications other than Manga Studio

Even though there are many different computer displays and tablets, we can be sure that when printing to the Internet, what we see is pretty much what others will see. This is one area where precise pixel measurements are very important. We'll have to crop, expand our canvas area, and/or resize our image easily and quickly. Unfortunately, Manga Studio is lacking in this area, as it was primarily designed to be an app only for printing. We're not saying that Manga Studio cannot do these things, but in the process, we lose much of what it can do as far as outputting files for printing is concerned.

The main issue here is that we're drawing larger images (because one of our goals is to have a hard copy printable version) than the images of the comic that will appear within the web page. The resolution is different; we're working at 300-600 dpi and most displays and tablets use various resolutions as we learned earlier. There are many different apps we can use as a way to post-process our comics. Some possibilities (that won't bust our budget) are as follows:

- **Sketchbook pro**: This is a modestly priced app that also has a free version that we can use. It's excellent for resizing and cropping. It uses a nonstandard interface, but with some learning, it can be used well with Mac OS and Windows.

- **ArtRage**: This is another painting app that uses a nonstandard interface (it resembles Sketchbook pro). It does have a trial version that can be used to see if it works for us. It can be used with Mac OS and Windows.

- **Pixelmator**: This is a Mac-only app and is truly a replacement for Photoshop. It's the app of choice of the author. It can resize and crop images very well in an easy-to-use interface.

The key thing to keep in mind here is the difference between **Canvas size** and **Image size**. **Canvas size** is what we draw on; **Image size** is the size of the image itself. If we make the **Canvas size** larger or smaller, it changes the size of what we draw on, not the drawing itself. **Image size** will scale the entire image up or down.

When we're using these other apps, we need to always use exported images from Manga Studio as our source files. This way, if we make changes to the art itself, it's done in Manga Studio and then exported out to these other apps for website processing.

It's good practice to create a folder to hold our exported images and then make a copy of that folder (and its contents) and work with the copied images to make changes. This way, if we mess up (and we will), we can just make a copy of the original file and carry on. It's better to have too many copies and not need them than to not have any copies when we need them.

Getting the word (and pictures) out

Now, we have our comic printed on paper or pixels. We need to tell people about it. Posting on a social art-sharing site (such as DeviantArt and NewGrounds) is a good start. Setting up a Twitter account just for your comics is another way. Google+ is fast becoming a more-than-adequate replacement for Facebook, and since it's tied in with YouTube, we could create a brief video about our comic and post it on YouTube and Google+.

We shouldn't expect to see an immediate response. It is like a plant. We're just planting the seeds now, and it takes time before the plant grows enough to have fruit.

When using social media, don't over-promote the work. This means just participating in threads and conversations that have little to do with your work. Then, share the rough sketches and finished work as a post or tweet. You'll find that with a bit of time, you'll gain followers and potential consumers of your art.

Another option is to check out local comic/manga/anime conventions. Local cons tend to be smaller, less expensive than other larger and established conventions. Most don't have too many big name guests. This means that there's less of a hurdle in getting some notice. When attending these cons, we need to be social so that we're friendly and approachable. Don't attend cons and expect to make money; we're there (for now) to gain attention and to make people aware of us.

Keeping the momentum

As if all in this chapter wasn't enough, we need to keep working on new issues, new stories, and new art. As Indy artists, we need to do it all: Creating the work, printing it out, and promoting it. Although people will take us seriously when we complete one issue of a comic, when we follow it up with a number two issue, they know we're here to stay.

Pop quiz

Q1. JPG is an excellent export format because it doesn't lose any information.

1. True
2. False

Q2. When exporting comics for the Web, we can export our art at more than 72 pixels per inch.

1. True
2. False

Q3. When using a home printer, it doesn't matter what kind of paper we use.

  1. Yes

  2. No

  3. Maybe, depends on what we're using the printout for

Q4. It's always worth it to have a print on demand order rushed.

  1. Yes

  2. No

Summary

Being able to output our art in ways that display it well and make us look good is as important as what we put into Manga Studio. We covered both printing at home and at external locations (copy stores and PODs) along with exporting for digital displaying. So, the reason why we spent so much time in creating those templates at the beginning of the book becomes clear. It makes printing and exporting our work that much easier.

Next is the final chapter where we look at Manga Studio 5 EX and other uses for Manga Studio. This should be fun. See you there.

11
One More Thing

In keeping with the trend of having a regular version and a pro version of the same, Manga Studio has Manga Studio EX. This EX (for Expert) edition gives us the ability to have one file reference to multiple pages, thus giving us stories. The other features allow us to perform batch processing and export files.

In this chapter, we will look at the following features of Manga Studio 5 EX:

- Story files
- Mass importing of files
- Mass exporting of files
- Batch processing, for example, adding layers to each page

We'll explore each of these and some more features in this chapter. We will get a good feel of the power that Manga Studio EX can give us to automate repetitive tasks and gain time for more drawing.

Manga Studio 5 EX

A few months after the release of Manga Studio 5, Manga Studio 5 EX was released. This was part of one of the updates of Manga Studio. The EX version isn't a separate program as it is unlocked by an upgrade license registration code. We can go to the **Manga Studio** menu and select **Register license** when we receive the license registration code, as shown in the following screenshot:

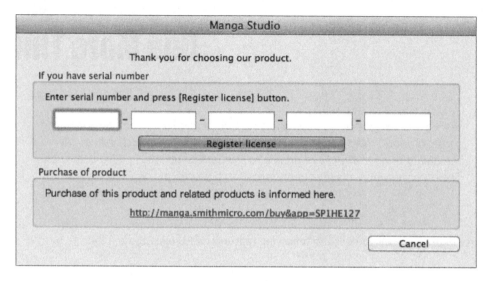

 As of this time (spring 2014), Celsys, the creator of Manga Studio, has denied Smith-Micro the ability to sell digital downloads of any Manga Studio 5 products. So any new purchases (and upgrades) have to be through a physical disc and box that will be shipped to you. Fortunately, updates and bug fixes are still distributed through downloaded files.

Once the code is entered, click on the **Register license** button. We'll be taken to a page-sized dialog where we can register through the Internet. Once that's done, the dialog vanishes and we should get a message box that says we need to restart Manga Studio to use the new features.

We should keep the old license code, as we can switch between the plain and EX versions of Manga Studio by just registering the other code and redoing this procedure.

 Although the interface of the screenshots in this chapter look just like those of Manga Studio, they are different from Manga Studio EX. So don't expect your dialogs to look like the ones shown here if you aren't using Manga Studio EX.

Once Manga Studio has restarted as Manga Studio EX, the interface looks basically the same, except for a **Story** menu. This is where we can set up a Manga Studio Story file, with the extension of CMC, which can contain well over a hundred pages. Other features of EX are batch import, export, and processing. In the **Interface** panel of **Preferences**, we can adjust the look of the interface to be either the light color we're used to or a new jazzy darker interface, which shouldn't be confused with the tone of most US comics.

While it may seem that features may be somewhat lacking with respect to an expert version of an app, they do save a lot of time, and will be more than worth the cost of the upgrade, especially if we're doing production work on a tight deadline where any time we can save allows us more time for drawing.

Stories

Instead of going into the Story menu, we can create a story file using the **New Document** menu item or the **New document control bar** button.

Time for action – starting a story

If you have Manga Studio EX, open it. If you don't have EX, then sit back, read this chapter, and see what it can do.

What we want to do in this section is to create a story. As far as Manga Studio EX is concerned, a story is a folder that contains many LIP files (the basic Manga Studio page files), and a CMC file, which is the Manga Studio story management file. The CMC file keeps track of which file is on which page (as we can move pages around in EX), how many pages are there in the story, and if pages are spread (two pages that are combined together to be one large page).

Just like a journey is begun with the first step, the first step in making our stories is to click on the **New Page** icon in the control bar. We'll get the usual dialog, but towards the bottom of the dialog box there's a checkbox labeled **Multiple pages**. Click on this checkbox to activate it and you'll get new options, as shown in the following figure:

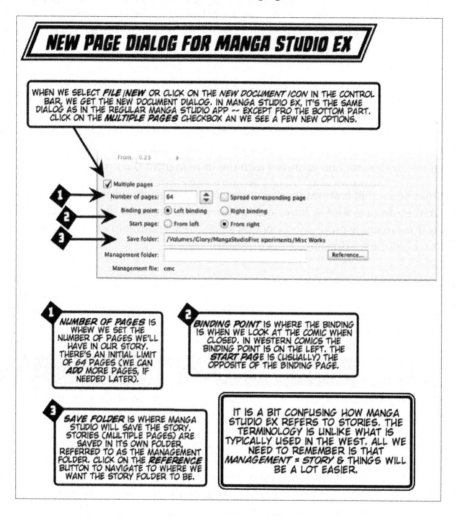

After getting more options, we need to perform the following steps:

1. We should have a rough idea of how many pages we want our story to be. Since this is an exercise, let's try to see the limits of what EX can do, so enter in **120** in the **Number of pages** section.

2. The **Spread corresponding page** checkbox should be unchecked.

3. As the preceding figure indicates, the **Binding point** and **Start page** options should be the opposite of each other for most cases. Since we're doing a western comic, the binding point should be **Left binding** and the start page should be **From right**. Grab a comic and look at the cover. What side is the staple (or binding, if it's a trade paperback) on? Yup, it's the left side. Now, open it. What side is the first page of the book on? It's the right side, isn't it? Sometimes, if we're in doubt, all we need to do is to look at a physical copy of something and things get cleared up.

4. The next section is somewhat upside down. As it is, the **Save folder** parameter will be updated when we choose the **Management Folder** value. Although we can type in this textbox, there's no real need to, since we can just click on the **Reference...** button and navigate to where we want to save our story.

5. Click on the **Reference...** button.

6. This brings up an open dialog box for our operating system. We can navigate to where we want our story to be, and create a folder for our story to be within. Let's name the folder OurGreatSeries.

7. Once we have our folder created, we can click on the **Open** button. This doesn't open anything, it merely selects the folder we created (or chose) in the previous step. We can see this because the **Save folder** textbox now reflects the path to where our story folder is.

8. In the **Management folder** textbox, we can type in the name of our story or issue number. We can just type in OGS Issue 01. Notice that below the textbox, the **Management folder** textbox now has OGS Issue 01.cmc after it.

9. We need to know that Manga Studio EX will now create a folder within the folder we chose/created when we clicked on the **Reference...** button with the name we put into the **Management folder** textbox. Within the management folder, a CMC file with the same name as that of our value in the **Management Folder** field will be created. It sounds confusing, but once we've created a few stories, it'll make sense.

10. Now, we go to the top-right part of the dialog box, double checking that the page size, active area, and Bleed are what we want, or that we have the page template we want to use selected in the **Preset** drop-down menu. Don't do this in a hurry. Take a few moments to make sure that all the information is exactly the way we want it to be.

11. Now we can click on the **OK** button in the top-right part of the dialog box.

12. Manga Studio EX will take a few moments to create all the LIP files for our story and the CMC file too. Once all the files have been created, we'll see a window with all the pages viewed as thumbnails. This is the Story Manager window; we'll take a look at it in the *Time for action – the Page Manager window* section.

What just happened?

In a dozen steps, we created a collection of files that Manga Studio EX will treat as a story. We discovered that by checking **Multiple pages** in the **New** dialog box. We are given options to set the number of pages that this story can have, where the story will live in our hard drive, along with the name of the folder and the CMC file that contains our story files and story information.

If we're observant, we should notice that even though we entered 120 for the number of pages for our story, it changed to 100 once we clicked outside the page number textbox. Usually, we'll get some form of alert if we enter in a number that's too large. Unfortunately, Manga Studio (all versions) will just change numbers to what it thinks it should be (as in the case for setting up **Bleed**) or the maximum (like with our setting the pages to 120) without any interaction with us. Without any alerts, we won't have any idea if the 100-page count is a limitation or just an arbitrary number. We can hope this limitation will be lifted or increased with an update that's released after this book is printed. But the important thing is that we can add many more pages if we want, and that's what we'll do when we see what the Story Manager window does.

Time for action – the Page Manager window

This is where a lot of the added functionality for EX exists. The Page Manager window allows us to see every page in our story. Once we've laid out and roughed in our story, we can consider the page thumbnails in the context of the story, and see how the story flows. This is great for us to get an idea of our story's visual structure, and we can now move pages around with ease.

Before we get into the Page Manager window, we'll be doing some deleting, creating, and moving of pages in this exercise. So be sure to either work with a blank set of pages or ensure all the pages with art in them are backed up.

Our CMC file (which contains information that makes the LIP files into a story) is present in its own window, as shown in the following screenshot:

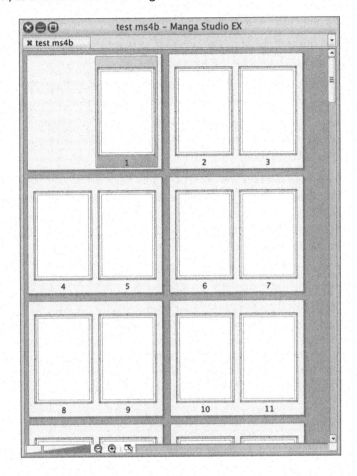

Now, we can see what the binding options look like. **Page 1** is by itself, on the right side of the two-page island. Each two-page island starts with an even numbered page. Look at a comic, and you will see that this numbering is correct for printing.

Let's add some more pages to our story by performing the following steps:

1. To make sure we are all seeing the same thing, navigate to **Story | Page Manager Layout** and select the **Left** option.

2. When we're in the Page Manager window, at least one page should be selected. All our actions will be based on the page(s) selected.

3. In the **Story** menu, we can select either **Add Page** or **Add Page (Detail)**, or right-click on a page and select one of the following options in the contextual menu:

   ❑ **Add Page** will add one page to the story. This page will be based on the page information that we entered (or template we chose) when we first created the story.

   ❑ **Add Page (Detail)** will open up a new page dialog, like what we've seen so far. Here, we can choose a different-sized page. If we're planning to print our story, it's best to only type in the number of new pages we want in the **Number of pages** textbox. If we are going to use our story in an online or digital format, we can change what we want to.

   ❑ For our purposes, let's just choose **Add Page**.

> As our story grows in page count, so does the time it takes for the story information to change and the CMC file to load when opened. If we find our story growing beyond 100 pages, we need to think about breaking down the story into two parts. This way, the CMC file will load up faster and the changes will be quicker. If we have a very fast computer and much RAM, reducing the page count may be unnecessary.

4. Once we select an option, we'll see a dialog which indicates that the page is being created and our story information is being updated.

5. When the dialog goes away, the window changes. Our Page Manager is now a part of the larger document window.

6. Let's take a moment to look at the window and see what information is being given to us, as shown in the following screenshot:

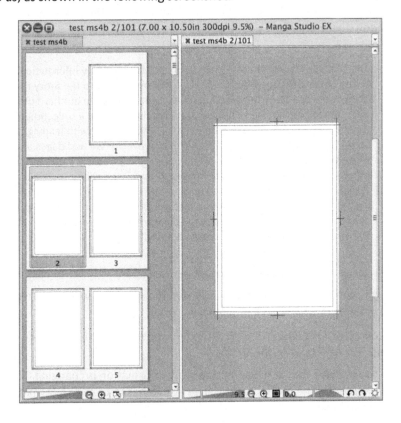

7. The **Page Manager** is on the left side of the Document window. We can change its size by clicking on the light gray bar on the right of the scroll area.

8. The section of the window that's active will have a lighter tab than the inactive section. The window title shows us the number of the page we're working on, how many pages are present in this story, the zoom of that page, and the resolution of the current page.

9. On the right pane is our page file. Notice that it reads as `test ms4b 2/101` in the tab. This tells us that we are looking at page 2 of a 101-page story that's named **test** `ms4b`. It's critical that we realize that this refers to the page's location in the story and does not reflect the filename.

The CMC file tracks the story page numbers, specific story information, and so on. To set that story information, we just need to go to the **Story** menu and choose the **Story Information** menu item. If we go to our hard drive and open the folder that we saved this story within, we'll see a collection of files named `PageXXXX.lip` (where the XXXX is a number with leading zeros, so the 15th page is `Page 0015.lip`). However, as we add pages and move them around, the filenames on our hard drives don't change, only the information inside the CMC file changes to match the changes we did in the Page Management window. We can trust the Page Manager to take care of such things for us. If we need to go into our story folder, the thumbnail for the LIP file should help us identify the page we want, or we could do this via the **Story** menu, and export the page from within EX.

10. We can click-and-drag pages to change their location.

11. Click on page 7 and drag it downwards. A vertical red line will appear on the right side of the page where we'll move page 7 to.

12. Let's drag the page down to page 10. When we see the red line on the right side of page 10, we'll release the cursor.

13. We'll see a dialog that tells us that the story information is changing. This will take a few moments. The more pages Manga Studio has to change information for, the longer it will take.

What just happened?

We learned about the Page Manager window, where Manga Studio takes the best part of a desktop publisher app and makes it work for comics. There's a lot information given to us by the tabs in the windows and the window title itself.

The layout of these pages is based on the selection of the menu item by navigating to **Story | Page Manager Layout**, where the following options are present:

◆ **Tab**: This will consider the Page Manager as its own tab. This is good if we're working on a single page and need as much screen space for our work as possible.

◆ **Left**: This will devote an area of the document window to show pages. We can resize the space this pane takes up and adjust the size of the thumbnails. The space for the pages will be on the left side of the window.

- ◆ **Right**: The Page Manager will be on the right side.
- ◆ **Up**: The Page Manager will be at the top.
- ◆ **Down**: The Page Manager will be at the bottom.

Using the **Page Manager,** we can add or delete a single page or many pages and also move pages around. We also learned that the CMC file keeps track of these changes, so that we can just focus on making our comic. This is so much easier than laying out a bunch of bristol boards on the floor, don't you think?

Have a go hero – story properties

We can go to the **Story** menu and choose the **Story Properties** menu item. We'll see a dialog similar to the following screenshot:

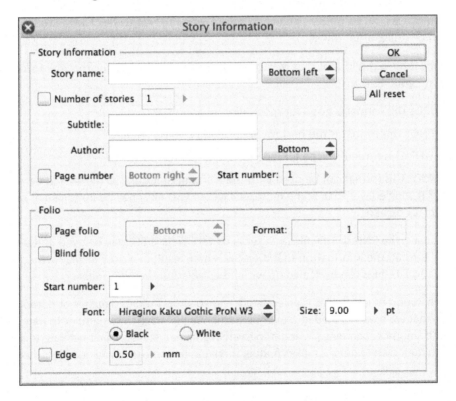

Here, we can set the **Story name** value and many other details of our story. Go and explore, and see what the options are used for here. How does the **Number of stories** field work? What is a **Page Folio** field? Also, don't forget to change the **Font** value to a western font that will match our comic.

Batch operations

Another important feature that Manga Studio EX offers is batch processing of files. These files need to be part of a story file, that is, a CMC file that opens up a Page Manager window. We can import a series of JPEG, TIFF, or PNG files into an existing story, or we could export pages from a completed story as JPEG, PNG, or TIFF files. Lastly, we can perform menu commands for an entire story. This means that we can add a specific kind of layer, or even apply an auto action to an entire page.

Import

If we set up our files as illustrated in *Chapter 10, Caring about Sharing*, we have a folder filled with PNG, JPG, or other file formats. If these are numbered in a sequence, and are either PSD (preferably a flattened, one layer, Photoshop file), JPG, PNG, or TIFF formats, we can import them in one run and have them placed, one on each page, in sequence. The amount of time this saves can be pretty significant, not to mention that while Manga Studio EX does it, we can be doing other things.

The file must be in the format that Manga Studio can read. This means that the following formats are good to use:

- **JPG**: This format is good for most references and photos.
- **PNG**: This format is the best for line art and rough sketches.
- **TIFF**: This format is used for color and fine-shaded drawings.
- **PSD**: This format can be used with the warning that the PSD file should be a flat, single-layer PSD. Some multiple-layered PSD files may be imported as solid black objects.

For most uses, the PNG or TIFF files will serve us very well. JPEG may be used, but because it is a Lossy format, the information that it discards may result in blocky displays when scaled up. PNG and TIFF files can be scaled up with less pixelation than JPEG files.

This batch import of image files is an excellent way to import rough sketches or notebook drawings that we have scanned into our computer. We just have to remember to name our scans with a number sequence in addition to an overall name. Also, don't hesitate to put these scans into their own folders; it makes finding them easier and backing up less of a chore.

Time for action – using the batch import

We'll need a set of at least three image files in JPG, PNG, or TIFF format. They should be numbered in a sequence. The filename can be something similar to `roughs_pg_X.png`, where X is a series of numbers. It helps to have at least three places for the number, so the third file would be `003`.

Next, we'll use the new story (and its files) that we created earlier in this chapter. Now we can navigate to **Story | Batch Import** and begin the action, by performing the following steps:

1. As soon as we choose the **Batch Import** menu item, we're thrown into a choose file dialog. We need to navigate to the place where the image files we want to import are present.

2. Once we find the folder where the files are present, we can click on the first image file. Then, we can hold down the *Shift* key and select the last image file. All the files between the first and the one we just selected by pressing the *Shift* key, and clicked on, will be selected.

3. Then, click on the **Open** button.

4. Now, we're presented with a **Batch Import** dialog box, as shown in the following screenshot:

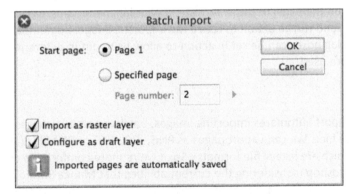

5. We want to begin the import with the first page of the story. If we want to start later, we can click on the **Specified page** radio button and enter the number of the pages there.

6. When **Import as raster layer** is checked, Manga Studio will be informed to treat the imported image as a raster layer. This will make it easier to make selections on this layer. If this option is unchecked, the image will be imported as an image object.

7. **Configure as Draft Layer** will set the layer as a draft layer. So, when we export the page or print it out, we can exclude this layer from being exported or printed.

8. Click on **OK** once the settings are what we want.

9. Now, Manga Studio will import one of the images per page until there are no more images. Manga Studio will let us know if it creates new pages for the images if the number of images we've selected are more than the number of pages we have in our story.

What just happened?

By being organized and having a plan, we will be able to import a series of graphic files into a sequence of our comic pages. The order that the graphic files were selected in is the order they are put into our comic pages.

One drawback is that the image that was imported is resized to fit into the page, so we'll have to go back to each page and scale the image object to the size we want.

Have a go hero – using the batch import

One thing about most automated processes is that if we're importing images that are of the same size, into pages, the imported images will be at the same place in each page. So, our challenge here is to see if we can put an auto action to use to resize and place our imported image on the page. In this way, instead of doing many steps, we just have to select the image object and run an action to resize the imported image. Remember that actions that bring up dialog boxes can be set in action to allow us to put in different information each time they are used.

Export

Just like batch import automates importing images, batch export automates exporting our pages into image files. We can export pages as PNG, JPG, TIFF, or PSD files (along with BMP and TGA files, which are legacy file formats). So, if we're more comfortable coloring our pages using Photoshop (considering the current abilities that Manga Studio has for coloring is a step down), we can export our pages in PSD. We can export pages in the TIFF format for lettering in ComicLife, to send to a print store, or to use the print on demand service.

Using the organization of folders that we explored in *Chapter 10, Caring about Sharing*, we should have an empty folder waiting for our exports. It bears repeating that being organized takes a fraction of the time it would take if we just put everything into one folder and had to sort through that mess. The less time we spend finding stuff, the more time we'll have for drawing, and that's the point of all this organization.

Time for action – using the batch export on our comic

We'll need to have a CMC file open, so that we can have a range of pages to export, and a folder that will be the destination of the exported pages. Once we have these two things in order, we can begin by performing the following steps:

1. Go to the **Story** menu and choose the **Batch Export** menu item.

2. We'll be shown a dialog box that is similar to the following one:

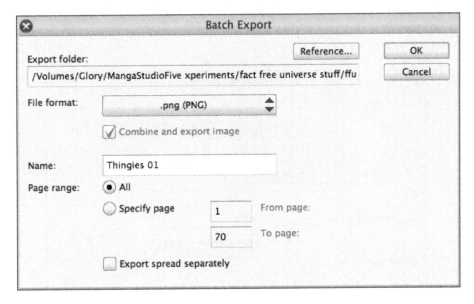

If we have the focus of the window on an opened page in the comic, Manga Studio assumes that we want to export that page only; this is why the **Page range** radio button has **Specify page** chosen, with the *From* and *To* range set to the page number of the opened page. We can click on **All** to export all the pages in our story.

3. The **Export Folder** section is where we choose where to export the pages to. As shown in the screenshot, Manga Studio will have the last location we already chose to export. If this isn't where we want to export the files to, we need to click on the **Reference...** button, navigate to the folder where we want to export the files to, and select the folder.

4. The **File format** area has a drop-down menu with the choices of export formats that we can choose.

5. The **Name** area will be the prefix of the exported files. In this example, the third page exported will have the filename `Thingies 01_003.png`. So, if we're exporting for the Web or for a digital reader, we should have underscores (_) instead of spaces in the name.

6. **Page range** can be all the pages or a specified range. If we've created a double-page spread, we can check the **Export Spread Separately** checkbox, so that the spread will be split into two files. If this isn't checked, then the spread will export as one file.

7. When we have the settings in this dialog box the way we want them, we click on **OK** and are shown yet another dialog box. This one's for the specific export format. Since we have chosen PNG, we'll see the PNG export properties, as shown in the following screenshot:

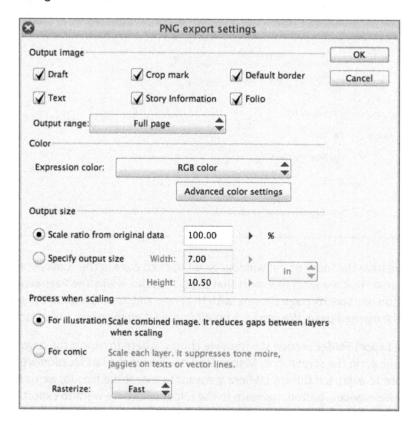

8. The top area is where we can choose which kind of layer will be exported. So, if we don't want to have our draft layers exported, just uncheck the box. This gives us a wide range of customization for our exports. This is another example where being organized pays off. If we set our rough sketching layers as a **Draft** layer (in the layer properties menu), this checkbox has a lot of power.

9. **Output range** will set how much of the page's image will be exported. Our choices are: **Full Page**, which will export the entire page, **To Offset of Crop Mark**, where the area up to the Bleed will be exported by the Manga Studio, and **To Inside of Crop Mark**, where the image inside the Manga draft area will be exported.

10. Once we've chosen our **Output range** value, we can select the color. Usually, RGB will serve us well. The other selections in the drop-down menu were covered extensively in *Chapter 9, Adding a Third "D"*. **Output size** is where we set the size of the exported image.

11. **Process when scaling** has two choices; **For Illustration** will be best for our purposes.

12. **Rasterize** should be set to **Quality**, unless we're exporting for lettering layout in ComicLife, where a low-quality export is acceptable. This is because we're just using the PNG file within ComicLife for reference, the PNG file won't be exported from ComicLife. This is covered in the ComicLife *Chapter 12, Along for the Ride*, which is an online chapter.

13. When we have the settings the way we want them, click on **OK** and Manga Studio will work on the export.

14. We can navigate to the folder in our operating system, see that the files are there, and preview them if our OS will let us.

What just happened?

We took our comic story and exported all the pages in one menu command. We went through dialog boxes that allowed us to refine what type of image format we want to export to and where the exported files will be saved. Furthermore, we refined our export to determine which types of layers we want included, and resized the export accordingly. The export dialogs were basically what we've been exposed to earlier, only this time we're operating on a set of pages and not just on one page.

Process

Quite possibly, the best feature in the EX package, the batch process, allows us to add layers, perform a menu command, and even perform an auto action that's applied to a range of pages or to every page in the story.

So, for the next exercise, create a new story file by clicking on the **New document** button in the command bar (or by going to the **File** menu and selecting the **New** menu item). Make this a five-page story, so it won't take forever to do the exercise. Name this story **ProcessTester**, or use a name that makes sense to you. Be sure to use the **Reference...** button to place this story into a folder that we're using for these exercises.

Got that? Good, let's get to it!

Time for action – batch processing a story

In order to keep this section simple, we're going to just add a new layer for rough sketches to the pages in the story we just created, by performing the following steps:

1. We'll get the option to process an entire page or the pages that we've selected. In the Page Manager window, we can select a single page, or multiple ones, by selecting one page and shift-clicking on another page to select all the pages between the two. If we hold down the *Command* key, we can select or deselect pages.

2. Now, right-click and select the **Batch Process** item in the contextual menu, or go to the **Story** menu and select the **Batch Process** menu item.

3. We will see a **Batch Process** dialog box, as shown in the following screenshot:

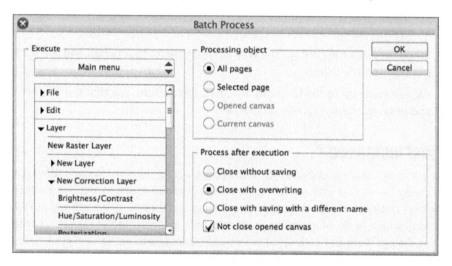

4. In the **Execute** area, we need to choose **Main Menu**. The other option is **Auto Action**, which we'll cover at the end of this exercise.

5. Click on the **Layer** item to disclose its contents.

6. We want to add a new raster layer, so click on that entry in the list. We can choose any item in this section, and it will be done on all pages (or the ones we selected).

7. In the **Processing object** section, choose the **All Pages** radio button. This is where we can either choose **Selected page,** the **opened pages** (called **canvas** here), or the currently active page.

8. In the last section, **Process after execution**, there are several options that we can choose. They're pretty much self-explanatory. As given in the preceding screenshot, we want the **Close with overwriting** option to be selected. This way, the new layer will be saved. The **Not close opened canvas** checkbox can be unchecked if we don't want to see all the pages we're processing. For five pages, it's not a big issue. But for 32 pages or more, it can stress our system a bit.

9. Now click on the **OK** button.

10. Now, we will get another dialog box, as shown in the following screenshot. This time, it is for the layer we're creating:

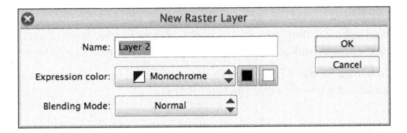

11. This is the same new raster layer dialog box we've seen many times. Give this layer a name, for example, `roughs`.

12. Change the **Expression color** option to gray. We could select **Color** or any other item in the drop-down menu.

13. Click on the black-filled square to the right of the **Expression Color** drop-down menu. Set the **Blending Mode** value to **Normal**. Then, click on the **OK** button.

14. The first page will be processed, that is, a new layer to our specifications will be created, and the page will be saved and closed. Then, we'll see a new dialog box, as shown in the following screenshot:

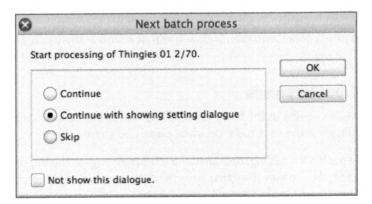

15. This dialog will appear at every page, unless we make some changes.

16. We have three options in the boxed area: **Continue**, **Continue with showing setting dialogue**, and **Skip**. The middle option will pop up the **New Layer** dialog, so we can change things for a page or series of pages. The last option will skip the current page.

17. We can select **Continue**.

18. The checkbox at the bottom of the dialog, **Not show this dialog**, can be checked, so that we can have Manga Studio add the layer to each page without any more interaction from our side.

19. Click on **OK**.

20. Manga Studio will then process the pages, adding a raster layer to each page, saving that page, and going on to the next, until it has processed the final page.

21. When Manga Studio is finished with the processing, open a random page in the story and see if there's a `roughs` layer there.

What just happened?

We selected the **Batch Process** menu item and added a layer to each page. In our example, we only had a five-page story, but imagine the time this saves us for a 32-plus-page story. This isn't just limited to adding layers; it pertains to the actions of the menu items that we can perform in each page. This means that we can apply a filter to our art in a selection of pages, or we can combine all the layers in a page, for all pages. Not only that, we can apply auto actions to pages.

Have a go hero – batch processing a story

Let's say we want to create a panel layer for each page in our story. First, we create an auto action that will do that. Then, we create a set of layers for roughs, pencils, inks, and colors inside the panel. This is similar to what we did in *Chapter 4, Roughing It*, when we created an auto action to create a panel with layers. Now, use that action in the batch process and see what happens.

Wrapping up the Story menu

We can now explore the rest of the **Story** menu. The first section of the menu is basically navigation; we can go to the next page, previous page, and so on.

The next section deals with adding, deleting, and importing pages. The import page allows us to import Manga Studio 5 pages (files that have the LIP extension) into the current page. This option also lets us import Manga Studio 4 pages (with the CPG extension). Be careful, since the dots per inch resolution may be different from the rest of the story.

The menu command, **Combine Pages**, allows us to create a double-page spread. This can be tricky if we're still working on finishing the page, since we can only add or delete pairs (or amounts divisible by two) of pages at a time now, because the two pages are now one. However, we also take up one island of pages in the Page Manager.

The last command, **Continuous Scan**, will allow us to scan multiple pages in one operation using our scanner. This may be a slow process, depending on our scanner, the amount of memory we have, and the amount of free disk space on our hard drive.

We should be confident enough by now to explore the rest of the options in the **Story** menu in Manga Studio. Combine pages, then move a pair of separate pages from after the combined pages, and place them before the combined duo. Scan in rough sketches of a short story using continuous scan. Be sure to be patient, since there are a lot of computations that are happening and there is no hourglass or spinning beach ball to indicate something's happening. Try creating a large page inside a story that has smaller pages. Be adventurous, you won't break Manga Studio.

Pop quiz

Q1. What file contains Manga Studio Story information?

1. All the files with the LIP extension
2. The file with the CMC extension
3. All Manga Studio files

Q2. We have to name each individual story page file

1. True
2. False

Q3. While exporting single layer image files, which format will not be a good choice if we're editing the exported file in another image editing application?

1. TGA
2. TIFF
3. BMP
4. JPG
5. PNG

Q4. When working on a long story of more than 80 pages, what could happen?

1.   The page numbers start over at page 64
2.   Changing page information can take a while to complete
3.   Manga Studio does not allow stories longer than 64 pages
4.   We'll have too much fun

Q5. In the batch process, we apply auto actions to each page.

1.   True
2.   False

Summary

Manga Studio EX, while costing more than twice the amount of plain old Manga Studio 5, has a lot to do with automating routine tasks. Importing files, exporting pages, and applying Menu commands and Auto actions to every page or a selection of pages saves us a lot of time and frees us to draw more. Really, this is what computers do best: repetitive actions that bore us to tears or cause carpal tunnel syndrome. Whether it's worth it to us to get EX is a personal choice, but now we know what's added and we can make an informed decision.

The improvements from the initial release to the current (as of this writing) version 5.0.3 are large and significant: adding Symmetrical rulers, an EX version, a basic kerning for text, and numerous bug-fixes. All these updates have added to the quality experience of using this very capable app for comic creation. Keep up with the updates and upgrades as they roll out. Go to the Runtime DNA Manga Studio forum for information and inspiration.

When I was instructing graphic design and apps, I used to refer to programs as being shallow or deep. Shallow apps were ones that had a single purpose and were easy-to-learn; they could be adapted to our purposes in a few days, if not a few hours. Deep apps were those apps, the basics (the surface of these apps) of which could be learned in a few days. We can get lost and go down many rabbit holes of discovery as we learn the depth and breadth of the nuances of an app's abilities, and that describes Manga Studio. We can learn the basics in a short time, and in this Beginner's Guide, we covered them with an eye toward going deeper into processes that apps can perform.

Never be afraid to wonder what this or that option in a menu or dialog box can do. If you have the time, then it's a learning experience. Time is never, never wasted. This is the secret of focused play: exploring with a sense of purpose and learning.

If we get frustrated and frazzled, it's time for us to push ourselves away from the computer and tablet. Go outside and take a brief walk. Perspective will come, and with the calm that it offers, understanding is sometimes a passenger.

Pop Quiz Answers

Chapter 1, Installing and Setting Up Manga Studio 5

Pop quiz

Q1	2
Q2	2
Q3	3
Q4	2
Q5	4

Chapter 2, Messing Around with Manga Studio

Pop quiz

Q1	2
Q2	2
Q3	2
Q4	3
Q5	1
Q6	2
Q7	3
Q8	4 and 7
Q9	1

Chapter 3, Formatting Your Stories

Q1	2
Q2	2
Q3	2
Q4	1
Q5	1
Q6	4

Chapter 4, Roughing It

Q1	2
Q2	1
Q3	2
Q4	1
Q5	7

Chapter 5, Putting Words in My Mouth

Q1	2
Q2	3
Q3	2
Q4	1
Q5	2

Chapter 6, Pencil Mechanics

Q1	3
Q2	1
Q3	2
Q4	1
Q5	2

Chapter 7, Ink Slingers

Q1	1
Q2	2
Q3	1
Q4	4
Q5	1

Chapter 8, Coloring the World

Q1	2
Q2	1
Q3	1
Q4	1
Q5	2

Chapter 9, Adding a Third "D"

Pop quiz

Q1	2
Q2	2
Q3	2
Q4	3

Chapter 10, Caring about Sharing

Pop quiz

Q1	2
Q2	1
Q3	3
Q4	2

Chapter 11, One More Thing

Pop quiz

Q1	2
Q2	2
Q3	1, 3 and 4
Q4	2
Q5	1

Index

V

Vanishing Point (VP) 211
vector 195

W

Wacom Tablet
  about 11
  control panel 20-27
  setting up, for usage with Manga Studio 5 20
Wacom Tablet Utility application 20
warm colors 272
watercolor 288
web-based digital comics 69
web comics 339
Webcomics 28
Writer's Café
  URL 93

Y

YouTube 343

Z

zoom tool
  using 97

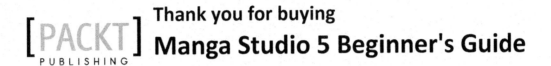

Thank you for buying
Manga Studio 5 Beginner's Guide

About Packt Publishing

Packt, pronounced 'packed', published its first book "Mastering phpMyAdmin for Effective MySQL Management" in April 2004 and subsequently continued to specialize in publishing highly focused books on specific technologies and solutions.

Our books and publications share the experiences of your fellow IT professionals in adapting and customizing today's systems, applications, and frameworks. Our solution-based books give you the knowledge and power to customize the software and technologies you're using to get the job done. Packt books are more specific and less general than the IT books you have seen in the past. Our unique business model allows us to bring you more focused information, giving you more of what you need to know, and less of what you don't.

Packt is a modern, yet unique publishing company, which focuses on producing quality, cutting-edge books for communities of developers, administrators, and newbies alike. For more information, please visit our website: www.PacktPub.com.

Writing for Packt

We welcome all inquiries from people who are interested in authoring. Book proposals should be sent to author@packtpub.com. If your book idea is still at an early stage and you would like to discuss it first before writing a formal book proposal, contact us; one of our commissioning editors will get in touch with you.

We're not just looking for published authors; if you have strong technical skills but no writing experience, our experienced editors can help you develop a writing career, or simply get some additional reward for your expertise.

Unity 3.x Scripting

ISBN: 978-1-84969-230-4   Paperback: 292 pages

Write efficient, reusable scripts to build custom characters, game environments, and control enemy AI in your Unity game

1. Make your characters interact with buttons and program triggered action sequences.

2. Create custom characters and code dynamic objects and players' interaction with them.

3. Synchronize movement of character and environmental objects.

4. Written in simple and step-by-step format with real life examples, this book is the only one in the market to focus on Unity Scripting.

Blender 2.5 Character Animation Cookbook

ISBN: 978-1-84951-320-3   Paperback: 308 pages

50 great recipes for giving soul to your characters by building high-quality rigs and understanding the principles of movement

1. Learn how to create efficient and easy to use character rigs.

2. Understand and make your characters , so that your audience believes they're alive.

3. See common approaches when animating your characters in real world situations.

Please check **www.PacktPub.com** for information on our titles

Cinema 4D R13 Cookbook

ISBN: 978-1-84969-186-4   Paperback: 514 pages

Elevate your art to the fourth dimension with Cinema 4D

1. Master all the important aspects of Cinema 4D.

2. Learn how real-world knowledge of cameras and lighting translates onto a 3D canvas.

3. Learn Advanced features like Mograph, Xpresso, and Dynamics.

4. Become an advanced Cinema 4D user with concise and effective recipes.

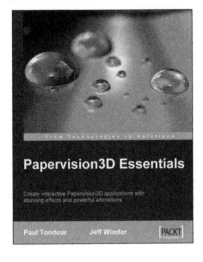

Papervision3D Essentials

ISBN: 978-1-84719-572-2   Paperback: 428 pages

Create interactive Papervision3D applications with stunning effects and powerful animations

1. Build stunning, interactive Papervision3D applications from scratch.

2. Export and import 3D models from Autodesk 3ds Max, SketchUp and Blender to Papervision3D.

3. In-depth coverage of important 3D concepts with demo applications, screenshots and example code.

Please check **www.PacktPub.com** for information on our titles

CPSIA information can be obtained at www.ICGtesting.com
Printed in the USA
BVOW09s2126220315

392725BV00005BA/74/P